AF470782

Mason's MOTORING MAYHEM!

To my wife, Sue, our daughter, Emma, and my stepdaughters, Jane and Clare, who have all brought me down to earth during my hectic life.

First published in May 2013 by Veloce Publishing Limited, Veloce House, Parkway Farm Business Park, Middle Farm Way, Poundbury, Dorchester, Dorset, DT1 3AR, England.
Fax 01305 250479/e-mail info@veloce.co.uk/web www.veloce.co.uk or www.velocebooks.com.

ISBN: 978-1-845844-39-4 UPC: 6-36847-04439-8

Mason's MOTORING MAYHEM!

Tony Mason's hectic life in motorsport and television

Tony Mason

VELOCE PUBLISHING

THE PUBLISHER OF FINE AUTOMOTIVE BOOKS

What they say about Tony ...

SIR STIRLING MOSS
"I have always said that 'Movement is tranquillity!' Well, Tony has certainly had plenty of movement over the years, but not a lot of tranquillity. I've known him more years than I care to remember and I know you'll enjoy this book."

NICK MASON OF PINK FLOYD
"Tony Mason ... sometimes accused of being my brother – more often my elderly uncle! He's an even worse drummer than I am, although much better at rallying and presenting motoring programmes on TV. His book should probably be nearly as good as mine!"

LEWIS HAMILTON, FORMULA 1 WORLD CHAMPION 2008
"Tony is good fun and a great guy."

KEN BRUCE, BBC RADIO 2 PRESENTER
"Tony has come a long way in his career; usually because he was lost! He's given us some great moments on *Top Gear* and other television programmes, and often reminded me of Wilfrid from the Bash Street Kids in the *Beano* comic."

DEREK BELL, FIVE-TIME WINNER OF THE LE MANS 24 HOUR RACE
"Tony is one of the rare breed of men that can sit next to an out-of-control driver for several days and participate for a lifetime with that same passion, and laugh about it."

LORD MARCH, GOODWOOD FESTIVAL OF SPEED FOUNDER
"Tony has played a big and hilarious role in British motorsport over the past four decades. This book is proof of that – not to mention the enormous amount of fun he has obviously had putting this book together."

ANDY GREEN, WORLD LAND SPEED RECORD HOLDER
"Tony is one of those enthusiastic characters that you enjoy meeting. Last time he put a microphone in my face I was climbing out of a rally car after an outrageously fast ride through the trees of Goodwood's rally stage. Tony used to do this full time, so I can confirm that he must be slightly mad!"

HANNU MIKKOLA, WORLD RALLY CHAMPION 1983
"I first met Tony many years ago before I could speak or understand any English. He still made me laugh! He has amazing stories to tell, including those about when he co-drove for me in New Zealand on his last rally."

Contents

Acknowledgements

Thanks a million!

Because of my hatred of computers and inability to 'Google' or send e-mails, I have had to rely on very many organisations, friends and acquaintances to help me put this book together. Everyone has been so supportive and I must have driven half of them mad when I showed my ignorance of modern technology. Despite all this immense help, I have to say that writing my autobiography is the hardest thing I have ever done. I hope you think it's worth it.

My very grateful thanks go to the following who have all helped. Some have supplied facts and figures, or memories, and others just great encouragement and enthusiastic support. Compiling this list makes me think this has every chance of being one of the longest chapters in the book.

My special thanks go to the following seven people from the worlds of motorsport, television and writing who have helped me enormously:

Mike Cable

Neil Henderson

Mike Preston

Bob Redhead

Graham Robson

Tom Ross

Stuart Turner

I am also indebted to the following who have helped in so many ways:

Louise Aitken-Walker
Carl & Conny Bailey
Don Barrow
John Bayliss
Fred Bent
Jon Bentley
Sam Berry
Jon Blackburn
Tom Blinkhorn
Mike Broad
John Brown
Stephanie Browne
Ken Bruce
Cindy Butler
Sam Childs
John Clegg
Paul Colbert
Jilly Cooper
Jenny Cornell
John Couzens
Ian Crammond

John Davenport
Ken Dodd
Ross & Lisa Dunkerton
Fred Gallagher
Jane Gladstone
Rod Grainger
Mark Griffin
Mike Griffiths
Mavis Hampshire-Fair
Dave Hill
Martin Holmes
Henry Hope-Frost
Alan Jolley
Pushpa Kasinather
Chris Knowles-Fitton
Karen Lamb
Justin & Bronni Le Fevre
Martin Leonard
Helen Loggin
Stephen Loh
Jonathan Lord

Sue Mason
Yvonne Mehta
Tiff Needell
Roger Oakley
Richard Pearson
David Penny
John & Gloria Penny
Richard Phillips
Lino & Peter Pires
Jim Porter
Vic Preston Jnr
Jemma Rapson
Harry Rhodes
Chris Sclater
Paul Slater
Tina Summerfield
Dave V Thomas
Lorraine Thornton
Sue Viggers
Mike Wood
Philip Young

I hope I have not forgotten anyone, but, if I have, my profuse apologies.

Photographs

I acknowledge the help of the following who have sourced and, in most cases, taken the photographs used in this book. All have kindly given permission for their inclusion in this book. Every reasonable effort has been made to establish and contact the copyright holders of all photographs. Any errors or omissions are inadvertent, and anyone who has not been contacted is invited to write to the publisher so that an acknowledgement can be included in any subsequent edition of this book:

Airston Photographic
Belinda McDougall
Bev Canning
David Skeffington
Derek Soden/griffinrally.
   com
Esler Crawford
Ford Motor Company
   Ltd

Goodwood Road Racing
   Company Ltd
Jack Wilson
Jeff Garnett
John Wolsoncroft
Jonathan Eales
Maurice Selden
McKlein

National Rally Productions
Neil Prunell
Speedsports
   Photography
Tony Large
Tony North
Tudor Photography
Xavier McCartan

Introduction

I know you'll find this hard to believe but I've been involved in motorsport for over 50 years. Mind you, I was still wearing short trousers when I did my first rally.

I've had an interesting and varied life but it never occurred to me to write about it until now. Being a jack of all trades (and master of none, of course!), I thought of my life as a bit of a hotch-potch of various activities.

I suppose I've had two or three careers running simultaneously at times, ranging from stand-up comedy to world rallying, which has led to a busy life. I've created a motor accessory business and taken to the road as a salesman, but I suspect I'm best known for waddling about on TV screens for twenty years and, as Terry Wogan said, making a career out of falling about in the mud! Mind you, Jeremy Clarkson said I had made a career out of winning one little rally!

However, I've certainly met a great number of interesting and highly successful people from all walks of life. I've enjoyed some success in motorsport, despite a few thrills and spills along the way, and I've experienced a lot of amusing incidents during my rallying and television careers.

I've travelled to some far-flung and very odd places around the world, visiting almost one hundred countries, and enjoyed some strange experiences in most of them, but I've always been pleased to return home to a happy family life which has kept my feet firmly on the ground.

I know one thing: I've certainly had a lot of laughs and excitement along my tortuous route through life.

Do you still want to read this book?

All right then, here goes!

∾ One ∾

Making a splash

By one of those accidental twists of fate, my career in rallying really started to take off at the very moment when it actually seemed to have sunk without trace.

It all happened fairly dramatically one morning during the 1971 RAC Rally of Great Britain. Always one of the toughest events in the rallying calendar, this was made worse than ever that particular year by severe Arctic weather, heavy snow having blanketed most of the UK. Conditions were so bad at times that only 104 of the 231 starters eventually managed to complete the course that started and finished in Harrogate, and which, for the first time, featured special spectator stages in parks and the grounds of stately homes such as Woburn Abbey.

I was in Ford Escort number 60 alongside Yorkshireman Peter Clarke, one of the top drivers in the British championship at the time. As co-driver, my job involved map-reading, navigating, and shouting instructions to Peter throughout the five-day rally, while occasionally taking the wheel when Peter needed a rest during an event that, in those days, went on non-stop day and night with only a few short breaks along its 2500-mile route.

We were doing well in the early stages, up among the leading British crews despite some rather ominous noises emanating from the gearbox. And when it came to the spectator stage at Woburn we were still managing to clock speeds in excess of 80mph as we hurtled along the roads leading through the famous Safari Park, where the wild animals must have wondered what on earth was going on.

Shouting "Hard Left!" as we hit a long, fast left-hand bend, I was aware of Peter's feet doing a bit of ballet dancing on the pedals along with some frantic gear-changing, and when I glanced up from my map I observed a huge crowd of excited spectators to the right, a huge oak tree to the left, and – even more alarming – a vast lake immediately ahead. Two wheels of the car slipped off the tarmac as the gearbox refused to accept third gear, and we skidded over the wet grass at undiminished speed, heading straight for the lake.

Having very nearly drowned in Lake Windermere as a child, and having barely been able to swim at all until my late teens, I have always had something of a fear of water. So the scenario that unfolded before my horrified gaze in the next few split seconds was, to say the least, unnerving. Safety organisations advise that in the event of driving into water one should remain calm and allow the water to seep in and fill the car until the pressure inside equals that of the water outside, at which point it should be possible to push the door open. But there was no chance of me keeping calm in the circumstances! My brain went into overdrive, I panicked – and had my door open before we hit the water.

As the car began to sink I felt the ice-cold, muddy water creeping up to my waist. At that point, I remembered the wild animals of the Safari Park, and, having noticed lions and tigers in the distance as we sped through the stage, conceived the rather irrational fear that something equally predatory might be lurking in the murky depths, and that a large set of open jaws might break the surface at any moment and clamp themselves around my head or various other important bits of my body.

That prospect was enough to have me clambering out of the car and onto the roof, still clutching my precious Ordnance Survey maps and my rally road book, desperate to stay out of reach of any advancing crocodiles. Peter, meanwhile, seemed more concerned about attaching a tow rope to the car as an RAC rescue Land Rover arrived on the scene. I let him get on with it!

As I sat there shivering on top of the half-submerged Escort that freezing morning, little could I imagine that this would be a positive turning point in my life. However, unknown to us at the time, the whole incident had been filmed by rallying's top film production company. It was featured that night on television, while the next morning photographs appeared in every national newspaper. So, in every sense, we'd made quite a splash!

More significantly, as far as my future career was concerned, the footage was seen and greatly enjoyed by Ford's director of motorsports, Stuart Turner, one of the most influential people in rallying. He wrote to me saying that he hadn't stopped laughing, and that Ford was delighted because it had achieved much greater press and TV coverage than Saab, which had actually gone on to win the rally!

Within a matter of months I was co-driving in the Ford works rally team, and twelve months later I went out and won outright the RAC Rally with Roger Clark, an achievement that completely changed my life. And this, in time, led to my career in television, not least of which was a 15-year span as a presenter on BBC TV's *Top Gear*.

Two

What a way to start!

For someone who has made a career in the world of motoring and television, I had something of an unexpected early life. For a start there was never any car in our family until I bought my own at the age of twenty, and neither of my parents ever learned to drive. Furthermore, there was no television set in the house for most of my young life, although one or two of our more affluent neighbours had flickering black and white devices that I used to watch periodically whenever invited. Nevertheless, I had a very happy childhood in a wonderful part of England, and my parents did everything within their means to give me an excellent start in life – and then it was up to me. As one of my last school reports said "He will probably succeed in the future but we're not sure in which field ..." I suppose that grammar school report should have given me a great deal of confidence as I set off into the big wide world. All I know is that I was determined to make my mark in life, be good at whatever I did, and, preferably, find my way into the limelight somehow.

My parents lived in their native north Lancashire, and from their house in the village of Bolton-le-Sands on the edge of Morecambe Bay they had wonderful views of the Lake District mountains and the Furness Peninsula, on which the famed shipbuilding town of Barrow-in-Furness is situated. I was a wartime baby, and my appearance into the world was celebrated by a fairly spectacular firework display, I understand! One night in 1941 the tranquil life of the area was shattered somewhat when Adolf Hitler decided to despatch a couple of his Luftwaffe bombers on a little outing to Barrow-in-Furness to clobber the famous Vickers-Armstrong shipyards there. Although some hits were made, there were obviously a few miscalculations, as the nearby small and genteel town of Grange-over-Sands received an assault as well. The conflagration lit up the whole of Morecambe Bay, and the inhabitants of Bolton-le-Sands were treated to a ringside seat. I often think that the German planes would probably never have made that mistake had their navigators been equipped with the wonderful Ordnance Survey map numbers 88 and 89, which would feature so strongly in my early days as a rally navigator.

I was born in the Royal Lancaster Infirmary on the 12th November 1941, although there is no blue plaque to celebrate the fact. Well, actually, there is a blue plaque on the wall now, but it announces parking charges and hefty fines for visitors overstaying their welcome! A few days after my birth in ward four I was transported with my mother, Hattie, and father, Donald, the five miles to Broadlands Drive, Bolton-le-Sands by a village friend of theirs in a black Vauxhall Ten, complete with wartime dimmed headlights. See, I was interested in cars at that early stage, but regrettably didn't manage to get the registration number! Having subsequently had a life-long association with the Ford Motor Company, which also gave me my greatest rallying success, I've always thought it was a pity that I should come into the world with the help of a Vauxhall! Still you can't alter history.

At this point you will no doubt be calculating how old I am now, and thinking that all of this cannot be true. It is, I am afraid to say. Anyone who thumbs through *Who's who on television* or similar publications and sees my entries will find that all of the above activities were occurring some four or five years before I was supposedly born which is, of course, quite an achievement! The reason for this confusion is that I entered the world of television at a fairly late stage in my life and discovered that most of the producers and BBC hierarchy thought I was at least ten years younger that I actually was. I didn't disillusion them, as I realised this could jeopardise my blossoming television career. What a cheat, I hear you saying! Well it worked, and I enjoyed twenty years 'on the box' entertaining viewers by bumbling about all over the place in an enthusiastic and cheery way that had been cultivated by very supportive *Top Gear* producers and Britain's greatest comedian, Ken Dodd, no less. More of all this later.

So, having got that little embarrassment out of the way, let's get on with the saga.

My father was an engineering draftsman by profession, and after a brief period working for Rolls-Royce in Derby had returned to work in Kendal in an engineering company manufacturing wartime military equipment. He commuted daily the twenty miles from our home by public service buses, which were all painted grey during the war. As an early bus spotter I do remember seeing one or two of these sombre looking Leylands parked in a depot before they were repainted red by Ribble Motor Services, which was then very prominent in Lancashire. My father worked long hours, and on return to Bolton-le-Sands each evening would don his uniform and do his *Dad's Army* bit in the Home Guard, often staying out most of the night. I vaguely remember tales of his escapades including the platoon stalking a supposed German paratrooper who they thought had landed in the woods near our village, only to eventually discover it was a horse. It had broken loose from its nearby field, and gave the platoon an almighty fright when it charged out of the undergrowth, knocking them to the ground. One village resident whose house was on the road alongside the bay constantly showed lights during blackout, and, after a great kerfuffle, was erroneously marched off to the police station to be handed over to the authorities as a spy – he was nothing of the sort, of course. The platoon was also instructed to manoeuvre large planks of wood into slots at every local bridge on the Lancaster to Kendal canal whenever there was an air-raid warning, in the hope of preventing possible flooding, which would prevent the canal emptying. This was heavy and difficult work, and once or twice Home Guard members fell into the canal, which amused those who didn't. It was, of course, then a working canal, with carthorses pulling big barges of coal and other materials during the day.

The best incident I can remember my Dad telling us about was at a family gathering at Christmas sometime after the war. It also concerned the Vicar of Bolton-le-Sands, one Reverend Ernest Shufflebottom, who was in the platoon. At the end of the evening's patrolling, the men would gather in the cellar of the Blue Anchor pub in the centre of the village, where they would enjoy the odd half-pint of Mitchells bitter whilst cleaning and fiddling about with their rifles. As so accurately portrayed much later in the brilliant BBC television programme *Dad's Army*, the platoon included all the local tradesmen, and inevitably there was chaos. Regrettably there was no gunsmith among the throng, an omission that eventually led to the local butcher, baker and candlestick maker, assisted by my father and the Reverend Shufflebottom, pulling a trigger at the wrong time, causing a bullet to pierce a large barrel of the aforementioned Mitchells best bitter, flooding the cellar floor. A few years ago at a BBC reception in London I had the opportunity to meet and talk with the late David Croft, co-writer and producer of *Dad's Army*. He was a charming man and a great delight to talk to, and I told him the beer barrel story. "Oh! I wish I'd thought of that for *Dad's Army*," he said "that would have been brilliant!"

I enjoyed my Dad's company, and over the years his engineering background was a great help as he was a very practical man and could mend toys, construct model railway tracks, and do all the other things fathers should do. Unfortunately his timing was not always the best, and many was the time that my sister, brother, and I were not able to touch our presents on Christmas morning as the paint had not dried! George Donald Mason was born in 1904 in the railway town of Carnforth in north Lancashire, where his father, also George, was a railway guard. Dad met and married my mother, Hattie, in 1929. She was born in nearby Lancaster, and was just 19 years old when she married. My sister, Maureen, was born in 1930; the war came along with me in the middle of it, and the third sibling, my brother, Stuart, appeared in 1946. We all had a normal, typical family life, and lived in the friendly village of Bolton-le-Sands where both parents took part in village activities, including the Garden Club, the Church, the Women's Institute, the Mothers' Union, and more. They had lots of friends, and the semi-detached house in which we lived had plenty of visitors, including numerous tradesmen's vans that appeared weekly. I even remember *Steptoe*-like rag-and-bone men with their horses and carts, and my mum scooping up the horse droppings with a shovel and putting them on the rose bed. The dustmen arrived weekly and used to open the front gate and another gate then pick up the one small metal dustbin before carrying it to the truck, returning the empty bin to the back garden through the two gates. Nowadays, things have changed somewhat on this front, with ugly wheely bins chucked onto pavements everywhere.

I remember the very early years of my life, mainly from the age of four onwards, and I recall appearing in fancy dress competitions at the village fete, once dressed as a sailor. The village school had a good stage and assembly hall where jumble sales, plays, concerts, and other attractions were very well attended. On one such occasion the entertainer Wilfred Pickles and his wife, Mabel, then popular radio broadcasters, appeared to open the fete or something similar, and I was selected to present some item to them. I can't remember what it was, but I can remember this man leaning over to shake my hand and tousling my hair. Come to think of it, this was the first 'celebrity' I ever met, and features as the first bit of name-dropping in this book. Don't worry, there will be plenty more.

My mother came from a large family, and I remember her telling me about her childhood, often speaking about her father, who I vaguely remember. Grandpa Fred was a clever man and had entered the then mysterious world of electricity.

He was employed to take charge of all electrical matters at the Port Sunlight factory of Lever Brothers, then starting its small soap manufacturing business on the Wirral Peninsular, near Liverpool. This would eventually become the now internationally famous Unilever Group, one of the world's greatest manufacturing companies. My grandfather was friendly with his employers, and was on first-name terms, calling the much-later ennobled Lord Leverhulme 'Billy.' He was offered a major shareholding in the company at one point, but declined it in favour of a salary increase. Every time I now see a packet of Persil, Flora margarine, Walls Ice Cream, or Marmite, I wonder if I might have inherited a slice of it all had things gone differently!

Grandpa moved to Lancaster as he had been offered the position of boss of the new Lancaster Power Station. He and his wife had five children, Jack, Fred, Chester, Hattie and Ruby, and lived in a house close to his workplace, which, at the time, was one of the most modern power stations in Britain. Evidently he was an important man in Lancaster, and mixed in the best circles.

Uncle Jack sadly lost his life early in the war in a Royal Navy submarine that failed to surface in home waters. It was one of the war's first major incidents, and Lancaster's first war fatality. Uncle Chester was one of the famous Red Devils in the war, parachuting into occupied countries, which, he once told me, petrified him at every jump. He later qualified as a chemist and eventually opened a shop in Caton, near Lancaster. Aunty Ruby married a Post Office telegram-boy who eventually rose to a senior position in Royal Mail, whilst Uncle Fred, a great humourist, eventually opened a fish and chip shop in east Lancashire and obviously prospered as he was the only member of the tribe to own a car in those early postwar years. He had a Jowett Javelin, which was quite an upmarket car in its day, and it was on Uncle Fred's knees in this very vehicle that, at the age of ten, I first took the controls of a car. This took place on the beach at Bolton-le-Sands, and it was the first great step in my motoring career.

In the early postwar years things were obviously very difficult, and although my father had a very respectable job there was not much money in the household. My mother kept a good home with lots of home cooking, and used household devices that were fairly primitive by today's standards. I remember a large bubbling Burco boiler – complete with mangle on top – in the kitchen, a grey Creda oven, a Ewbank carpet sweeper and not much else. A roast joint of meat would last all week, washing would be done on Mondays, and my mother would cycle to the village shops to bring back whatever she could afford, including warm, freshly-made brown bread. If this is starting to sound like a well-known television commercial I do apologise, but it was true. I can still remember the smell of it.

At the age of four I became the proud owner of a small number of Dinky toy cars, which my mother bought for me by saving parts of her very limited housekeeping money. They would be purchased from a small shop in nearby Carnforth or from two marvellous shops, Lawsons of Lancaster or Edmondsons of Morecambe. To me these were the most wonderful, magical emporia I could imagine, and Mr Topham and Mr Edmondson in their respective shops let me carefully take the model cars out of the boxes to examine them before deciding which model I should select. I suppose I was giving them a sort of road test.

I also received a small red bicycle for my fourth birthday, which had proper inflatable tyres and a bell. I soon mastered the art of bicycle riding and was rapidly off down Broadlands Drive, which was then unsurfaced. Needless to say, I hadn't quite mastered the art of opposite lock or sideways driving on gravel, so I frequently fell off and returned home to have knees patched up with sticking plasters before returning to the road. Within weeks I had created a small undulating track over some piles of soil on a bit of nearby waste ground, and, with other kids, started a primitive form of BMX riding. I was very competitive and would like to win, although I can't imagine how we timed our laps as no-one had a watch. I remember my first days at the Bolton-le-Sands Church of England primary school and my mother walking the half-mile to the school gates with me (there were no large 4x4 vehicles commandeering all the roads around schools then, as they seem to today).

I was soon considered by my parents to be proficient enough to make my own way to school on my little red bike, parking it carefully in a shed behind Mr & Mrs Storey's village shop. They made ice cream in this shed, and, very occasionally, I would be given an ice cream in a cornet when collecting the bike after school. However I never quite mastered the art of cycling and ice cream eating at the same time, so I usually arrived home covered in the stuff.

I quite enjoyed infants' school, and progressed satisfactorily thanks to the efforts of Miss French who was tall, thin, and slightly frightening, and would deal with any bad behaviour by whacking the backs of the hands of offending pupils, using a twelve-inch wooden ruler. I have to admit to receiving this punishment on more than one occasion.

❧ **Three** ❧

Wheels and water

The first of my life-changing moments came in 1951, when I was ten, and the third postwar Monte Carlo Rally took place. Broadlands Drive adjoined the main A6 road between Carnforth and Lancaster and it became known that cars starting from Glasgow on their hazardous route to Monte Carlo would actually pass our road end. Obviously, I didn't know what a rally was, but my Mum, quite rightly, thought that I would enjoy it, so took me to see the cars passing early one evening. I was completely captivated by these amazing cars coming past at regular intervals among the trundling Leyland, Foden, Albion and ERF lorries making their way down from Scotland. The rally cars were Rileys, MGs, Jowetts, Austins, Sunbeam Talbots, Hillmans, and Jaguars. But not only that, they had roof racks carrying shovels and spare wheels, yellow headlights to make them legal when they got to France, and two or three people in each car wearing wartime leather jackets. And, most importantly, they had huge numbers on the doors and extra spotlights.

We stayed for two hours and my poor mother must have been frozen, but I would not return home, even though my Dad's dinner had not been cooked. When we did get home, I instantly unearthed my Dinky collection from my toy-box and selected all the appropriate models, then converted them into rally cars by painting numbers on the doors, using little tins of Humbrol enamel that I had previously used when making model aircraft from plastic kits. I went further and put mud on the cars, and I actually biffed in the wing of one with my Dad's hammer, having noticed that one the cars I'd seen had obviously had a contretemps with something on the icy roads in Scotland. I couldn't believe what I had witnessed that day, and went to bed the happiest I have ever been. That was it! I was going to be a rally driver when I grew up. Forget the fire engines or big lorries. In fact, when I grew up I did drive rally cars, but also drove fire engines and big lorries, thanks to *Top Gear*. Dreams can come true!

In 1952, *The Lancaster Guardian*, our local newspaper, ran a children's painting competition, and the headmaster at Bolton-le-Sands primary school, which I attended, encouraged me to submit an entry as I obviously had some artistic talent. I laboured long and hard, and eventually produced a painting entitled 'Monte Carlo Rally,' which portrayed a variety of cars, yellow headlights shining, descending from snowy French mountains. Pride of place in the painting went to a dark green Bristol 401, and I later discovered what I believe to be the actual car at the Bourne Classic Car Show in Lincolnshire, which I opened in 2006. It is now owned by former European saloon car champion Warwick Banks, who I now know well and who recently let me drive it. On the 1952 rally that featured in my painting, it was driven by Warwick's father, Bill.

Beyond my wildest dreams and to the great pleasure of my parents, my painting won the competition and my photograph appeared in *The Lancaster Guardian*, no less. I quite enjoyed my first taste of fame, and it helped me psychologically as I had something of an inferiority complex in my very early school years, being much shorter than the average boy of my age, and not liking football or fighting. I had also had a major deflation during morning assembly one day, when the ferocious headmaster, Mr Parker, decided to judge all the new pupils' singing abilities. He lined us up and asked us to sing the hymn *Fair Waved the Golden Corn* over and over again. He then proceeded to call us over to the upright piano he was thumping and thrust his large bald head into each of our chests to hear our vocal ability. When it came to my turn he listened for about five seconds, elbowed me away and said "You're a grunter!" I was mortified, and I think I cried.

The incident was far from over, however, as I made the mistake of saying "My father is a very good piano player and says I'm a good singer." With that I was unceremoniously plonked on a table alongside the piano while Mr Parker thumped away to the tune of hymn number 339. I had to sing several verses alone whilst the rest of the school stood and sniggered. It was a bad experience and since that day I have rarely sung a note, usually mouthing the words of the National Anthem or *Happy Birthday* when necessary, hoping no-one would notice. Of course, Mr Parker was probably right, and my voice had already been damaged by making incessant car noises when I was playing with my Dinkies or riding my mud-spattered bicycle. It was only during my years in television that I realised I had a distinctive (and probably awful) voice which people instantly recognised. At the height of my limited fame on television I would often receive the question "Is that Tony Mason?" when speaking to call-centres to talk about electricity bills, or whatever. I am pleased to say, it has even come in useful and profitable for the odd voice-overs.

So, my early childhood in the immediate postwar years was following a not unusual but varied pattern. I went sledging in the deep snow each winter, skating on the canal at the end of our garden, and played in the dark, dank, air-raid shelter that my father had previously constructed beneath the rhubarb bed just before the war. With other friends of my age I would patrol the village and find empty Tizer bottles, which we would take to the fish and chip shop to claim the deposits on them, spending the few pence on chips. We would often sit on a bench at the junction of the A6 and the road to Morecambe and watch the traffic. I became expert at identifying all the vehicles that came along, and when darkness fell I became the star performer in our little troupe as I could identify cars by the position of their lights. I loved seeing the big trucks trundling back and forth between the Lancashire towns and Scotland. The high-spot of our traffic spotting was at the time of 'Scottish holidays,' when hundreds of coaches would transport people to Morecambe for their two weeks' annual holiday. On one occasion, in 1956, we were joined by various adults who gathered to see a large black limousine containing Russian leaders Bulganin and Khrushchev passing from Morecambe towards the north. What on earth these two communist leaders were doing coming to Morecambe, I really cannot imagine. Another little excitement for our 'gang' was to go to Bolton-le-Sands station to train spot and, somewhat dangerously, put pennies on the main line to see them squashed flat.

In my school holidays I used to enjoy watching a local builder and his men construct new, semi-detached houses on the field opposite our house, in Broadlands Drive. I had mixed emotions about this development as the builders were obliterating the off-road bike tracks that I had created, but there were other attractions. An ex-World War II glider was placed near the building site to be used as a store area for the builders. This was a great location to play in, as you can imagine.

I became quite friendly with Mr John Cottam, the builder. He let me help him and taught me how to mix cement, lay bricks, fit floorboards, and even climb the various long ladders to the top of the half-built houses. Health and safety? What's that? Mr Cottam, who was a friend of my parents, let me go with him in his Austin 10 and trailer to collect building materials from Lancaster and Morecambe. At one point he acquired a new bright green Austin A40 pick-up, and I would sit upon bags of cement or whatever in the open back of the vehicle as it sped along between jobs. Again, health and safety?

In 1950, I remember a picnic with a difference when we travelled by train to Barrow-in-Furness to witness the launch of a great liner, the Chusan. Along with thousands of other people we sat on a huge grass bank, enjoying our alfresco lunch and cheering loudly as the big ship slid majestically into the sea between Walney Island and Barrow.

I was quite a shy child and had a few close friends, but was encouraged by my parents to widen my circle of friends by joining a youth club that was being created in the old boys' grammar school on St Michael's Lane in Bolton-le-Sands village. I can remember a Dansette record player blaring away and various soft drinks being offered, and some very embarrassing and ill-at-ease dancing. The evening was supervised by some parents or members of the Women's Institute, and was all very genteel and innocent although I do remember my first clumsy kiss with a girl called Cynthia. Gosh! This book is getting racy!

Back at home there were great happenings, as my Dad had decided to build a boat. Not a simple little rowing boat for the adjacent canal, but a 16-foot long clinker-built yacht, which he planned to sail on Lake Windermere. He constructed a large wooden and canvas shed at the bottom of the garden in which to build the boat, and also erected a strange device he called a 'steaming chest,' into which he placed planks of wood that would be bent into the required shape to suit the curvature of the boat. Where the steam came from I do not know, but it did. He would labour long into the night having returned from his job in Kendal. Lord knows how he had the stamina. Maybe I inherited a bit of this gene, as I was always able to do without sleep when rallying.

Eventually, the 'Golden Hind' was finished, and, with the help of half of Broadlands Drive, launched into the canal with my mum breaking a bottle of something on the bow, which didn't do a lot for the magnificently varnished wood over which Dad had laboured so long and hard. The boat was moored temporarily at the end of our garden and the following weekend was taken to Carnforth, near the gas works, where there was some contraption that could 'hoik' the boat out of the canal and onto the back of a local greengrocer's lorry to be transported to Bowness-on-Windermere, where Dad had acquired a berth in a large boat shed. With still no car in the family, (much to my chagrin), Mum, Dad, Stuart and I would travel by Ribble bus on route 68 (Lancaster – Keswick) taking well over an hour to get there and sail in the boat. I mention the bus details because, by now, I was an avid bus spotter and indeed a member of the Ribble

Enthusiasts Club. On a *Top Gear* item about a vintage bus rally from Southport to Blackpool, which I presented some 40 years later, I was re-installed as an honorary member of this august organisation and given a new shiny badge to prove it.

By the age of nine or ten my Dinky Toy collection had grown massively, and I had managed to acquire over twenty double-deck buses which I painted into my own colour scheme of red – not dissimilar to the mighty Ribble colours – and, of course, put my name – Mason's Motor Services – on each side. I also put advertisements for Capstan cigarettes, Cadbury's chocolate, Ilford films, Horlicks, and Chivers jellies on the sides, just like real buses. Advertisements had started to appear on the sides of buses at this point but not on the Dinky models produced by Meccano Limited in Liverpool. Thinking it would save me some time I wrote to Mr Roland Hornby (yes, he of Hornby trains, also produced by Meccano) and suggested he should put advertisements on Dinky buses. I also suggested he should consider other models of cars that were not yet in the Dinky range. I developed something of a rapport with Mr Hornby and corresponded regularly, rather pompously giving him my advice. The great man must have thought I was a complete pain in the arse, but, thinking it might be a way of getting me off his back, wrote and offered me the chance to visit Meccano and see the factory in which he manufactured his products. He said I could take a friend so I selected David Schofield for this great honour, not least because his parents had a nice new Standard Vanguard car and could therefore transport me the fifty or so miles to Binns Road, Liverpool.

David was a very good friend, and his devoted parents had a huge Hornby Dublo model train track in a special room in their house, where I used to spend many hours. Incidentally, following our trip to the Meccano factory, advertisements did eventually appear on Dinky buses, and this gave me a lot of credibility at school, although no doubt most boys didn't believe that I had instigated this, just as many readers will probably not believe some of the amazing happenings that occur later in my life and will be recalled later.

Both sets of my grandparents were still alive at that time, and we would frequently visit them. Grandpa and Grandma Mason lived in an end-of-terrace house in Carnforth, and we went there with other members of their family for little soirées from time to time. My Dad was a very good self-taught pianist, although he could not read a bar of music. He could play 'by ear' and having heard a tune once could instantly remember it. He was good enough to once achieve the accolade of appearing on the BBC radio programme *Workers' Playtime*, and played regularly at local dances. I wish I'd managed to emulate him, but I was obviously musically inept for I could not pick it up. He encouraged me to learn the trumpet and the banjo, but to no avail. Both my sister Maureen and brother Stuart learnt to play the piano satisfactorily.

Nevertheless, I contributed to the little musical gatherings at my grandparents' house by performing as compère and comedy artist. At 14 Alexandra Road in Carnforth there was a big bay window with long thick curtains in front of it. This acted as a little stage, and I was very partial to standing behind the curtains then entering through them just like one would in a proper theatre. Then would follow recitations from various family members, much piano playing, and I would precociously impersonate great stars like George Formby and Arthur Askey by attempting to sing their songs (very badly!). Show business was calling.

Whilst in Carnforth my Dad would often take me to the local barbershop to have my hair cut by Mr Albert Marshall, who was also a part-time fireman, and who would frequently leave clients mid-haircut when he had an emergency call. He would leave the shop and run down Market Street to the fire station, his white overall billowing behind him as he ran. I observed this little procedure several times and found it highly amusing.

I must have been a horrible child, as I had visions of grandeur from an early age. On return from a primary school prize-giving, clutching my copy of *Biggles in the Baltic* with which I had been presented, I pondered on the career to follow in order to be invited to present prizes there in the future. I also spent a long time, from an extremely early age, practising my autograph for further use.

I certainly had eyes on show business and listened avidly to comedy radio programmes like *Variety Bandbox*, *Variety Fanfare* and *Educating Archie*. My parents regularly took me to see shows at the Winter Gardens theatre in Morecambe – then one of the greatest variety venues in Britain. We saw big stars of the day including legendary names like George Formby, Frankie Howerd, Josef Locke, Albert Modley, animal impressionist Percy Edwards, Wilson, Keppel and Betty, 'Two-ton' Tessie O'Shea, and Gracie Fields. My Dad knew someone in the orchestra at the Winter Gardens, so we would sometimes go to the stage door and meet the stars. I remember Gracie Fields being very nice, chatting to my parents and giving a friendly tousle of my hair. If you remember Wilfred Pickles did the same in the last chapter. It's no wonder my hair eventually fell out in later life with all this 'tousling' going on!

Probably my greatest moment as a comedy fan was to see on stage at the Winter Gardens no less an act than Laurel and Hardy. Towards the end of their hugely successful film career they made three tours of Britain, and in May 1947 duly appeared in Morecambe, across the bay from Stan Laurel's birthplace of Ulverston, which they later visited. In all honesty I can't remember their act in any detail (I was only six), but I do remember being completely fixated when they first came on stage accompanied by their familiar theme tune, dum, de dum, dum, de dum, didly dum ...

Morecambe's Winter Gardens flourished from the turn of the century, and the stage was graced by some of the greatest stars of music hall, variety, music and theatre over the years. Edward Elgar, no less, visited the theatre as part of the Morecambe Music Festival before the First World War, and the Halle orchestra also appeared there. Predictably popular entertainers there in the fifties were comedians Morecambe and Wise, not least because Eric Morecambe took his stagename from the town and was often seen locally. His parents lived in nearby Hest Bank and Eric would often be seen walking along canal banks or on the beach alongside Morecambe Bay.

I was very lucky to meet Eric a few times during the late sixties and early seventies when he would visit his parents, George and Sadie Bartholomew, and would occasionally enjoy a quiet drink in one of the local pubs near their village. He drove an Aston Martin at the time and was not particularly interested in cars, but inspected my Mini-Cooper in the pub car park. He was fascinated by the 'flexy' navigation light dangling from inside the roof, and proceeded to speak into it, using it as a microphone! He was a very funny man, as we all know, and seemed to enjoy being rude about my 'little Mini.'

In the early fifties my sister Maureen, by now a state-registered nurse at Royal Lancaster Infirmary, had met and married Edward Parker, a young RAF pilot from Carnforth. I thought Ted was great; he was interested in cars, Ribble buses, trains, and could fly a jet plane. What else could a man want? I instantly decided that I wanted to be a pilot when I grew up and the stage would have to wait. Nevertheless, I did join Bolton-le-Sands Players a few years later and acted as assistant stage manager, scenery painter, and general dogsbody, but also appeared as the French jockey in the farce *Dry Rot* and as 'the boy' in *A Christmas Carol*. Big stuff!

My younger brother, Stuart, liked more serious matters, and joined the choir at the local church. He was the 'brains' of the family, and achieved a first at Oxford before becoming ordained as a priest. We never really saw eye-to-eye on many things, and more or less lost touch before his early death at his home in the Orkney Islands in 2006.

After her marriage my sister Maureen followed her new husband to his first overseas posting in Hong Kong, which in those days was quite a major assignment. She was booked to travel on a troopship, the Dunera, from Southampton, so my mother, brother and I accompanied her and a huge cabin trunk by train to Southampton. It was a great adventure to be sure, and I well remember standing on the docks and marvelling at the size of the vessel. Obviously, many tears were shed before we waved goodbye and headed for London, where Mum, Stuart and I would spend the night, taking in all the sights on our first ever visit to the capital.

I remember being completely overwhelmed by the size of the place, and walking for miles trying to find the rather downmarket hotel that Mum had organised in good faith. We were billeted in cold and draughty attic rooms at the top of hundreds of stairs; I found it quite frightening, and was pleased to waken the next morning and realise we had not been murdered in our beds. I decided that I did not like London, its tube trains, or even its buses, which were mostly AEC's instead of sturdy Lancashire-manufactured Leylands. I have never really changed my opinion about London, surprisingly, although I have obviously spent a great deal of time there over the years. Never would I have imagined that, at the height of my TV exposure in the nineties, I would hail a taxi in the West End and be greeted by the driver "Hello Tony, where are you going, mate?"

Our family had few holidays, although we did once go to a Lake District B&B in Ambleside, and on another occasion rented a caravan on the banks of Lake Windermere. This, in fact, nearly saw my demise, and at this point this rambling story could have come to an end and you'd have a hundred blank pages to look at!

Lake Windermere can be beautiful in many respects, but has a reputation for being unpredictable, as winds blowing through the 'funnels' between the mountains can easily turn into a squall. A local saying goes "Sail the seven seas, then sail Lake Windermere." During the caravan holiday we were joined by a friend of my parents who brought along his own yacht. He invited me to go with him for a short sail across the lake whilst my parents were otherwise engaged making lunch. I donned a small life jacket and set forth with great excitement.

It was a nasty dull day with overcast skies, and, inevitably, one of Windermere's famous 'squalls' arrived as we were five minutes into our little trip. Within minutes the small 'Enterprise' class yacht was being pitched about in a most alarming way. There seemed to be a bit of panic in my father's friend's behaviour as he leapt about from one side of the boat to the other, pulling ropes and trying to turn the rudder. I suspected that all was not too well, but hung on to my seat for dear life and said nothing. Then it happened! Within seconds the yacht lurched in the air and fell over as a great wave appeared from nowhere. Needless to say we were both pitched into the lake, my father's friend at one end and me floundering at the other.

Being a non-swimmer I was very frightened, but was assured by my father's shouting friend that I would be fine as I was wearing a life jacket and would float happily whilst he righted the boat by fiddling around with ropes, sails, rowlocks and other nautical things. Now this is where he was wrong, for I started to sink and remember going deeper and deeper into darker water and actually getting to the bottom of the lake where I could vaguely see green weeds swirling about in the freezing water. I cannot remember how deep it was but I seemed to be there for ages and felt dizzy and sick with panic, gulping down water. I assume I tried to wave my arms about to regain the surface but as a non-swimmer I probably did all the wrong things.

Suddenly there was a 'whoosh' as a large black figure grabbed me, pulling me up vigorously whilst mud and weeds swirled around. To this very day I can still remember the horrid taste of the water. I was still conscious, but only just, and had swallowed a great deal of water. I was then aware of various black arms pulling and tugging me, and was unceremoniously manhandled onto the deck of a boat – but not the boat I had so hastily exited some few minutes (which felt like hours) before. I remember people pummelling me while I was spurting water like a beached sperm whale then further coughing, spluttering, and being sick, and hearing a lot of instructions being given by a man. With the luck of the devil I had survived this great near-death incident, as some Sea Scouts and their Scout Masters were on Lake Windermere as a training exercise, or some such, and had observed our little drama. Presumably they thought it a good opportunity to put into practice their life-saving skills, and, possibly, get another badge for their uniforms.

Anyway, the long and the short of it is that I survived to tell the tale, but I have been frightened of water ever since. I eventually learned to swim when I entered Lancaster Royal Grammar School some time later, but to this day I seldom go out of my depth in a swimming pool or in the sea. Latterly I have been employed by P & O Cruises to entertain passengers on their magnificent ships as they sail around the world. I enjoy the trips, but seldom look over the side!

I should tell you that the reason I didn't float as expected during the lake incident was that I was wearing oversized wellington boots, which filled with water and dragged me down despite my small life jacket, according to the Sea Scout master who saved my life.

Four

Growing up

L ife was a lot simpler in the early fifties, but it was amazingly exciting for me as my interest in all motoring matters increased when major British car manufacturers introduced their marvellous new streamlined models.

My favourite car was an Austin Atlantic, a stylish car produced to capture the massive American market. I had two Dinky versions, one of which survives to the present day, and appeared in my hand during a *Top Gear* road test some forty years later. Incidentally, the car was a great failure commercially. When researching for my television item, I remembered that Stirling Moss had achieved a major endurance record driving the car in America. I asked him what he thought of the Austin Atlantic. "It was the worst bloody car I've ever driven!" he said. So much for my taste in cars.

I had by now graduated from my small red bicycle, on which I won my class on a road safety rally in nearby Carnforth (I suppose you could say this was my first rally award), and was the proud owner of a Phillips Kingfisher, complete with the new-fangled 3-speed 'derailleur' gear. I virtually lived on my bike, and ventured further afield, spending time at local garages, watching mechanics and petrol pump attendants at work.

In my best Walter Mitty fashion, of course, I had assumed the role of a rally driver. Rally plates were fitted front and back, extra spotlights were added, with one of them converted to a yellow beam by adding yellow cellophane from an old Lucozade bottle; I felt this was essential for foggy conditions. Now, you may wonder what I am talking about here, as the brand is now a popular sports drink sold in a variety of small colourful plastic bottles. In those far-off days, Lucozade was a glucose recuperative drink sold mainly in chemists, in one size of glass bottle, wrapped in yellow see-through paper. Mum had added to my rally driving hallucination by knitting me a bobble hat (as worn by all self-respecting rally drivers in those days) and a matching sweater – all in kingfisher blue. I must have looked a right berk!

My interests extended to all forms of transport, and increased daily. I started to collect Ian Allan 'spotters' books, and scoured my parents' *Daily Mail* for any photographs of cars or planes, which I would paste into a scrap book (often before Dad had read the newspaper, which didn't go down too well!).

As well as cars, I also loved buses, big lorries, farm vehicles, and aircraft. I received occasional letters from my pilot brother-in-law telling me of his exploits in Hong Kong including an incident when he skidded off the runway in his Gloster Meteor jet and ran over a wild pig, which emerged from the wreckage unscathed after five days! I was very excited on the 10th of March 1956, when

Mason's Motoring Mayhem!

Peter Twiss achieved a new world air speed record of 1132mph in his Fairey Delta jet plane. Needless to say, I wrote and congratulated him and received a nice letter in reply, which I have kept to this day. This was a prized possession indeed, and I took it to school, allowing specially approved fellow pupils to have a secret look at it.

There was still no sign of a car in the Mason household, so I spent a lot of time with friends whose parents had cars, including David Schofield. His father had a new Standard Vanguard that I used to wash every Saturday morning. Obviously his dad, Percy, thought he was on to a good thing here, and welcomed me into his house in Bolton-le-Sands at all times.

It was with the Schofield family that I made my first ever flight in an aeroplane. They were going to the then 'exotic' island of Jersey for two weeks' holiday, and asked my parents if I could accompany them. We flew from Blackpool Squires Gate airport in a Douglas DC3 Dakota of Lancashire Aircraft Corporation in August 1954, and, of course, I was mesmerised and instantly decided I should become a civil airline captain rather than a fighter pilot. During the holiday we also made a day trip to Dinard in France in a Jersey Airlines de Havilland Heron, where David and I were amazed to find French Dinky toys on sale – there were Simcas, Peugeots, and Citroëns, and Mr Schofield generously bought each of us the car of our choice.

We had a wonderful holiday. We hired bicycles and spent a lot of time at the Jersey Motor Transport bus station where the old Leylands and Dennis buses were turned around using a massive turntable that the drivers and conductors pushed by hand. Eventually we were assisting them in this chore.

The holiday was marred somewhat when David and I were attacked and bitten by an Alsatian dog, fell off our bicycles, and had to visit the Jersey Hospital outpatients' department. There was later a great kerfuffle when Mr Schofield, an astute businessman, attempted to sue the dog's owner, which, on reflection, possibly contributed to the holiday fund! I am still wary of Alsatians and other large dogs, incidentally, which might have been something of a handicap to another of my boyhood dreams – becoming a lion tamer.

Travelling circuses were a great part of my young life and an extra dimension of show business, which was never far from my dream careers. Huge lorries, each pulling two trailers, would travel the length and breadth of Britain throughout the year, and whenever they came to Lancaster or Morecambe I would be there watching the 'Big Top' being erected, seeing elephants pull the great poles into position. The sights and sounds of the circus fascinated me, and my parents would always take us to see the performances. The lights, the noise, the smell of the sawdust, the wild animals, the trapeze artists, and the clowns with their exploding car were beyond belief.

To see Chipperfields, Bertram Mills, or Billy Smart's circus on the move was a sight to behold. The huge convoy of dozens of trucks would take an hour to pass as the vehicles, containing wild animals and all the circus paraphernalia, trundled slowly along. Occasionally the elephants would be sent ahead by special railway trucks on goods trains, led in a procession through the town between the circus site and the station at both ends of their journey. One year, the next stop after Lancaster was Carlisle, which entailed the procession of lorries passing over Britain's most feared and difficult main road, Shap Fell in what is now Cumbria. A very good friend of mine in later life, Morecambe Car Club early member Bob Baxter, of Baxters' Morecambe Bay Potted Shrimps fame, recalled coming upon the back of this procession in his new sporty Jaguar. Bob had a colourful turn of phrase, and you can imagine his description of his plight in having to pass this lot in a hurry.

By now, you may think that my life was one long playtime. In fact, I was encouraged by my parents to do as well as possible at school and acquire other skills along the way. My parents used to play cards with friends, but I never enjoyed this activity, other than playing a game called 'Speed,' which featured cards bearing the photographs of cars, ships, trains and planes. I was given a small garden of my own within our garden, taught the rudiments of carpentry by my father, and, as mentioned earlier, encouraged to take up a musical instrument. I didn't really excel in any of the above, regrettably.

There was great excitement in Morecambe in 1959 when the local newspaper, *The Visitor*, revealed that a major film was to be made in the town. *The Entertainer* was written by John Osborne, and told the story of a struggling second-rate comic, played in the film by no less a star than Laurence Olivier. Extras were wanted, and would be paid £1 per day. Needless to say, I was onto this immediately and pedalled furiously on my bike to join a massive queue of people at the auditioning room at a church hall in Morecambe, later in the week.

After an entire afternoon spent queuing, I was miraculously selected along with many hundreds of others. Filming would take place a month later on Morecambe promenade, at the open-air swimming pool and in the Winter Gardens theatre. Stardom beckoned and I became very excited about this, but somewhat deflated when the film was finished and shown at the local Odeon some months later. The shots in which I appeared featured for milliseconds only and could be missed completely if one blinked! Nevertheless, my brief appearance was enough to enable me to 'dine out' on my far-from-starring role for many years. Let's face it, not many people can say they appeared in a film with the man widely acknowledged to be Britain's greatest actor of all time. Well, actually, a few thousand Morecambrians could say exactly the same thing, if they enjoyed name-dropping, like I do, I suppose.

I mentioned earlier that my mother used to take me to see the Monte Carlo rallies passing our road end. This became an annual occurrence each January, and, in later years, I went by myself to watch this magical procession. Also watching, along with a number of villagers, was Leslie Rigg, who, unknown to me, was a rally enthusiast and chairman of Morecambe Car Club. He gave me an expert commentary, telling me who was driving what. He obviously noted my great interest.

It was Leslie Rigg who really started my career in rallying when he invited me to join him and his wife, Marian, in their car to go marshalling on a local rally one Saturday night. I jumped at the chance, as you can imagine.

After a short drive from Bolton-le-Sands, we positioned ourselves on a lonely moorland road on the southern edge of the Lake District and waited for the rally cars to arrive, hopefully at one minute intervals. None arrived at the appointed time, but, some ten minutes later, all hell broke loose when two Triumph TR3s appeared at once. Both cars sported a battery of blinding lights on the front and they screeched to a halt with engines revving, while the navigator of the first car opened the door shouting "Give me 11.04!" Confusingly, the navigator in the second car opened his door and also shouted "11.04." It all seemed pretty chaotic to me but as Leslie was engaged with the first car I tried to attend to the shouting man in the second one. I leaned in, looking at the watch in the small sealed plastic case that was being offered for my attention. I thought the clock said 11.06, but because this shouting man insisted on 11.04 I wrote that on his timecard and signed my name on a rally document for the very first time.

This whole procedure would, of course, become very familiar to me in the future when I would be performing the role of navigator. The aim of all navigators is to stay on schedule or lose as little time as possible, hence the navigators 'shouting up' a time that had just preceded the actual minute shown on the watch. A minute or two later other cars arrived and were duly attended to by Leslie and, once or twice, by myself. I should mention that much more sophisticated methods of timing exist today, including computer chip-clocks, timing beams, and much more.

Although a bit flustered by my marshalling duties, I then experienced one of the magical moments that seem to occur in my life from time to time. The sight and sound of the rally cars thrilled me beyond belief but there was another ingredient to consider – an amazing odour. The smell of a hot, oily engine together with exhaust fumes and steaming mud (not to mention cow shit!) on the hot exhaust pipe was quite a cocktail! I inhaled this and knew instantly that I was hooked. It was like a drug – the 'rally smell'! At that moment I knew that I wanted to go rallying more than anything else in the world.

Although I was still at school, I became a member of Morecambe Car Club and really enjoyed attending its monthly meetings held at the Midland Hotel in Morecambe. I knew no-one except Leslie Rigg, and stood quietly at the back of the room watching films of continental rallies that the club had borrowed from Castrol or Shell. I would often have to leave early to catch the last bus home, which meant I seldom saw the end of the films. I must surely be the only car club member ever to travel by bus to meetings, as I had no car.

Morecambe had other connections with rallying, as one of Britain's well known annual national rallies finished in the town. Then, as now, rallies were graded into different categories, ranging from small club events up to full-blown internationals. The national series featured major events all over the country, many with various starting points before an easy 'run-in' section to converge on a common route. The Morecambe National, run by the Lancashire Automobile Club, was one such rally, and was always considered one of the toughest as it featured the demanding roads of the Lake District over which competitors had to average 30mph. This might not sound very much, but with all the twists, turns, and junctions only the very best drivers and navigators could get anywhere near this average. In fact many organisers 'tweaked' the time sections, making it necessary to go flat out for most of the night to be in with a chance of success.

In the fifties and sixties, clever organisers came up with various new timing systems and more intricate navigation requirements. The all-night rallies over public roads became virtual road-races, contravening all the rules and regulations laid down by the Royal Automobile Club who controlled all motorsport in Britain. There were, of course, far fewer cars on the roads in those days so rallying was not as dangerous as it sounds as the events took place in the night.

Most rallies also featured special speed tests on private land, and, in the case of the Morecambe National, some of these took place on the pedestrian promenade, which became a great spectator attraction as cars negotiated the course with much tyre-squealing and engine-revving.

I remember watching these tests, in particular the 1960 event, which was won by Anne Hall and Val Domleo in a maroon Ford Anglia. The Huddersfield housewife, as Anne was known, beat all the men at their own game. I became a great fan of hers and would eventually number her among my closest 'rally friends.'

In the mid-fifties I got to know Garry and Jean Helliwell, who had moved to the village from Southport. Garry was a dentist who had a great interest in cars, and I would spend a lot of time with them and their three young boys to whom I gave many of my Dinky model cars. Occasionally I would babysit for them, and on one occasion was invited to go with them on holiday to Abersoch, where I temporarily overcame my great fear of water and actually learnt to water ski.

Garry joined the Morecambe Car Club and my monthly bus trips to meetings became a thing of the past, for he kindly gave me a lift in his new Singer Gazelle, at first, followed by a succession of Volvos. He was a good friend, and gave me some early driving tuition in his cars on private land, long before I could legally drive.

The dreaded 'eleven plus' examination caused me to take life more seriously and I started to worry in case I failed it. My parents left me in no doubt that, should I fail it, my progress and success in life would be limited. I have always had a fear of failure, which has been prominent in my mind throughout my career in motorsport, business, and television. I think this has spurred me on.

I really did worry about my eleven plus, and it was probably the first major worry I ever had; I've had quite a few of one sort or another since then, I can tell you. Fortunately I passed the dreaded exam, and remember the elation in our household when the news arrived.

In 1953 I was duly kitted out in the uniform of the Lancaster Royal Grammar School, and set off from our house to the nearby bus stop for the first of my many daily journeys to the county town of Lancaster, and this great seat of learning. Fortunately I had three or four close friends from primary school starting with me, but I was surely entering a strange and different world. I was placed in the 'second' stream, indicating a reasonable eleven plus result, and embarked upon subjects that included French, Latin, biology, physics and chemistry, in addition to the usual ones like history, geography, and mathematics, as well as rugby, cricket, athletics, cross-country running, and lord knows what else. It was daunting to say the least.

Lancaster Royal Grammar School had a very good reputation, as it has now. It was a semi state-funded school under the control of governors, and had very high standards and strict discipline, not to mention corporal punishment. Boys not wearing their caps at the approved angle would be reprimanded, and the slightest misdemeanour would warrant a 'sheet' – that is, the instruction to write a part of the school rule book in good writing on two sides of a sheet of foolscap paper. These would be handed personally to the Headmaster after assembly the next day. Other punishments included detention after school for an hour, and a whacking from most masters using sticks, slippers, or whatever came to hand.

The standard of teaching was very high, as was sports instruction, with the school winning many rugby and cricket championships as well as other trophies at inter-school sports. We won't go into my sporting activities at school, if you don't mind, as I was pretty useless at such things. I never knew quite what to do in football at primary school, other than kick the ball in whatever direction my foot was pointing. At Grammar School I played rugby (very badly) and found it a very rough affair, being pummelled and sat on by sweaty bodies. Athletics had no chance as my legs were too short, so I was usually last in races, and if hurdles were involved I was in even more trouble as any miscalculation could really make my eyes water! Cross-country running required stamina that I seemed to have, but I wasted this possible opportunity of major success by hitching a lift on a tractor that happened to be on our route one day. Obviously I was found out, as some little sneak (who is probably now a much respected retired architect, accountant, or dentist, and a current Rotarian) reported me. I was whacked, of course, by the sports master, who I remember had a particularly nasty, smelly gym shoe. Cricket petrified me, as I once saw a boy hit on the head by a cricket ball and carted off to hospital. I won't mention swimming, of course, as I was still frightened of water after my Lake Windermere drama, although I have to compliment the school for actually teaching me how to swim. I remember an early school report from the sports master who said I had learnt to swim satisfactorily, but I had the style of a wildebeest migrating across a flooded African river. There were other sports at Lancaster Royal Grammar School, but I'm afraid I can't remember them. Of course, I never admitted any of the above when I later rubbed shoulders with numerous sporting greats at various functions, receptions, or at the studios of *A Question of Sport* (for which I wrote some of the motorsport questions).

I know school days are meant to be the happiest days of your life, but I cannot say they were for me. I achieved adequate results and enjoyed English, French, geography, biology and art, but I did not enjoy maths and went through school without understanding one iota of calculus or trigonometry. I really blame the same maths teacher I had for all my years at LRGS, as I posted the lowest marks ever recorded at the school in the mathematics GCE O-level. I think the five marks I got were for correctly putting my name at the top of the answer paper! My career could have gone in a much different direction had I been mathematically inclined, as I was interested in medicine and, of course, flying, both of which need some knowledge of the subject.

Many 'old boys' of Lancaster Royal Grammar School have gone onto great things, and I used to sit in the grand hall of the school looking up at the gold-lettered honours board recalling the success of past pupils. There were judges, cabinet ministers, surgeons by royal appointment, bishops, professors of this, that and the other, and chiefs of the armed services. I realised that the only way I would get my name on that board would be by becoming a sign writer.

Nevertheless, some years later, after my win of the RAC Rally of Great Britain and my television presenting activities, I was invited to speak at the LRGS Old Boys' reunion dinner, where I met many of my former masters who, in conversation, confirmed that my maths master was "bloody useless."

Apart from the academic side, there were other important activities at school including all those sports mentioned and the Combined Cadet Force. The CCF was optional, and thinking I might pursue my idea of becoming a pilot I 'signed up.' The purpose of the CCF was to give pre-military training, and it was run by masters who had all seen active service in World War II. My parents thought it would be good for discipline, and encouraged me to join.

I was duly accepted and measured for my army uniform and supplied with all the bits and pieces including large black boots. I brought all this clobber home and tried on everything for the benefit of my parents and other onlookers on our road, some of whom suppressed a giggle as I marched – sorry, clumped – up and down for the benefit of my parents and their Kodak Box Brownie camera. As I was approximately 4ft 5in tall at this point, it must have been an amusing sight indeed. All I know is that the rough, hairy khaki material was extremely heavy and uncomfortable, I could hardly lift my feet wearing the heavy boots, and I felt a bit daft in the black beret they had provided. I think it was a size too big and I felt like a French onion seller! When I travelled by bus to school on the CCF day each week I had to travel in uniform, and overheard quite a few remarks from the conductors and passengers on the buses. I may be wrong but I think I heard the comment "Make way for Little Hitler" from a bus conductor on one occasion. I felt somewhat embarrassed, as no other schoolboy using my bus route had joined the CCF.

Needless to say, I did not star in my mini military role. I found it difficult to keep up with the others when marching, and if I was on the back row of the platoon had to scurry and run to keep up. I once dropped my rifle, and as punishment had to hold it aloft and run up and down the hundreds of steps of the Ashton Memorial in a large park near the school. The Ashton Memorial is in memory of Lord Ashton of James Williamson & Sons, once Lancaster's biggest employer, manufacturing floor coverings including linoleum, known universally as 'lino.' After ten minutes of running up and down the steps of his Lordship's memorial I wished he'd never bothered inventing the bloody stuff. Younger readers may not know what I am talking about here, but linoleum was by far the most popular floor covering in the civilised world at that time. I do hope you are finding this book educational!

My greatest claim to fame in the CCF at Lancaster Royal Grammar School occurred in the rifle range, built on the edge of one of the sports fields of the school. We all had to lie on our stomachs and point guns towards the end of the hut and fire at various targets that magically appeared when Captain Melinsky (also a teacher of history and divinity) pulled a rope. I can't remember the details, but we had to load and eject bullets and reload and do everything when instructed. I didn't! Next thing I knew an extremely agitated Captain Melinsky was pulling me by my ear, apoplectic with rage. I had nearly killed him! I don't know whether I was asked to resign or was chucked out, court martialled, or whatever. I do know that this was the end of my military career.

I suspect that Mr Melinsky was not too enamoured with me before the rifle range incident, and he probably already thought of me as being a cheeky little twerp. Once, during a divinity lesson, he asked the pupils to state a difference between animals and humans. There was no response from the class, so he proudly announced "Animals can't pray, but humans can." To the slight amusement of the rest of the class I cheekily asked "What about the praying mantis?" I was rather pleased with my witty remark, but all it resulted in was an extremely accurately aimed piece of chalk which pinged onto my head and brought this particular bit of religious instruction to an abrupt end.

However, my interest in motoring continued during my time at Lancaster Royal Grammar School, and I may have learnt a lesson or two about driving. Not all the masters owned cars, but I remember our Latin master Mr Black had a

Ford Model Y, a prewar car. 'Jack' Black was a large ungainly man who, one late afternoon after school, could not start the Ford despite many turns of the crank handle at the front of the car. Again, younger readers may not understand this last bit, but don't worry.

As I may have mentioned, Lancaster Royal Grammar School was situated in East Road on the outskirts of Lancaster at the top of a great hill. It was always an ordeal, if one was late, to run up the hill, but it was no problem going down. Well, not for us pupils. However, it was a different matter for Jack Black who couldn't start his car, and so pushed it – with the help of one or two pupils – from the edge of the side road on which it was parked to the main road at the top of the hill.

Mr Black then stood on the running board on the side of the car, leaned through the open window to steer the car, which was obviously in neutral gear, planning to open the door and slide into the driver's seat and engage gear, at which point the engine would fire up and he would be off for his tea. Regrettably, things didn't work out like that! It appeared that the door of the Ford had locked itself, so the procession of school boys walking homewards down East Road were treated to the sight of a red-faced Jack Black, his black gown flowing, and his car gathering momentum down the road as he leaned through the window clutching the steering wheel and trying to get in through the locked door. He failed, and the Ford plummeted into one of the many trees on East Road, and unsurprisingly our Latin master fell off in a great steaming heap. Amazingly, Mr Black survived without injury, but it was a marvellous moment in my education which I was privileged to observe. It was Keystone Cops, Laurel and Hardy and Fred Karno's Circus all rolled into one, and tickled my rapidly developing sense of humour.

It was after that splendid incident that I made another major decision with regard to my career in motorsport. Lancaster Royal Grammar School was an all-boys school with a mix of boarders and day boys. I always had the feeling that we day boys were an inferior breed, but I expect that was my natural inferiority complex coming out. However, before and after school there would be huge processions of boys going to and from the Lancaster bus station for transport between various surrounding towns and villages.

It was a panic in the mornings, but after school it was a leisurely stroll through Lancaster city centre, often via Woolworths, to the bus station. There, one evening in 1959, I noticed the newspaper seller with his pile of Lancashire Evening Posts and his boards announcing: "LOCAL DRIVERS' MONTE CARLO RALLY SUCCESS."

My eyes focused on this, and I instantly forgot all the Latin, French and dreaded mathematics homework that I was about to start thinking about and discussing with other boys on the bus home. I found the one or two pennies required and purchased the newspaper. I then read of the success of two locally based Morecambe Car Club members, Bobby Parkes and Arthur Senior, who had driven their Jaguar to win their class, team award and take the 'Best British' trophy on the Monte Carlo Rally.

That was it! I was determined to similarly hit the newspaper headlines by getting to the top in rallying. Again, another of my 'Little did I know' moments, but I would eventually co-drive for both of these talented drivers after only a few years.

Five

Home and away

As I entered the sixth form at Lancaster Royal Grammar School I realised that I had to think seriously about a career. After various meetings with the careers master and mediocre O-level results, I realised that my dreams of becoming a pilot or anything medical had gone, and university was out of the question. Obviously, any form of entertaining was not a serious consideration as a 'proper job.' Nor was anything to do with radio or the embryonic world of television.

Art was one of my best subjects at school, along with English, geography and economics, and I had developed a keen interest in the world of advertising and marketing. I spent a lot of time creating advertisements for popular brands for my own enjoyment, and even subscribed to *Advertisers' Weekly* – a trade magazine for the profession. For one of my sections of the GCE O-level paper I designed and produced a poster featuring racing driver Stirling Moss recommending BP petrol. As a 13-year-old visiting the Aintree race track in Liverpool in 1954, I had collected Stirling's autograph, which I had obviously kept safe and sound, and I included it in my poster design, practising signing his autograph time and again for the benefit of accuracy.

Many, many years later when I entered the world of *Top Gear* I would, inevitably, meet Stirling Moss and interview him a number of times. We struck up a good rapport, and I now like to consider Stirling and his wonderful wife, Susie, as friends. Not long after they became Sir Stirling and Lady Moss I regaled them with my story of the BP poster for the art exam, and said I had practised his autograph in my design work as part of planning my career. "What career were you planning?" asked Susie. "Probably a forger, by the sound of it!" said the great man.

I had two boyhood heroes from 1958 onwards, but unlike most schoolboys of my era, these were not footballers, cricketers, or film stars. Stirling Moss obviously featured because of his enormous racing and rallying ability, and his high media profile. The other represented my interest in the world of show business, and was the irrepressible young comedian from Knotty Ash, Ken Dodd. I marvelled at his ability to communicate with his audience, having actually seen him on stage quite early in his career.

I first met Ken Dodd in 1964 when, for some unaccountable reason, he became a member of Preston's Longton and District Motor Club, and I was asked by the Club's leading light, Gavin Frew, if I would like to attend a function at the Odeon in Preston where Ken was presenting prizes. He was already a huge star by then, and was shepherded from his car into the Odeon by the largest and burliest members of the Motor Club, including top local driver Roy Mapple with whom

I was competing in rallying from time to time. I tagged along with his entourage, although I can't imagine I would have been much use at fending off the crowds as I was very small and puny in those days.

Ken stayed for some time after his presentation, and I had the chance to meet him briefly. I also met him again after various shows, including a memorable visit with my wife, Sue, and daughter Emma, who was six when Ken was appearing in pantomime. For such a big star he gave us so much time, and, of course, gave Emma the obligatory tickling stick. However, I got to know him much better when I entered the world of television with *Top Gear* as you will read later.

I still find it quite astonishing that today I should have a good relationship with my two main boyhood heroes, and it is another of my examples of dreams coming true which, you will find, are scattered throughout this mighty tome.

Away from these superstars I was having to buckle down to getting a job so sent letters to all the major companies in Lancaster and district. I was offered a sales office job at James Williamson and Sons, the manufacturers of floor linoleum, but was also offered a position as traffic clerk in a proper advertising agency as a result of the efforts of another person in the village of Bolton-le-Sands, John Thrower. He was also in the advertising profession, and he and his wife Pat were members of the Bolton-le-Sands Players, the amateur theatrical group that had given me minor parts in productions.

There was a problem, and I realised I was going to have to take a major step into the unknown; the advertising agency in question was in Liverpool. It was too far to travel daily, so 'digs' would have to be found, but more help was on its way from friends Garry and Jean Helliwell, mentioned earlier. I was offered lodgings in their home town of Southport, from where I could commute daily by train.

I joined SC Peacock Ltd, a leading provincial advertising agency and was offered the princely sum of £6 per week for my troubles. It was a dream job for me, and entailed keeping records and checking progress of all new jobs for the clients, which included several then-popular brands like Royal Lemon Meringue Pie, Richmond Pork Sausages, Meccano, Red Heart Dog Food, and numerous major local retailers and car distributors. I was in constant contact with all the staff in the company, as well as all the consumer and trade press and the new independent TV companies. I really loved every minute, and, I believe, became a popular member of staff, congratulated by the bosses on my great attention to detail. There were also several nice young girls in the agency who seemed to enjoy my company, but regrettably none of them lived in Southport, so relationships did not develop any further than mild flirting during the day. When filming *The Race of Champions* in 1995 for BBC in Gran Canaria, I bumped into a lovely lady in our hotel who introduced herself and her husband. It was Glenda Charnley (her former surname) who had sat at the next desk to mine some thirty-five years before at S C Peacock. She still looked as attractive as before, and she and her husband and I had a pleasant evening reminiscing. Glenda said she could not believe I had achieved such a high profile TV career, as I was such a shy boy. I wouldn't kiss her at the Christmas party, she said. I must have been a fool.

One of S C Peacock's clients was NEMS Record Store in Liverpool, owned and run by Brian Epstein. You may remember that Mr Epstein achieved a much greater claim to fame, for in 1961 he met and subsequently signed up to manage four youths appearing as a band at the nearby Cavern Club. I am now about to indulge in another bit of name-dropping for, one morning, I was asked to visit Mr Epstein at NEMS, carrying out some menial task like delivering artwork, and who should be in his office but the then relatively unknown Beatles. Pleasantries were briefly exchanged before I was ushered out, but they did show slight interest in my appearance there and in the parcel I was delivering. It's a pity I didn't get them to sign the receipt for delivering the parcel. It would be worth a few quid now, I reckon.

Each Friday evening I would leave the agency and take a train from Liverpool's Exchange station north to Lancaster and home for the weekend for much bike-riding and catching up with friends, including members of Morecambe Car Club. I was put in touch with one member by the name of Arnold Roberts, a farmer from Garstang. He wanted a navigator for an evening rally in which he had entered his Triumph Herald Coupé. You're ahead of me now, but this was another major happening in my life; I was about to compete in my first ever rally.

I was introduced to 'my driver,' and some weeks later was transported by my mentor, Leslie Rigg, to a large transport cafe in Garstang for the 6.00pm start of the 'Mild and Bitter' Rally. I was, of course, excited but somewhat apprehensive. However, I was armed with the appropriate Ordnance Survey map, a number of 2B pencils, and a 'Romer,' which is a simple device to enable you to plot map references for all of the points you have to visit. I had previously read several books on how to compete in rallying, so I had a clip board, a map board, and a clock in a plastic case, just like those that baffled me on my first rally marshalling expedition some months before.

I plotted all the map references, and we lined up among the forty or so cars. I had marked the route we should take on the map using my 2B pencil (with a rubber on the end, of course) and when the start marshal had signed my route card and entered our precise time of departure, we set forth along the old A6 road. Within a few miles we were looking for a minor 'yellow' road. I was quickly picking up the terminology and jargon, and knew that navigators describe the colour of the roads on the map: red, brown, yellow, or white. I also knew that 'white' roads could be surfaced or rough and muddy and should be avoided unless instructed to use them. In fact, as I would learn, a good navigator will build up a huge knowledge of 'goers' and 'non-goers,' and mark these white roads appropriately on the map.

Despite one or two hesitations at junctions my new friend Arnold and I were proceeding satisfactorily. The car was bumping around the lanes near the Trough of Bowland, along a few muddy tracks, and I began to smell the marvellous magical odour that had captivated me on my first marshalling expedition. You remember? Mud and farm yard effluent on a hot exhaust.

Things suddenly started to go awry, however. I felt a bit queasy because of constantly altering my field of vision, looking at the map one minute then looking at the road ahead. In addition to this my driver was puffing at a strongly smelling pipe and the inevitable happened. I asked that we should stop immediately, and opened the door to vomit. Arnold was very understanding, and obligingly stopped a few miles further on for a repeat performance. For navigators, travel sickness is an occupational hazard, I'm afraid. However, nearly everyone overcomes the problem the more experienced they become.

We continued on our merry way, and observed lots of cars going the opposite way to us or approaching from side roads, or, horror of horrors, approaching a control from the wrong direction, incurring a big penalty. Three hours after our start time we arrived at the finish at a pub, where timecards were handed in so results could be calculated. We then sat, waited, and mixed with other competitors who, in those pre-breathalyser days, were enjoying a few beers. After my earlier nausea I refrained from drinking alcohol, but I would certainly make up for this omission on future evening events after I had overcome my travel sickness problem. As another aside, when I had graduated to full night rallies it was not unknown for bars and hotels to be opened after breakfast, and the odd foaming pint consumed whilst waiting for results.

The results of the Mild and Bitter Rally were eventually announced, and a large scorecard stuck on the wall that showed we had placed second in the novice section and had made few serious mistakes, apart from the inevitable delays caused by my 'mal de rallye.' My first rally had been a relative success, and I was congratulated by one or two senior Morecambe Car Club members who identified me as the boy who came by bus to stand at the back of meetings.

I wouldn't say drivers were clamouring for my services, but over subsequent months I had further trips of a similar length and won the novice class on one, despite more travel sickness. Soon I was a so-called 'expert,' and invited to accompany one of Morecambe Car Club's top drivers, Bill Willicombe in his Austin-Healey 'frog-eye' Sprite. Small trophies were now being won, and I was working hard at my rallying, preparing maps and talking to other navigators about map reading. In fact, I was starting to eat, sleep and breath 'rallying' and discovered *Motoring News*, a weekly newspaper that covered motorsport in detail including many rallies both large and small. I was fascinated by this marvellous publication and achieved a new ambition – to get my name in *Motoring News*.

Thanks to my avid reading of *Motoring News*, as well as any rally books I could lay my hands on, I realised that I would need to have all the right equipment for map reading if I was to succeed. I knew about maps, clipboards, average speed tables, and other bits and pieces, but it was to the lighting department that I turned my attention.

All rally cars are fitted with a 'flexy' light, dangling from the inside top corner of the roof, which is vital for plotting map references and fiddling about with other paperwork. This is the driver's responsibility, of course, but the navigator has to provide more illumination in the shape of a map-magnifier. I found to my bafflement these came in a variety of designs, so I sought advice from those in the know and learnt that an 'Eolite' was considered the bee's knees. It had a powerful magnifying lens and a rheostat, which enabled the user to vary the brightness of the light bulb by twiddling a little knob on the top. The whole thing was about the size of a large coffee mug. There was only one problem: Eolites had been manufactured for use by RAF navigators during the war, so they were very scarce indeed.

I searched army surplus stores and junk shops to no avail, before hitting on the bright idea of advertising for one in my now beloved *Motoring News*. The small classified advertisement appeared in due course but, sod's law, there was a typographical error in the advert. The 'o' had been omitted, so I received details of Lotus Elites! The advertisement was rectified, and I then received just one reply, so I sent off a cheque for a couple of quid. When it arrived I felt like a proper navigator.

As Eolites became scarcer, one or two other contraptions were introduced. One was called the 'poti' which became the generic name for such devices, but, far and away, the best one to appear was the Don Barrow light. Multi-championship winning navigator Don gave a lot of thought to designing his plastic moulded product. It had changeable base plates with varying map scales, and a handle (which the others hadn't), and became very popular. Don still manufactures these lights, selling them along with other navigational device like 'Romers' for plotting map references, but, as I also later designed such a device, I'm not going to publicise his!

Fully equipped with all the appropriate navigational clobber, I was now fully prepared to compete in rallying. I was so keen to succeed that I practised plotting map references incessantly, and even took my Eolite magnifier to bed to get used to reading maps in the dark. Yes, I know it sounds a bit sad, but it's a fact. All in all, life was good and I was enjoying my new-found hobby.

My enjoyment was short-lived, however, when my mother was admitted to Blackpool Victoria Hospital to undergo a minor heart operation. It was considered a fairly straightforward procedure by the family doctor and hospital surgeon, but sadly there were complications and Mum did not recover well. She had a type of stroke, partly losing her speech and the full use of her leg and arm on one side.

My father, brother, and I visited her in Blackpool as often as possible but with great difficulty, as my father worked in Kendal, I worked in Liverpool, and Stuart "was on his way to Oxford University." It was a very unhappy time for all of us and we all knew that Mum would be an invalid for the rest of her life. She returned home with a lot of medication and recovered slightly over the next year, but never lived life to the full again.

Six

The beginnings of mayhem

Back on the rallying front, things were progressing well. I was asked by the top local female driver, Pauline Reddy, to navigate for her on a major new all-night rally taking place in the north-west on the 5th November 1961. The Kirkby Lonsdale Motor Club's Devil's Own Rally would feature quite difficult navigation, and a 200-mile road section around the lanes east of Lancaster and on into the Trough of Bowland.

I was obviously on good form that night, and coped with all the navigational demands admirably. Pauline was a superb driver, and had the added advantage of knowing all the lanes we were traversing, as her job involved visiting all the farms in the area, testing milk. The night was wet and foggy, which didn't please all the people having Guy Fawkes' night bonfires, but we were happy and seemed to have a good rapport. This is, of course, an essential part of rallying – the driver and co-driver/navigator must like and respect each other in order to succeed. After a full night of difficult rallying, I was pleased to find that Pauline and I won the event by eleven minutes from the next car. It was my first big win, and naturally I was elated.

However, there is another little twist to the story; I mentioned earlier that one of my ambitions was to get my name in *Motoring News*. I had, therefore, precociously telephoned *Motoring News* and asked to speak to the rallies editor. I advised him of the forthcoming Devil's Own Rally and asked if he would accept an article from me. The rallies editor at the time was one John Brown, a former Oxford student and a brilliant rally navigator and organiser. Thankfully, he had heard of me (very vaguely, I suspect) and commissioned the article on the Devil's Own Rally for the princely sum of £1-15s.0d. For the benefit of any younger readers of this book (if there are any!), I am talking about pre-decimal currency, but I think you'll get the point that I was being paid peanuts.

Fate had played its hand again; my first-ever article in *Motoring News* was to feature my name in the opening paragraph in heavy print. I duly wrote the article, posted the hand-written words to *Motoring News,* and it appeared in print. I offered to write articles on many other northern events, including local Morecambe Car Club rallies, and was accepted as a correspondent. This had two enormous benefits: I could ensure my own name appeared in *Motoring News* (usually in the first couple of paragraphs!) and I could also approach and converse with all the other competitors (including well-known names like John Sprinzel, David Seigle-Morris, Pat Moss, Reg McBride, Don Barrow, Phil Simister, Graham Robson, and others) to solicit their views on the previous night's rally.

John Brown went on to organise some of the best rallies in Britain. He won the RAC Rally of Great Britain in 1961 alongside one of the greatest rally drivers of all time, Sweden's Erik Carlsson. We've had a lot of contact over the years, and I value John's friendship which all started with that innocent phone call in 1961. To be honest, John has, for many years, been encouraging me to write this book, so now you have someone to blame when you take it down to the Oxfam shop.

Away from rallying, I was progressing well in my job in Liverpool and studying hard for qualifications in advertising and marketing, attending evening classes in the famous Royal Liver Building. Now aged seventeen, I decided to take driving lessons and signed up with the British School of Motoring in Southport, taking six lessons in quick succession. It was a good place to take the test as there were lots of wide streets but no hills, other than a railway bridge near the station. I passed the test driving a Hillman Minx, and can still vividly remember that the examiner wore a blue mackintosh that smelt of vinegar.

On the job front great progress was being made, and I was 'head-hunted,' to use modern terminology. I was offered a job in the marketing department of a much larger advertising agency in Manchester. Osborne-Peacock had no association with S C Peacock in Liverpool, although there had been in the distant past, apparently. I would be working on lots of major accounts including Cussons Imperial Leather soap, 1001 cleaner, Vosene shampoo, Vimto, Currys and Great Universal Stores. It was an exciting time with new products being developed all the time, and I was part of a very busy department, making many new friends.

I arranged digs in Timperley, near Altrincham, and commuted to Manchester by train. I remember my Scottish landlady who provided my breakfast and evening meal, and I also remember sitting in the freezing lounge with her, watching the new programme *Coronation Street* on the small black and white television. The lady had purchased a new electric fire with two bars that were never turned on as she was convinced that the flickering red bulb under the artificial coal was emanating heat! As she was protected by several layers of shawls and woollen half-gloves, she could not see the necessity of any more heat. I would often go to bed early to keep warm.

Among the staff at Osborne-Peacock was a former fellow Lancaster Royal Grammar School pupil, Mike Harrison, who was employed as a copywriter. We enjoyed each others company and very soon decided to leave our respective lodgings to share a flat in the Chorlton-cum-Hardy district of Manchester, which made life much more enjoyable.

My interest in rallying continued apace, and I was competing as a navigator a great deal as we entered the sixties. Road rallies took place all over Britain, and I started to venture further afield than my native north-west Lancashire. Many of the toughest rallies took place in Wales and were demanding in every sense. The roads were hilly and twisty and the maps difficult to read, so it was a true test of the ability of the crews. It was a steep learning curve for me, as practically all my rallying had taken place in the north-west, where I had built up a good knowledge of the roads and become very proficient as a navigator, winning local events and, indeed, taking the Morecambe Car Club navigators' championship (the first of many). I also won the drivers' championship as well, once, but I'd better not sound too much of a clever Dick!

Among the very best crews in British rallying were a number from the Manchester area, and I began to get to know them as I competed in the most competitive road rallies as part of the *Motoring News* Rally championship. Still living and working in Manchester, I was able to meet many of them at meetings of the successful Knowldale and Cavendish Car Clubs. I also discovered that the leading lights of the Cavendish Club would meet up for a drink at the Brocklehurst Arms in Macclesfield on a Thursday evening, to discuss the following weekend's rally.

I was welcomed to these little get-togethers, and felt very privileged to be among such notable drivers as Reg McBride, Phil Simister, and Frank Grange, and the quite brilliant navigator Don Barrow, who would win the *Motoring News* championship four times as well as the RAC Rally championship. I got to know all these people well, and Don and I remain good friends to this day.

Back on the work front, I was continuing to study for my exams and making good progress in the Manchester advertising agency. Osborne-Peacock moved from an old-fashioned building in Piccadilly to new offices in Television House where Granada TV also had offices. Many evenings, some of us would go to a bar beneath the building for an early evening drink after work. These were sociable occasions, and I can remember one of the older executives telling us about his wartime experiences in the RAF when he had been an orderly on a small transport plane flying to North Africa. The plane had a special compartment with a bunk bed in it, which on one occasion contained Winston Churchill, no less. Churchill stayed in the bunk the whole trip and summoned the orderly by ringing a bell. He popped his head out of the curtains and growled the very few words "I want some soup, I want it hot, and I want it now!" before briskly closing the curtains. These were the only words uttered by Churchill to my colleague on the entire trip. Another occasional attender at these little soirées was a young actor called William Roach who had recently joined the cast of the new Coronation Street where he remains to this day.

My interest in cars and all motoring matters was increasing, and I was entrusted with the marketing director's new Ford Anglia, which I drove as much as I could, travelling all over the north-west on market research projects. Life was marvellous as I honed my driving skills, but I was a little too exuberant at times and the inevitable happened. I entered the underground car park of Television House far too quickly on one occasion and scraped the entire side of the car on a concrete pillar. The boss was livid, as one might imagine, and I was reprimanded in no small way.

My next driving incident was even more extreme and embarrassing. I had been allocated the new 'pool car,' another Ford Anglia, for a full week. I made the most of this by racing back to north Lancashire to marshal on a local rally one evening, and practicising rally techniques around Derbyshire on another night. I had new freedom, so took a girl out one evening to demonstrate my prowess behind the wheel. There was a sprinkling of snow and it was quite icy, but I managed to return the young lady safely to her home in Cheshire before returning through the lanes towards our Manchester flat. I misjudged a fast bend on a bleak moorland road and 'lost' the rear of the car. I over-corrected with the steering wheel, and the car spun wildly in the darkness before sliding backwards into a rock face, severely modifying the rear of the Anglia. Thankfully the car was drivable, so I gingerly drove home with my tail between my legs. I didn't sleep that night, worrying that I might lose my job.

Facing the marketing director next morning was not a pleasant prospect, but I made sure I was at work early, long before any of my colleagues would arrive as I did not want them witnessing my downfall.

My reputation as a budding rally driver was in tatters and the boss man was incandescent with rage. He marched round his office, arms flailing, and called me a bloody hooligan. He said I was a pathetic driver to have had two crashes in two months, and marched me off to the car park to inspect the damaged car, which I'd craftily reversed into a dark corner so no-one would see it. He marched around the car, fuming, and said "This will cost a bloody fortune to repair – you'll have to pay for it!"

I didn't enjoy our walk back up to the offices, and not a word was said by either of us. I returned to my own office very sheepishly while the boss stormed off to see the managing director. Things were getting serious. I braced myself for his return and sure enough, he reappeared and said "You're bloody lucky mate, we're going to dock your wage by £50 and you'd better go out to find a panel beater for a quote."

It was the beginning of the sixties, and as I now had a driving licence I needed some wheels, so I foolishly took up the offer of a friend in my home village of Bolton-le-Sands and bought his Norton 500 motorbike. I don't know why I did it because I had never had the slightest interest in bikes. It was a speedy machine, and I soon discovered that I was not cut out for this sort of thing when I crashed through a hedge and into a field near my village. I was not injured badly, but a bit bruised here and there. I soon disposed of the bike, and didn't sit on another one until I filmed the Isle of Man TT races some forty years later. I was meant to close the *Top Gear* programme by saying a few words before riding off into the setting sun as pillion to the TT winner Phillip McCallen. So petrified am I of motorbikes that it was agreed I would dismount after saying goodnight to the viewers, and another person of similar stature (yes, there was someone out there, can you believe?) would be put into my jacket and helmet, and filmed screaming along the road. Never believe everything you see on television!

I had swapped my dreaded Norton 500 for a prewar MG PA that had steering problems, and I frightened myself to death driving around the villages of north-west Lancashire. I was not a good mechanic, but tinkered with the car alongside a friend who lived down the road, and knew more about engines than I did. I kept the MG for about three months before selling it to the friend who enjoyed the mechanics bit. I then purchased a red 848cc Morris Mini from the chairman of the Morecambe Car Club, Colin Briars. I paid £360 for 588 GRM, which, incidentally, is exactly the amount paid recently to my dentist for two fillings. How things have changed.

John Baxter, the friend who bought my MG, seemed to accumulate various cars, and informed me that he had acquired a Bond Mini. For the benefit of those who are not familiar with such things, I should tell you that this was probably the cheapest car on the road, with one wheel at the front and two at the back. It had a canvas roof, a short bench seat for two, and a Villiers motorbike engine attached to the front wheel.

There was a problem: the Bond had broken down on the road by the shore at Bolton-le-Sands. John had walked home and persuaded his father to let him borrow his Armstrong Siddeley to tow home the three-wheeler. I was appointed as driver of the Bond Mini. We went down to the Bond with a long tow rope, and set forth along the mile-long and very straight Pasture Lane, which led from the shore back towards the village.

The big Armstrong Siddeley was soon in full flight. John was driving very quickly and the little Bond was rattling along behind, although it was a very low car and close to the ground so he could not see it in his mirrors or through his back window. There was a right-handed bend at the end of the mile-long straight and I dread to think what speed we were doing. The little Bond was literally bouncing along, the front of the car lifting in the air, not unlike a world record-breaking power boat on a lake. I was beginning to think there could be some problems as I had little control over what was going on.

As we approached the bend I attempted to turn the steering wheel but nothing happened. The single front steering wheel was only in contact with the road intermittently and I had absolutely no chance of following the big Armstrong Siddeley round the bend. I went straight on, up a bank and demolished a line of fencing as I continued to be towed at a high speed, still being attached to the towing car.

For the first time in my life (but certainly not the last) I experienced the sensation of turning over. It was quite dramatic as the windscreen and canvas top were demolished with glass flying everywhere. I had to crouch down (or was it up?) to be lower than the dashboard, otherwise I would have been decapitated. My friend in front continued at great speed, unabated and unaware of my predicament. The Bond was now being towed while being upside down with me doing everything to stay unharmed inside. There was enormous noise as the long fence continued to be turned into matchwood with bits flying in all directions. It really was frightening, and I feared for my life.

A road junction thankfully appeared so the Armstrong Siddeley stopped and, at last, John looked out of the car and saw this upside down clump of metal on the end of his tow rope. The Bond three-wheeler was a light car so he managed to put it the right way up without assistance and I emerged with relatively few cuts and bruises.

There is an even more frightening aspect to all this, as the 50 yards of fencing that we had demolished was at the side of the main West Coast railway line, and, had the tow rope become disconnected, I would inevitably have been catapulted onto the busy railway track itself with unimaginable consequences. My motoring career was certainly becoming incident-packed at this early stage, but this would not be the last time I turned over in a three-wheeler as viewers of the Reliant Robin world championship, shown on *Top Gear*, may remember. More of that later.

Seven

Back on home territory

The so-called 'swinging sixties' were hectic, exciting and enjoyable for me, as they were for most people in their twenties. My years away from home to work in Liverpool and Manchester had widened my circle of friends and provided a bigger world to investigate but most of my activities still centred on the north-western area in which I was born and to which I would return every weekend, if only to depart for some rally in another part of the country.

I exchanged my little red 848cc Mini for my first Mini-Cooper, and eventually a much more powerful Cooper S. I drove the cars incessantly and became more and more proficient at handling the rapid front-wheel drive car, scurrying around the north Lancashire and Lakeland lanes as quickly as possible, mastering the car's handling on all surfaces. Late at night I would drive over well known bits of road, occasionally coming unstuck by skidding through a hedge, or, on one or more occasions, parking it on its side on a bank. Amazingly severe damage was avoided, although I inflicted damage on myself when I hit a bank, pushing the front corner of the wing onto the tyre. I decided the best way to pull the metalwork off the tyre was to fasten a strong tow rope between the front wing and a sturdy wooden gatepost, or what I thought was a sturdy wooden gatepost! I then put the Cooper S in reverse, revved the engine, and let in the clutch in order to 'jerk' the wing off the tyre. Well that was the theory, anyway. What actually happened was that the gatepost broke in half and the bit attached to my rope zoomed up in the air and crashed through my windscreen! On another occasion I became stuck in a snowdrift and had to stay there, sleeping in my car, until a farmer rescued me at six in the morning.

Looking back I must have had a fixation with motorsport and driving. I was reminded of this many years later when I met one or two former girlfriends at the Morecambe Car Club 50th anniversary dinner where I was guest speaker. It was nice to meet them, of course, and brought back happy memories, but they reminded me that my idea of a good night out was to select a pub in the Lake District, the furthest distance from home, then race flat-out to and from it, causing them to feel quite queazy for most of the evening. On return, any amorous intentions of mine disappeared out of the window.

We had quite a good social life and a group of us would regularly meet-up at the Cross Keys in Slyne, the Redwell at Arkholme or the Fenwick Arms in Claughton, all in the countryside north of Lancaster, and we would charge from one pub to the other, usually with a bit of a race to get there before closing time, which was 10.30pm in those days. I still see some of our troupe, particularly Bruce Murgatroyd, Graham and Mary Payne, David Alderson, and Dave Rayner, and we shudder when recalling the various minor incidents that befell us during our travels.

By far the most spectacular of our misdemeanours concerned Frank Shepherd and Ron Turner, who one wet night were returning home in their Mini, no doubt at substantial speed, when it lost grip on a wet narrow lane alongside the Lancaster Canal. The car bounced through a hedge before plunging dramatically into the canal's murky waters, becoming fully submerged. The hapless pair were extremely lucky and rapidly extricated themselves, leaving the Mini in its watery grave with headlights still blazing and orange indicator lights flashing. They sheepishly walked home, planning to return next morning to sort out matters but during the night were alerted by the Police as they received a call from a somewhat inebriated man, on his way home from the pub on foot, who reported seeing a submarine in the canal!

I became much more involved in Morecambe Car Club and was appointed to the committee, eventually taking on the role of secretary before reaching the dizzy heights of chairman. I started to organise small auto-test meetings, and introduced guest speakers at the monthly meetings at the Midland Hotel, the first being works Triumph rally driver Roy Fidler, who I would get to know very well in later years.

In 1963, while still working in Manchester, I offered to organise Morecambe Car Club's major rally, the Illuminations, which usually attracted over a hundred entries from all over the north and even further afield. Almost single-handedly organising a 200-mile rally, with all the paperwork involved, as well as contacting the police and other authorities, was a huge assignment, and, looking back, I don't know how I did it. I had to plot the route in detail using my own knowledge, explore new roads in the Lake District, then to publicise the event and produce the regulations to be sent to prospective entrants.

Even then it was a monumental task to organise a full-night rally (now it is even harder) but I took on this mighty task despite having no car for most of the time, living in far-away Manchester during the week, and having no telephone at my parents' house where I lived at weekends. I really can't see how I managed to do it, but I was lucky to have support from various members of the Morecambe Car Club who helped when called upon. It took a good eight months to get everything organised, but when the 30th November came round and I stood in the foyer of the Midland Hotel looking at 100 rally cars parked on the nearby promenade and 200 competitors milling about in the hotel prior to the 10.00pm start, I really did wonder if I'd bitten off more than I could chew. After all, I was still only 22 years of age.

The Illuminations Rally itself was extremely demanding, and possibly a little bit too difficult for some crews, but there were no complaints from competitors and the whole thing went very well with few problems, and a lot of very tired crews arriving back in Morecambe on Sunday morning.

To say I was relieved was an understatement, and I basked in the glory poured upon me by the senior members of the club including the chairman, one Leslie Rigg, the man who introduced me to rallying. I've always been something of a worrier and, despite the general euphoria, realised that there was something else to worry about: the rally would be reported in the nationally circulated *Motoring News* and *Autosport* magazines. Would they be critical of the event, which was far too demanding in reality? Only two crews managed to get round the route without incurring a 'fail' for being more than 30 minutes late. This was practically unheard of.

The following Thursday I scurried off to purchase my copy of *Motoring News* and held my breath. There was a long report describing the route, detailing everyone's problems, and congratulating Reg McBride and Don Barrow in their Ford Anglia for winning by losing only 53 minutes of time. *Only* 53 minutes! Reg and Don later told me that it was one of the hardest 'thrashes' they had ever done! And they should know, as they went on to become multiple *Motoring News* championship winners, and were generally regarded as the best road rally crew of all time, with wins the length and breadth of Britain. The *Motoring News* report hailed the rally as "A great success and a first-class event with slippery, muddy and treacherous roads galore."

However, there was another worry on the horizon! The next day would see the respected *Autosport* magazine on the newspaper stands. I knew that the report would have been written by the much feared Graham Robson, a top class rally navigator with a great rally pedigree, having been competition manager of the Triumph rally team among other things. He knew more about rallying than I would ever know, and being a very forthright person, never minced his words. Not least among my worries was the fact that Graham, navigating Phil Simister's Ford Cortina GT, had most unusually 'wrong-slotted' on the maze of little roads near Staveley, north of Kendal. They lost no less than 17 minutes in time because of this, a rare occurrence for the talented crew.

Incredibly, Graham Robson's report was very complimentary about my route and referred to my "comprehensive local knowledge and great organisational ability." He mentioned all the competitors' unanimous praise for my efforts and said what a good chap I was. Praise, indeed, from the man who went on to become Britain's most prolific motoring author.

My Illuminations Rally should have taken place in August of that year, but the minister of transport, Ernest Marples, introduced a national speed limit of 50mph on all roads in England and Wales (other than motorways and those with a permanent speed limit) for five peak holiday weekends. The idea was to reduce accidents and the RAC duly imposed a 25mph maximum average speed for rallies, making it impossible to run a competitive road rally. The August Illuminations Rally had, therefore, to be cancelled, but every cloud has a silver lining: I was quoted in a *Daily Mail* article headed "Marples puts the brakes on Britain's rally drivers." It was the first time I had hit the nationals.

Speaking of press reports, I should mention that I was now reporting many events for *Motoring News*. After competing in an all-night rally I would return home, often not until Sunday afternoon, look at my scribbled notes, and duly write a lengthy report in longhand on foolscap paper. This would then be posted to the *Motoring News* office in London. Royal Mail was a different animal to the one we now know and don't love, as there were Sunday collections, and letters would almost certainly be delivered the next day. However, to guarantee my reports reaching London first thing next morning, I came up with a cunning plan, as they say.

A super-safe method of guaranteeing my article arriving at the *Motoring News* offices in the first post (thus ensuring I got a prominent position in the newspaper) was to put an extra pre-decimal half-penny stamp on the envelope and take it to Lancaster Castle station before 8.00pm. At that precise time the long and brightly lit Royal Mail train would arrive from Glasgow, en route to London, and would stop at the platform in Lancaster for just two minutes whilst post from a local sorting office was hurriedly loaded onto the train. Much more post would previously have been collected in sacks from metal gantries alongside the track by large hooks protruding from the side of the train as it sped by.

I would scurry down the platform and put my envelope, bearing its extra half-penny stamp, in a post box on the side of the train before the great English Electric Diesel engine would roar into life and haul its carriages full of mail-sorting postmen to the south. Looking back, the whole mail-train performance was quite remarkable, very reliable, and ultra-efficient. It was an amazingly advanced system, but it all went wrong one night, the 8th August 1963, when the train was stopped at 3 o'clock in the morning at Sears Crossing between Leighton Buzzard and Cheddington on the Bedfordshire/Buckinghamshire border, and the Great Train Robbery took place. Many people think that this audacious crime was committed purely for the millions of pounds of cash on the train, but it might not have been. There was something else the robbers wanted to get their hands on!

Needless to say, my 2000 word report never arrived at its destination as it had been carted off with the rest of the booty. I still wonder if the robbers knew my finely-crafted words were on board the train, nestling among the many millions of used £5 notes.

I was very annoyed that my hard work had been in vain, and even more annoyed that my payment from *Motoring News* of £2-17s-6d (£2.87p to you) would never be paid! Some forty years later I passed through Brazil on my way to Rally Argentina and seriously considered calling on fugitive Ronnie Biggs, one of the great train robbers, who happened to live there, to see if he still had my article or, at least, could give me my £2-17s-6d!

In the mid-sixties I knew I had to progress in advertising, and applied to various agencies in London. I was offered a few positions and decided upon a job as media buyer at Napper, Stinton & Woolley, doubling my salary to over £1000 per year. I had mixed feelings about leaving the north, but realised I had to make a move. I resigned as chairman of Morecambe Car Club, said my fond farewells to friends and relatives, and prepared to 'do a Dick Whittington' and go to make my fortune in London. Underneath, I felt a little apprehensive, and I tried only to think of the good things that might develop. I still had twinges, and wondered if I was doing the right thing.

For some years I had been rallying with Bob Lamb, an appropriately-named local butcher who owned a number of shops in Lancaster and had a successful business supplying hotels and restaurants in Morecambe and the Lake District. Very occasionally I would help Bob out on a Saturday so he could be sure to get away to rallies in which we were competing, and I knew quite a lot about his business.

I would often take deliveries in one of his vans, and remember an incident in a minivan in which I was transporting large trays of that peculiar northern delicacy, tripe. For those not familiar with such products, tripe is the lining of a cow's stomach, and has a very slippery consistency. I was hurrying, of course, and worrying about being late for our rally so no doubt going quicker than I should have been. Suddenly the traffic lights changed and I slammed on the brakes of the little minivan. There was an enormous clatter, and the tin trays of tripe slid forward on the shiny wooden floor of the back of the van, ramming into the rear of the front seats. The slimy white tripe was ejected from the tin trays and flew in the air. Bits of it hit my head and dangled from my ears, other bits dangled from the interior driving mirror, and half a hundredweight of the stuff descended into the footwell, most of it wrapped around the foot pedals and my feet! It was a real mess.

I didn't report this little incident to Bob, as he would have insisted on destroying or at least rewashing the tripe, which would have delayed our departure for the rally. I hastily scooped up the slippery tripe and attempted to refill the various tin trays, wiping off as much dust and fluff as I could, hoping no-one would notice.

Whilst on the subject of Bob's minivan, I should mention that he and I actually competed on an evening rally in it. Yes, really! We were due to compete in his Sunbeam Rapier, but it was in the local Pye Motors' garage being prepared for a bigger event, so we took the minivan and actually won. He had thoughtfully removed the tin trays and sausages that, one hour before, had been dangling from hooks in the back.

Bob Lamb and another successful butcher had decided to expand their businesses by investigating the then unheard-of market of pre-packed meat. They even considered producing pre-packed cooked dishes like cottage pie and other similar items. Out of the blue, Bob asked me if I would like to join his company to develop this exciting new market which could, of course, lead to much greater things. This was a great dilemma for me and I didn't know what to say. I thought about the pros and cons for a couple of days and solicited the views of one or two friends, and eventually decided to take a risk and get involved in the new project. I then wrote a letter to the London advertising agency to say I wasn't joining them, and felt a great weight being lifted from my shoulders. I will never know whether I did the right thing or not but often wonder what might have been. I think about it often as a walk down a supermarket aisle looking at all the thousands of ready meals now on display! In fact, it was quite a struggle to establish our products and to gain distribution, although I persevered for a few years. In my heart of hearts I probably realised it had not been a great career move, and had probably been influenced by the fact that I could continue rallying. But this, of course, would lead to greater things eventually.

As a navigator I was quite successful, and had certainly built up a great knowledge of the northern roads, so I began to move away from the area more and more, concentrating on *Motoring News* events, mostly in Wales. Odd trips to Scotland, Derbyshire, and even Devon were included in my itinerary. I was regularly asked to navigate for Bill Willicombe, Bob Lamb, and Roy Mapple, with occasional rides with other north-western drivers including Tony Payne, Roy Kirkham, Leo Jemson, Bobby Parkes, Colin Briars, Les Cowan and his son David, a remarkably quick driver aged just 17. We had successes galore, and my collection of silverware started to increase. My outings further afield included trips with Frank Grange of the famed Cavendish Car Club, mentioned earlier, and other drivers including Chris Knowles-Fitton, Mike Bowyer, John Francis, Norman Harvey, David Friswell, Bobby Parkes and George Beever.

Considering the number of rallies in which I was competing I escaped relatively unscathed in terms of incidents. Obviously there were the odd off-road excursions incurring body-panel damage and occasional bruises and scratches.

Gated roads were used a great deal in those days and I was a master gate-opener. I practised opening gates quickly, and on rallies would be assisted by my drivers who would tell me which side of the gate had the handle and which way it opened.

On more than one occasion I slipped and fell into deep Lakeland ditches full of water, once managed to catch the back bumper of a Sunbeam Rapier as I slammed a gate shut (thus holding up all following competitors, much to their chagrin), and on another occasion closed a metal gate in front of a heavily braking Ford Anglia that was following us as the leading car. As the Anglia stopped, all four of its spotlights protruded through the spaces between the bars of the gate. The car then settled back on its suspension and the driver realised it could go neither forwards or backwards. I won this rally by thirteen minutes, but didn't stay around at the finish as I do not think I would have been very popular.

During the very early seventies the M6 motorway was extended north from Carnforth to Penrith, and the route cut through our prime rallying country. This presented extra problems for navigators who, if they had any sense, would traverse the area on a Saturday afternoon and makes notes on their maps before nightfall as small lanes would suddenly disappear in a sea of mud before continuing on the other side of the motorway foundations, prior to a bridge being built. On occasions new bridges would have been built and we would use them, although I remember flying across a newly built bridge with David Cowan in his Mini-Cooper only to find there was a three-foot drop at the other side. It was like a scene from *The Italian Job* as we flew gracefully through the air.

Competing with Tony Payne in his Hillman Imp one night we had a similar incident when we had to cross a dual carriageway that was being constructed near Kendal. The levels of the two carriageways differed considerably, and we drove onto the grass in between the two to discover a practically vertical five-foot drop down which we slithered in the darkness. We survived to go on and win the event, the Garstang Rally, despite our little drama.

I was involved in a much more spectacular crash one night whilst navigating for Mike Bowyer in his Ford Cortina on a Welsh *Motoring News* Rally. As ever, the steep and narrow lanes were covered in wet leaves and mud, which was not the perfect surface for road adhesion. At high speed Mike 'lost' the Cortina, and the rear end slid into a bank, propelling us towards the opposite bank which pitched us into the air, rolling several times. There was a lot of noise, broken glass everywhere, and the roof of the car was flattened as the car rolled over and over. More importantly for me, my precious Ordnance Survey map had fallen from my hands and was dragged along the road, shredding it.

It is a strange thing but, as anyone who has been involved in any similar incident will tell you, everything goes into slow motion as the accident develops. I saw the roof come down and lowered myself slightly in the seat as the car slid down the steep hill, upside down. Suddenly there were no more noises of metal scraping on the tarmac, and Mike and I struggled out of the car. It was dark and we had lost all the lights and couldn't even find a torch. However, a following rally car soon appeared and the combined efforts of this crew and other following crews manhandled the remains of our Cortina to a wider bit of road. These following crews then ensured we were not injured before going on their merry way. I cannot remember what happened next, but a breakdown truck eventually appeared, and we were transported to the midnight petrol halt of the rally where we made phone calls galore. Remember, there were no mobile phones in those far-off times.

A more amusing incident occurred in another Welsh lane during the hours of darkness. Among the most popular cars in rallying in the sixties were Mini-Coopers, as they were nimble, speedy and small, and felt really at home in narrow lanes. One of the best Mini drivers was Roy Mapple, who hailed from the Blackpool area. He was a very quick and talented driver and experienced few major incidents, but miscalculated a tightening right-hand bend and understeered into a narrow ditch. I was navigating for Bob Lamb in another Mini-Cooper S and came upon the ditched Mini with Roy and navigator Jeff Smith trying to lift the car out. We stopped and Bob joined the other two, whilst I had the bright idea of warning following cars who would soon be arriving at the blind bend. I therefore opened the driver's door of the beached Mini and stood on the door sill, pointing the movable roof light towards the entrance of the bend, assuming this would slow the cars down. Within seconds, yet another Mini screamed into the corner; the driver, Cec Offley, braked heavily and put the car into a spin, the rear of his car coming perilously close to clobbering the Mapple Mini. In fact, he was only inches from it; so close that the rear bumper of Offley's Mini literally ripped the back off my shoes as I stood on the door sill. I was half an inch away from serious injury. The other participants in this drama, Mapple, Smith and Lamb, ran in all directions, but the excitement wasn't over yet, for Offley's Mini then hit the open door of Mapple's orange Mini, and said door shot into the air literally flying over the top of the rapidly retreating Bob Lamb. Mapple eventually collected the door and threw it on the back seat of the Mini-Cooper, then drove for the rest of the night with the crew very nearly freezing to death. Looking back, it is one of the most hilarious rally incidents I've ever been involved in, but could have been considerably worse for all concerned.

Road rallying was accepted by most country dwellers, and they were all aware of the passage of any event as clubs meticulously carried out PR work beforehand. Most farmers were amenable to up to 120 cars passing along tracks over their land and, occasionally, driving between the buildings in their farmyards. This was not the case on the Coventry-based Godiva Rally in the early sixties, when a farmer took a great dislike to a number of cars that 'wrong slotted' into his Welsh farmyard instead of joining a nearby muddy track. I remember it well, as I was navigating for John Francis of Cheltenham in his 1071cc Cooper S, a car in which we had recently won the Hunter's Moon Rally in Gloucestershire.

As we entered the yard we saw one or two people hovering about and a closed gate ahead of us. I was about to disembark to open the gate when a very irate farmer in a brown smock ran towards me and hit my half-open door with a long-handled woodman's axe. I could see the metal glinting as it sliced through the door, only inches from my knee. "Turn around!" I shouted to John, who executed a speedy reverse spin to exit from whence we came. To our horror we saw that the exit gate had been shut by various members of the mad farmer's family, who started to attack us by throwing a huge bucket of dirty water at our screen, followed by the mad axe-man lopping off one of our spotlights!

Amazingly, for no apparent reason the assembled gathering realised they had had their fun with us so opened the gate to let us out and wait, presumably, for another victim to appear.

Mason's Motoring Mayhem!

There was great camaraderie between competitors in these evening and night rallies, and all participants were amateurs and remarkably good sports who would help each other if required. The drivers would always lend parts or tools to other drivers, if necessary, but the navigators tended to be more guarded about passing information to their rivals and would jealously protect their maps, seldom letting other navigators have sight of them, as they contained valuable information about the state of roads and tracks.

There was one great exception to the above. One of the very best northern navigators, Bob Redhead from Barrow-in-Furness and I became close personal friends, and our friendship extended to comparing the routes we had plotted on our maps before the start of each event. We would each have our own bits of local knowledge and willingly impart this to the other party. Bob and I were considered by other competitors as bitter rivals, and they were right, for when the rally started we would fight for supremacy in a fair but competitive way. It has to be said, however, that much of the silverware went in our direction.

Bob and I joined forces to organise the Illuminations Rally for a number of years, and were proud to elevate it to the status of one of Britain's best rallies, becoming a part of the *Motoring News* championship and winning the coveted Ecurie Cod Fillet trophy a few years later, when Fred Bent and Stephen Bye were at the helm.

This little incident with Peter Clarke changed my life.

Sideways as usual! Roger Clark's speciality.

Good training for my future TV work.
Wrap up well!

Just think! If things had turned out
differently, I could have won the
Grand National.

Mason the artist, aged 11. My passion for rallying started with my award-
winning painting.

Watch out Lord Olivier! I'm 'the boy' (second left) in Dickens' *A Christmas Carol.*

It's the way I tell 'em! A dreadful stand-up comic in Morecambe.

My first little Mini had a hard life.

Water, water everywhere! My Mini-Cooper S at home in the Lake District.

My first navigators' championship win. Driver Bob Lamb is next to me, then club chairman Leslie Rigg, and the Mayor and Mayoress of Morecambe, no less.

With Bill Willlicombe in his Austin-Healey Sprite, and more water.

We'll take the high road! Bill and I would soon get completely lost in the
middle of Glasgow.

Not a gypsy encampment, but the start of a Lakeland forest stage on my first RAC Rally in 1962.

With Bob Lamb in his Humber Sceptre, starting a rally in Yorkshire.

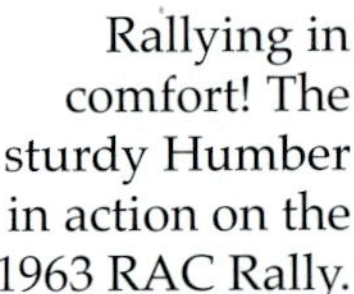

Rallying in comfort! The sturdy Humber in action on the 1963 RAC Rally.

With Phil Simister in his Cortina on the 1964 RAC Rally.

Just for a change! A road section shot of Bob Lamb and me on the 1965 RAC Rally.

Road rallying with David Cowan in 1968. Please note that the dented front wing had nothing to do with my navigation.

The closed roads of the Circuit of Ireland were a new experience for Tom Beaumont and me in the Volvo PV 544 in 1968.

An appearance on stage with Britain's tallest man, Christopher Greener. I'm on the right!

Club rallies also had special stages. Here I am in Bob Lamb's Cortina on the Filldyke Rally.

Roy Mapple and I had an action-packed RAC Rally in 1966. This is one of our
more peaceful moments.

Our first international class win. With Bob Lamb on the 1968 Scottish
Rally.

Young David Cowan driving carefully in his dad's new Escort RS on the Welsh Rally.

Fellow Morecambe Car Club member Mike Preston and I went to watch the Targa Florio in Sicily in 1971. This is the first sighting of a Mason cap.

Some glamour at last! Racing driver Gillian Fortescue-Thomas tried her hand at rallying.

With Peter Clarke on the British championship Mintex Seven Dales in Yorkshire
in 1971.

A year later and my first trip with
Roger Clark in a works Escort on
the 1972 Seven Dales.

Guess what? We won!

An unusually bleak bit of Scotland. This is Peter Clarke and me in 1972 on the
Scottish Rally.

Mud, mud, glorious mud. The first
stage of the 1972 RAC Rally with
Roger Clark.

Flat out in the Yorkshire forests on the
1972 RAC Rally with Roger.

I double-checked every bit of paperwork as we held our lead on the RAC Rally.

Service areas are a little more organised these days. In 1972 they were bedlam.

Leaving a stage on the 1972 RAC. I haven't had time to remove my helmet.

The spoils of victory. We never saw these trophies again – they went to the RAC Club in London.

At last! After our last-minute dramas we finally made it to York and won.

Ford's publicity machine went into overdrive, with huge posters in the windows of every Ford dealer.

Every new Ford sold had this sticker in the back window.

Prints of this Robin Owen painting were very popular, even appearing as jigsaw puzzles.

Every national newspaper carried this full-page advertisement.

Even my employer, K Shoes, got in on the act.

Oops! HRH Prince Michael of Kent overdid it on the Seven Dales Rally in 1973. You'll notice I was first out!

Eight

It's shoe business!

One of the biggest employers in the Lake District in the sixties and seventies was K Shoes Ltd. The company was started by Somervell Brothers in 1842 and, over the years, had grown to become one of Britain's leading shoe manufacturers. The K brand was very well known, and was, at the time, the only single-letter product name in the world. A short pause here, while you try to think of another one and prove me wrong!

One evening, while perusing the local newspaper, I noticed a job advertised at K Shoes which seemed just up my street, for the company wanted an executive to work in its busy advertising department at its factory in Kendal. I applied and, after interviews and short-listing, I was given the job, sharing an office with assistant advertising manager Chris Stott.

It was good to be back in advertising, and the advertising manager encouraged me to complete my studies, giving me quite a lot of assistance. I soon passed the last of nine papers and was duly appointed a member of the Communication, Advertising and Marketing Foundation. That final paper was one of the most difficult – advertising law. It was necessary to be factual and not waffle (my speciality, as you may have noticed), and I thought I stood little chance as one was expected to quote dates of obscure court cases, concerning suspicious products and bogus advertising claims. I passed this paper with flying colours after a lot of guessing, and my pass surprised me, quite frankly. Mind you, I did notice that another candidate called Mason failed this one paper abysmally. I bet he had a shock when the results were announced.

Shortly after joining K Shoes I was sent off to learn about the footwear industry as part of a training scheme operated by this very professionally run company. I was despatched to spend time in different departments in the factories, travel with representatives on their rounds, and was even sent off to work as an assistant in the company's own K Shoe Shops for several weeks. I really hated this latter experience and spent most of the time in the London shops where I remember kneeling on the floor in a servile way before a variety of customers, within inches of their smelly hot feet, before climbing ladders to obtain further pairs of shoes, most of which would be rejected after being tried on! The only bright spot in this rather mundane few weeks of my life was when comedian Tommy Cooper entered the shop looking for a pair of size 14 shoes. He tried on a few and then proceeded to stride about the shop trying them out which, of course, had all the other shoppers in stitches. He didn't buy any.

There were two K Shoe Shops in Oxford Street in London's West End, and once I was asked by the manager to take 20 pairs of shoes from one to the other. The approved manner of transporting boxes of shoes is to pass a single thick strap around them and carry one bundle in each hand. All was well on my little expedition along the very busy street until I was required to cross the road. There were not as many pedestrian crossings around in those days, so I had to take my life in my hands and dart among the passing taxis and buses, clutching my straps full of shoes in my little hands. I reached the safe haven of a traffic island in the centre of the road, regained my breath, and set off for the next sprint among the traffic.

I do not know why, but halfway through my manoeuvre one of the straps loosened and ten boxes of shoes fell onto the road. Needless to say, all the shoes fell out of their nice grey boxes and scattered all over, the shoe box lids and tissue paper packing material blowing about among the traffic and pedestrians. It was mayhem, but eventually a kindly bus driver stopped, allowing me to gather up all my merchandise and try to repack everything prior to presenting myself to the company's most senior manager at 324 Oxford Street, pretending nothing had happened.

Apart from the above minor incident, I really liked the work and the people at K Shoes, and collaborated on projects with the advertising manager, Brian Hufton. He and I would often travel in his Hillman Hunter, and I was offered to take the wheel a lot. It transpired that Brian was a nervous passenger but obviously approved of my driving, which was, of course, a little more tempered than when in my Mini-Cooper S. It would be fair to say that Brian enjoyed good food and drink, and we travelled the length and breadth of Britain to put on fashion shows and promotions demonstrating footwear. I certainly learnt to find my way around menus and wine lists, if nothing else!

The K Shoe shows were held in all major cities around the UK in large hotels or small theatres, and we would often be accompanied by a number of models for several days, staying overnight and enjoying the facilities of top class hotels. For a young red-blooded unattached male in his late twenties, these little outings certainly had their attractions, as you might imagine.

It was not only shoe business but also show business for me, as I took to the stage with the lovely models to demonstrate new amazing waterproof suede 'Aqua Skip' shoes. They were revolutionary, and I would demonstrate their stain-proof qualities by pouring all sorts of household products, including Ribena, gravy, Worcestershire sauce, cooking oil and even hydrochloric acid over the shoes. I introduced a bit of 'patter,' of course, which amused the audience and, more importantly, some of the girls.

Each year K Shoes held an important three day event for all its major customers, mostly independent shoe shop proprietors and buyers from major stores. It was a lavish affair featuring several major attractions, including, on more than one occasion, the band of Her Majesty's Royal Marines. The tallest man in Britain, Christopher Greener, appeared in one show wearing specially made size 20 K shoes. I went on stage with him, barely coming up to his waist. We made an odd couple for sure! There was music, lights, and effects, and the whole function was held on the upper floors of the prestigious Café Royal in Regent Street, London.

I was asked to perform my K Aqua Skip demonstration, and as I had by then been appointed sales promotion manager, I became involved in all aspects of the shows. This included ensuring that the shallow trays on each catwalk were adequately filled with water, through which models would paddle in their suede Aqua Skips to the music of *Singing in the Rain*. Are you beginning to wonder where on earth this 'motorsportish' biography is going? Don't worry. It gets better!

At the end of each day I would affix a long hosepipe to a fire hydrant and slowly refill the trays. Until one evening, that is, when most of the participants had departed. I attached one end of the hosepipe to the fire hydrant, and unwound it from the reel affixed to the wall on the top-floor landing. I pulled it to the farthest point, but it may have been a pull too far, as there was a clank and whooshing sound from the landing, and a certain lack of water emerging from my pipe. On return, I found a huge torrent of high pressure water jetting out of the hydrant horizontally. I rushed towards it to try and turn it off, but the jet hit me mid-chest and propelled me across the landing. It was like something from a Norman Wisdom film as I tried to reach the hydrant and was jetted away again. I was eventually joined by another colleague who, when he had finished laughing, turned off the hydrant. By now the torrent had soaked the expensively carpeted landing and stairs of the Café Royal on two floors and, of course, Café Royal staff appeared, one of whom summoned the fire brigade, whose engine sped down Regent Street with blue lights flashing.

I feared for my job, but the K Shoes and Café Royal hierarchy took a very charitable view and considered it an accident. Thankfully, they never asked which handle I had pulled down. There were two brass handles close together: one was marked 'Lock on hose-pipe,' the other 'Release hose pipe.'

Apart from the above, I had some great memories of this part of my life, and enjoyed organising sales conferences in various Lakeland hotels (and sampling all the facilities prior to booking), and on one occasion taking photographs of K Shoes displays in every shoe shop between Lands End and John O'Groats. There was a bit of drama associated with my visit to a small market town in Devon, where the local shoe retailer was next door to a branch of Barclays Bank. It was early evening and my flashing photographic bulbs were noticed by some local worthy, who notified the police that a young man was taking photographs of the bank. More flashing blue lights!

Among the staff in the advertising department at K Shoes was a talented artist by the name of John Watton. He was a gracious, family-loving person who edited the K Shoes magazine, *The Eyelet*. I was fascinated to learn that he had been imprisoned in Colditz Castle for some years during the war (which, itself, indicated that he was a brave man, having been recaptured after escaping from another prisoner-of-war camp). I have since seen his name mentioned in books about Colditz, and it appears he was involved in preparing passports, uniform buttons, and other items for escapees. He never talked about his experiences, although I persuaded him to give a short talk at the local Carnforth and District Round Table, which I had joined, along with fellow local rallymen Jim Pye and Tony Payne. All John talked about were the lavatorial habits of the different nationalities of prisoners!

Although it may sound as though my work at K Shoes consisted of gallivanting all over the country, I should mention that I was at my desk in Kendal many days, enjoying my journey to and from the town in my Mini-Cooper S, and having the occasional bar snack and drink at lunchtimes in a local country pub with colleagues or, occasionally, with one of the many unattached secretaries that worked in the same building. Our department produced all the K Shoes catalogues and other material, much of which was printed by Kendal's local newspaper, *The Westmorland Gazette*. On one occasion I was invited into the print manager's office and noticed a grey-haired man slouched in the corner puffing his pipe, whilst I discussed our printing requirements with Harry Firth, the manager. At the end of our very short meeting Harry introduced me to his other visitor, Alfred Wainwright, the celebrated fell-walker whose best-selling books were all printed by *The Westmorland Gazette*.

Through the haze of blue smoke I had a little chat with Mr Wainwright, and asked how much work went into preparing the copy for his popular books, which consisted entirely of reproductions of his hand-written manuscripts and his illustrations. He said something along the lines of "if a job's worth doing, it's worth doing properly," and said he felt there was not enough attention to detail from most people today. I suspect Mr Wainwright could be very grumpy and suddenly got the impression that he had had enough of me and I had outstayed my welcome. Anyway, we shook hands and I received a sort of smoky smile. I am glad I met one of the Lake District's legends, and often thought of him as I rallied at break-neck speeds over famous passes close to his favourite places that he described so well in his genteel way.

Not content with my enjoyable K Shoes work and my regular rallying and other motorsport activities at weekends, I then embarked on yet another project – to take to the stage again. An amateur band known as the Syd Patterson Concept occasionally played at various sales conferences and shows for K Shoes, and the splendid Mr Patterson (a Kendal chiropodist by day) informed me that he had agreed to perform nightly at the Broadway Starlight Room in nearby Morecambe for a summer season. He had seen my performances at the K Shoes events and asked me if I would be interested in compèring and doing a bit of comedy there. Of course I said "yes."

Morecambe's reputation as a popular holiday resort was on the wane by the late sixties, and the Broadway Starlight Room was not the most salubrious of venues, I have to tell you. In fact, it was as far away from the famous New York Broadway as you could get. Nevertheless, I turned up and met the other acts and Syd told me what he wanted. One of the acts was a very good young comedian who was a local schoolmaster by day – his stage name was Jim Bowen, and he went on to become a top comedian and famous face on the ITV series *Bullseye* and other programmes. We got on well and after the shows would often go for a Chinese meal together with some of the other performers, but all of us realised that we were not pulling in the crowds (not that there were such big crowds in Morecambe to pull in, anyway).

There were various guest artists at the Broadway from time to time, but by and large the whole season was a struggle, and I remember one wet evening when there were just eight people in the audience! I reckon half of them had only come in to keep out of the rain while waiting for a bus! Although I did have further small 'gigs' to do (one of which was at a strip club), I began to realise that if I must go on the stage, rally stages were less scary!

Whilst I did not know the Lake District as well as Alfred Wainwright, who I mentioned earlier, I certainly knew all the roads and tracks and managed to get round them a lot quicker than he did. There were regular evening rallies as part of the Morecambe Bay championship, with events organised by the Furness and District, Westmorland, Kirkby Lonsdale, and Morecambe Car Clubs, and I managed to win all of them at one time or another. Many full night events also came to the area, including the Jeans Gold Cup from Liverpool Motor Club, the Bolton Midnight, the Keswick, the Preston, the Garstang, and further north the Hadrian (which actually included a section along the famous wall), and in the west the Derwent Rally, which I won with Peter Clarke in an Escort, narrowly beating a very young Malcolm Wilson who was navigating for Keith Thomas in a Ford Cortina Mk2. It was a club stage rally, and Peter and I could be accused of 'pot-hunting' but we were using it as a shakedown prior to competing in the RAC Rally a couple of weeks later. Malcolm, of course, went on to great things as a driver in British and World rallies, and for the last 12 years has run the entire Ford World Rally Team from his huge and magnificent headquarters in his native Cockermouth. He never forgets the fact I beat him on that rally, or that I appeared as guest speaker at his local motor club dinner dance at the Moota Motel, with one of the first of my many, many after-dinner appearances. The act did eventually get better, Malcolm.

Nine

Memory lanes

You must remember that in the sixties, about which people of my age speak so fondly, there were few 'proper jobs' in motorsport. Rallying, in particular, to which mast I was undoubtedly pinning my colours, had even fewer people employed professionally. There were team managers at most of the big British motor manufacturers (who often did other jobs as well) and mechanics who, again, often did other work between rallies. There were motoring journalists, of course, but few who specialised in rallying matters, and there were some other people with enviable jobs, working for oil, tyre, brake, and plug companies, whose main purpose was to dispense cheap or free products to rally teams and a few favoured amateur drivers. Again, they would combine this with similar activities in racing whilst working in a department generally concerned with marketing – itself a new word in business vocabulary.

All of this meant that I had little thought of being employed in rallying as a job. It was purely a hobby, and one in which I managed to find an inexpensive way of participating. Although I struggled and scrimped and saved to buy a car, and eventually competed in minor events as a driver, I soon cottoned on to the fact that the cheapest way into the sport was to buy an Ordnance Survey map and a pencil! Duly equipped, I continued on my path, becoming more proficient in the map-reading department and offering my services to anybody and everybody who would take me along in their rally car. I have already mentioned many of my escapades with my cronies in Morecambe Car Club, and these incident-packed outings continued, although I was travelling further afield as well.

One such outing was with Bill Willicombe in his Austin-Healey Sprite. He invited me to accompany him on the Scottish Sporting Car Club's Highland Rally at Easter in 1962. This event had a great history, a three-day affair beginning in Glasgow before moving to the Highlands. The rally consisted of road sections, defined by what seemed like thousands of map references, and complicated navigation problems featuring spot heights, which were very difficult to make out among the hundreds of brown contour lines that abound on maps of mountainous regions. There were further barmy instructions featuring 'herringbone' designs, intended to show you which roads to ignore in order to find the right route. As you have probably surmised by now, I hated every minute of my navigational work on this event, which was only relieved when intermittent 'driving tests' on private land, hill climbs, and even forest stages took place. If you feel you would like to learn more about navigational trickery, don't ask me, please!

I probably should have found out more about the Highland Rally beforehand by reading one of several specialist books that teach you how to cope with such horrors. Of course, I could have said no to Bill's invitation, but I was keen to expand my rallying repertoire and enter my first 'foreign' rally.

My Scottish adventure didn't begin in the most salubrious way, and in fact, looking back it was probably a pretty disastrous and embarrassing start. As it was a major Scottish sporting event, the obligatory Scottish piper piped, Scottish saltire flags were waved, and we descended from the start ramp to travel down Sauchiehall Street or some such thoroughfare. Within seconds I was completely confused, and couldn't make the route instructions marry up with the cobbled streets that then existed in Glasgow. It was all very confusing to a young lad from Morecambe who had never, ever, started a rally in a big city before. In fact, I'm not sure I'd ever been north of the border to Scotland.

In panic I asked Bill to pull over to the kerb while I asked a local person to tell me the way to the east of the city. "Follow that tram," I was told (yes, they actually had old-fashioned, clanking trams in those days!). Now, can you imagine a sporty, spotlighted Sprite – the pride and joy of its driver – proceeding at approximately 10 miles per hour behind a clattering tram that stopped every now and again to disgorge passengers? I could feel Bill's temper rising. It rose even more when the dreaded tram, having disposed of all its passengers, then turned left into a tram depot and we were lost again.

I now feel very sorry for poor Bill who was much older than me – probably old enough to be my father, in fact. He didn't explode, but I could tell he wasn't too pleased, and there was a bit of an atmosphere in the car, to say the least. Unfortunately there's worse to come, so stick with it.

By the second day things had settled down somewhat, but the odd mistake was being made, including our visit to the same control near Stirling not once, not twice, but three times. There was a maze of farm tracks that all looked the same and we should, of course, have only visited the control point once. The marshals found it hilarious, and I could see steam rising from Bill's red face on our third visit. I got out of the car to hand the timecard to the marshal (an unnecessary act, in itself, as he would only record another 'fail' on it), when I suddenly heard a revving engine, wheels spinning on gravel, and my rally car had disappeared without me. Bill had had enough!

This is the first and, thankfully, only time this ever happened to me (or, for that matter, probably anybody else), but it was a shock. Bill, who admitted to having a 'short fuse' and some problems with his nerves as a result of being a Japanese prisoner of war towards the end of the war, could be excused. He soon returned and apologised. We both saw the funny side of it and pressed on with the rally, eventually finishing half way down the results. I never competed in the Highland Rally again. Are you surprised?

Although I avoided the Highland like the plague, I did enjoy other rallying visits to Scotland, and became very friendly with lots of rally folk north of the border. More adventurous drivers like Tom Paton, Jimmy McInnes, and Andrew Cowan (who went on to reach dizzying heights when he won the London–Sydney Marathon in 1968) used to make occasional forays south to compete in major English events. Bob Lamb and I reciprocated, taking his lumbering Humber Sceptre up to Kilmarnock for a night rally (on which we came second) and back up to the dreaded Glasgow where we entered the four day Scottish International

Rally in a Cortina, then an Escort. We won our class in the 1300cc Escort, I recall, but were then demoted for some piffling technical homologation matter.

I won't get into matters of this sort for I find them difficult to understand, being far too technical for me, but I know that we had not cheated. The car was totally legal, and some over-zealous, pompous far-too-full-of-his-own-importance scrutineer was wrong. All rally competitors have had a similar experience, I am sure, but it still leaves a sour taste in my mouth after all this time.

Come to think of it, I had another similarly unsavoury experience in Scotland that I shall tell you about; but please, don't think I've anything against the Scots, who are fine people with far more than their fair share of motorsport glitterati (just think Jim Clark, Jackie Stewart, Innes Ireland, David Coulthard, Allan McNish, Andrew Cowan, Jimmy, Colin, and Alister McRae, Louise Aitken-Walker, Dario Franchitti et al). In 1971, I co-drove for Peter Clarke (yes, he of Woburn Lake fame) in his Escort on the Snowman Rally in faraway Inverness-shire. We won, if I remember rightly, but there was a bit of a commotion when we were demoted because of some inaccuracy in navigation instructions, or in the application of a timing penalty ... I can't remember. Anyway, quite wrongly, we were demoted and we were livid. We protested, but it was chucked out by the stewards. We were really pissed off.

On returning home to our safe havens south of Hadrians Wall, I fired off a letter to my beloved *Motoring News,* disputing the organisers' decision and putting forward the facts as I saw them. Unbeknown to me, I was not far from being brought into the Ford fold and to having a close involvement with the works team. I very nearly blotted my copybook, for I received a curt telephone call from Stuart Turner, no less, the Ford motorsport boss. He said it was not the done thing to bleat to the newspapers, looking for sympathy. I never, ever wrote another letter to any publication.

Prior to the above little incident, I was embarking on a lot of motorsport activity in the sixties at club level and on bigger events, with a wider collection of drivers. Regular northern rallies were my favourites, and never an event went by without me being offered a ride. I navigated for Roy Kirkham, a daring driver from Blackpool who had a history of fairly spectacular incidents, including a major smash in Holland's Tulip Rally in which he was badly injured when his Sprite left the road in the French Alps. He gained another claim to fame when he rolled another Sprite on the tortuous Hardknott Pass in the Lake District, from the edge of one hairpin down to the next one 20 feet below. He regained the road, minus windscreen and other bits and pieces, but continued merrily on, losing less than half a minute in time! He always drove on the limit, and usually won if he stayed on the road. I navigated for him a couple of times. We won once, and were winning another all-night event in the Lake District when I failed to notify him of a sharp right-hand bend on the moors of Lowick in the southern Lakeland fells. We were within sight of the finish when we sailed off the edge of the road and into a great bog below. I can honestly promise you that this was the only bend I failed to notify Roy about during 200 miles of very precise map reading. I felt a real twazzock, I can tell you!

Very sadly, Roy Kirkham lost his life in 1969 when his speedboat hit something at high speed whilst crossing Morecambe Bay after a lunchtime visit to the Ship Inn on Piel Island, near Barrow-in-Furness. On board were two of his great friends and fellow car club members, Leo Jemson and Jeff Rostron, who also lost their lives. I had navigated on rallies for all three of them during the previous few months, and felt very saddened.

On a happier note, Hardknott and Wrynose passes continued to entertain us almost weekly, and will always be remembered as one of the finest and most difficult rally sections in the world. Whilst not having the distances or height of the famous Italian and French mountain passes, these twisty Lakeland roads were a major challenge and really sorted the men from the boys (and in some cases the women from the boys, eg Pat Moss and Anne Hall). Usually four minutes would be allowed for the Wrynose pass, just east of Ambleside, then six or so along Wrynose bottom before Hardknott, for which another four minutes would be allocated. Hardknott was the most difficult with numerous steep, tight hairpin bends, one of which has a gradient of one-in-three, allegedly the steepest in Europe. Many are those who misjudged the distances – usually in misty low cloud or snow – and slid over the edge.

As a change from my own never-ending list of off-road excursions, I would like to mention a rare incident concerning probably the finest Lakeland-based rally crew of Frank Davies and Bob Redhead. Frank was a talented mountaineer, owning the well-known Climbers' Shop in Ambleside, but could 'pedal' a rally car with equal skill. I know, as I once co-drove for him in his Mini-Cooper S on the RAC in 1968, but we ended up on the end of a tow rope after a mechanical failure, so I won't go into that any further! I will say it was a hell of a long tow back from the Welsh Dovey Forest to the Lake District, and when we arrived at an M6 motorway junction on our way home, we suffered the indignity of the tow rope breaking in front of a huge number of spectators who had gathered at the roundabout to watch the rally cars. Needless to say, they cheered and jeered with great gusto.

Back to the Hardknott and Wrynose passes – Davies made a rare mistake on Wrynose, leaving his braking fractionally too late at the top of the 2000ft high pass. Ever so gracefully the Cooper S dropped its two front wheels over the bank side. Bob Redhead, unused to such activity, clambered out of the car and tried to push it upwards and back onto the track – obviously an impossible task for one person. Roy Mapple and I then arrived on the scene, and, as we were in the same team, offered assistance. While Bob and I huffed and puffed and slithered about to no avail, the mighty Mapple manoeuvred himself under the front of the sump guard and 'shouldered' the car back onto the road while Frank quickly gained grip and showered us all with mud. It really was the most amazing show of strength I ever saw in my entire rallying career, which has often featured visits to ditches where superhuman strength suddenly presents itself.

In an earlier chapter I mentioned seeing headlines in the local newspapers about a Monte Carlo Rally success by a local driver, Bobby Parkes. It was about this time in the early sixties that I answered the door of my parents' house in Bolton-le-Sands to see an immaculately dressed gentleman wearing an expensive-looking dark overcoat and a trilby hat. I thought he was selling insurance or, worse still, might be a bailiff. "Hello Tony," he said, "My name's Parkes, I think you know of me. I'm sorry we've never been introduced before now, but I travel away a lot and don't usually attend Morecambe Car Club meetings. I know you are becoming well-known as a good rally navigator, so would you possibly be available to navigate for me on some selected British rallies? I will pay for everything, and I've just bought a rally-prepared Cortina GT."

I think I spluttered "Oh, yes that will be very nice, I'd like to come with you." This resulted in five or six good rally outings, and I have to say that Bobby was the smoothest driver I ever accompanied. Considering the drivers I later sat alongside, including the mega-brilliant Roger Clark and Hannu Mikkola, that is saying something.

Bobby and I competed together on various rallies, including the Night Hawk event in Yorkshire, which we were leading by about half a minute at the very last stage, the notorious Oliver's Mount hill-climb circuit at Scarborough. It had been announced that the winner of this fast tarmac stage, more used to hosting motorbike racing, would receive a case of champagne. Bobby Parkes enjoyed a drink or two, and was fully aware of this prize. "I do like champagne," he said in his refined voice before the start. "If we win, it will be six bottles each, you know."

So saying, Bobby and I started the stage and I must say he was driving like a man possessed. We slid and skidded round corners, but did it all with great precision and perfection until we reached the top of the hill where we arrived at a fast right-hand bend leading us to the finish line. And that's where it all went wrong, for Bobby (already licking his lips in anticipation of the champagne) 'lost it' and the Cortina skidded to the left. We mounted a bank, on top of which was a long hawthorn hedge. The flying Cortina straddled this and we ran along it for fifty yards or more, with the hedge becoming uprooted and flying over the top of the car. We eventually regained the road just before the finish line, but lost the champagne to Jack Tordoff in another Cortina. Bobby never forgot this or forgave himself.

Different rallies, drivers, and cars came and went with varying results, but I was usually somewhere among the silverware. In fact I had quite a big collection, with over a hundred tankards at one point. Pint and half-pint tankards were standard fare during the sixties, along with silver ashtrays and loads of little silver cups that looked like glorified egg cups. The national scene was great, but I started to get the first whiff of jealousy from some of the other navigators on the local scene, who often accused me of 'shouting up' times and bullying marshals on club rallies. Jealousy and envy are terrible things, but, apart from the above example, I never ever experienced it again in rallying. It was a different matter when it came to television, however, as I shall tell you later on.

One noteworthy incident was an unforgivable mistake I made competing on a rally in North Wales. I was navigating for David Cowan in his Cooper S, and we had built up a healthy lead by the halfway point in the early hours of the morning. Having filled up with petrol, we drove to a lane near what I thought to be the 'out' control, where we would need to clock in about 20 minutes later. We decided to have a bit of shut-eye before taking our handsome lead into the second half of the rally, which I had plotted on the map and looked quite easy. One hour later we woke up and saw car lights through the trees a few hundred yards away. I had stupidly taken the wrong lane, running parallel to the one where the control point was situated! Never have I felt such a fool, and never have I had to make such abject apologies to a driver. I didn't enjoy writing the *Motoring News* report for that rally, I can tell you. Young David was very good about it, but, inevitably, put it firmly in his repertoire of rally anecdotes for many years to come.

Ten

More memory lanes

Many books have been written about club rallying escapades in Britain, so I hope I may be forgiven for giving the odd chapter or so to mine. As I was rallying for thirty or forty weekends a year with different drivers, these incidents did seem to come thick and fast.

On a night rally in Cumberland (as it was then known) many fords were included in the route, not in itself particularly unusual, but on this wet March night there had been heavy rain so the short water crossings were deeper than usual. All competitors' cars would have good waterproofing so no major problems were foreseen. I could, at this point, launch into a rather pompous few words on the art of driving a car through deep water. You know the sort of thing: keep medium revs, build up a nice bank and gulley of water in front of the radiator grill, etc, etc. However, I won't. You haven't bought this book (and I hope you *have* bought it) to learn how to drive, but to learn how *not* to drive.

The King's Meaburn ford near Appleby was different. It had a concrete bottom, about 10 feet wide. The idea was, obviously, to keep on the concrete and make a bee-line for the other side. I forgot to mention that I was navigating in a 'frog-eye' Austin-Healey Sprite in the hands of one Bill Willicombe. Yes, he of the Highland Rally pandemonium. I should mention here that Bill was always sartorially perfectly turned out, wearing neatly-pressed cavalry twill trousers, polished brown shoes, and a smart Les Leston rally jacket. Overalls were never worn on events in those days, and the rally jacket was very new to the scene. Les Leston, by the way, was a successful and famous racing and rally driver who was among the first to own a motorsport accessory shop, and certainly the first to market a dark blue, mildly-quilted short jacket. (This last bit is for the benefit of younger readers, I should add, and other similar things may pop up again.)

Leaping off at a tangent, I want to mention that I was invited to be guest speaker at the Hong Kong Motor Club's annual dinner and prize presentation in 1977. It was a great banquet, as you might imagine, and afterwards I was asked to present lots of magnificent trophies. I have to say this Hong Kong display made the average British motor club 'do' look like a village jumble sale. One large trophy was for the driving test champion, and I very nearly fell off the stage when the name Les Leston was called out. He had emigrated to Hong Kong a few years earlier, and he seemed in very good form, although he admitted that performing handbrake turns on the promenade in Kowloon wasn't quite as exhilarating as breaking lap records at Brands Hatch.

Back to Mr Willicombe and the low-slung Sprite. As we entered the ford we thought things were a little odd, as the famous frog-eye lights went beneath the surface of the water. Some water actually splashed against the small windscreen through which we both peered. The Sprite continued to trundle through the water and the engine seemed fine if a little spluttery. However, halfway across it stopped spluttering. In fact, it stopped altogether. Worse was to come, for the fast flowing stream (which was more like a raging river) pitched up the little car like a floating sycamore leaf and we sailed backwards, off the concrete track, and downstream in the darkness. It was actually quite frightening, and not unlike a scene from the film *African Queen*! I helpfully suggested switching on the reversing light so we might see where we were going but this comment went down like a lead balloon with my driver! By now, water was seeping into the car and Bill's cavalry twills were looking somewhat less pristine. There was suddenly a shudder and the floating car stopped abruptly, nestling in the large bushes at the side of the stream. Stream, did I say? It was a bloody raging river.

By putting the car in first gear and turning the ignition key we made a bit of progress moving back towards the ford exit; then a man appeared at the side of the bank and threw a rope. Thankfully another man, wearing large fisherman's waders, leapt into the water and attached the rope, on the other end of which was a Ferguson tractor. You'll notice I'm getting in all the classic motoring names of the era! Anyway, we got out in one piece and various willing local garage mechanics helped dry out the Sprite's engine and off we went, about twenty minutes late and a lot wetter. We finished the rally, I think, and were no worse for our experience although Bill claimed he had rheumatism ever after. It would be ten years until I again entered water in a rally car, as described in chapter one.

Motoring News championship rallies were the best road rallies in Britain, and there were up to twenty different events each year. They varied slightly from year to year, but the backbone of the events were the 'classic' ones in Wales, the north-west, or Yorkshire. There were also rallies in such far-flung places as Inverness (one year only, in 1964), Devon and Cornwall, Kent, the north-east, and East Anglia. I tried to do as many as possible, and, of course, each brought its various dramas and disasters.

Trips to Wales were always a challenge, especially as it was often a four hour or more trip down from the north-west. The M6 motorway from the Midlands to the north had not been built, but as the sixties wore on there were bits of it appearing. This helped our trips, although hindered us on one occasion when the route of a rally included a section of new motorway on the run-out section from the start. We were not used to motorway junctions with roundabouts and great blue signs, and I'm sorry to tell you that I misread a junction and proceeded to navigate Bob Lamb's Humber Sceptre the wrong way up the M6 back towards the north. What a fool! And what a bigger fool to admit this to others, who ensured it appeared in *Motoring News* the following week.

Another M6 catastrophe for Lamb/Mason and the Sceptre occurred on our way to start the *Wolverhampton Express and Star* Rally, nearing the then lower end of the M6 somewhere near Stafford. The Sceptre had a major engine malfunction, the details of which I cannot fully remember, but it was certainly terminal, and poor Bob had to phone back to Lancaster for his local garage to come down and tow him home (no service crews in those days and I don't think the RAC or AA had great trucks to get you home). Alright, I know I'm getting on a bit, but I'm not going to mention AA patrol men on motorbikes with sidecars, saluting members. Don't worry!

We had been driving down from the north in convoy with Frank Davies and Bob Redhead, and after a road-side conference it was agreed that Bob Lamb would stay put, but I would go on to compete in the rally in the Davies/Redhead Mini-Cooper S. I was gathering points in the *Motoring News* championship navigators' section, whereas Bob Redhead was concentrating on northern events and not contesting the *Motoring News* championship, so he, amazingly generously, offered to take the back seat in the Mini and I would occupy the front, thus nominated to claim points. First of all, can you imagine a three-up Mini careering around the tight and twisty lanes of mid-Wales for eight hours, and the discomfort for all concerned? Secondly, can you imagine the tripartite conversations and arguments going on, with two navigators attempting to mislead the driver in different directions?

We actually completed the route, and had a relatively successful night in a rally that featured a great amount of mud, drizzle and rain (ideal rally conditions, of course), and which finished at the infamous 'Flannel Factory' near a network of difficult junctions always feared by navigators, including Bob Redhead who, despite his magnanimous gesture in giving me his seat, was pleased to avoid navigating that final bit of the route! I just want to say that I navigated this last bit perfectly, despite Redhead's mutterings from the back seat. Alright, I know I'm a clever arse. Sorry!

I spent a lot of time navigating Minis and accompanying various drivers of note. I navigated Norman Harvey from Cardiff in his 'Goldfinger' Mini-Cooper S (so called as he had painted it gold, for some strange reason). We had a healthy lead in the Sunday Mercury Rally in Wales by the halfway petrol halt, and I was looking forward to my first win in the principality when Norman became ill with severe sickness and migraine, and we had to retire. I was annoyed, but rallying is a team effort and such is life.

Another leading Mini driver was David Friswell, a regular winner of *Motoring News* events. As he lived in the Midlands, I travelled down by train from the north to meet him for the start of the Shunpiker Rally. We started from Coventry before attempting a special stage on Cannock Chase.

I knew David was a very fast driver, but I didn't realise quite how fast. We set off like a rocket, over gravel and soil tracks, across this area of barren grassland. I was reading the notes we had been given as best I could, and also looking out for arrows on sticks placed near the junctions. We were touching 80 or 90mph on one fast but bumpy track among the gorse bushes, when the car leapt off the track and into long grass. David struggled to keep the car going in a straight line, and would have easily regained the track had there not been an unexpected and unbelievable obstacle. To our shared horror, we spotted what appeared to be a very large manhole with brick edging, but no cover on it! We hit it at speed, fortunately, otherwise the car could have nose-dived into the pit.

The Mini's front left wheel was sheared off and the car stood on its nose and sort of 'tottered' at high speed through the rye-grass. It didn't go end over-end, but wasn't far off doing so, and we were both relieved when we came to a standstill. We clambered out, gathered our belongings, put on our rally jackets and wondered what to do. We watched all the following cars driving safely past (at somewhat lower speeds than D Friswell, I should add), and, after the last car passed, waited for a rally official to collect us. Surprisingly, we then saw a Triumph 2000 rally car driving slowly through the stage. It was a retired rally car; in fact, the highly fancied works entry of Roy Fidler and Graham Robson, which had expired somewhere near the start, causing their retirement at an even earlier point than ours. They stopped, inspected our car and the scene of its demise, then shuffled things about in the back of the Triumph and gave us a lift to the end of the stage. I really can't remember what happened then, but as it was only early evening I suspect that we drowned our sorrows in some handily placed public house, awaiting a breakdown truck. That's rallying!

I hope you will forgive me if I gallop through my early rallying career in a non-chronological order, but I don't want this book to be a list of my successes (or lack of them!). I never kept a precise record of everything in which I competed and I can't quote too many facts and figures. I can remember the accidents, incidents, mistakes I made, and all the amusing things that happened. I rallied many, many weekends in the early years, as I have mentioned, and hawked myself around getting rides with a great variety of drivers. It's only just occurred to me, but I was performing a bit like a prostitute. Well, not in that way, of course, but you know what I mean! It's really not surprising that ordinary sensible people think we rally folk have lost our marbles, is it? Who, in their right minds, would want to drive all night, flat-out, over twisty, slippery lanes, or, even worse, over muddy and rocky tracks? And what about snow and ice? No problem, of course, just another challenge. Drivers take all of the above in their stride and I've always been amazed how they can cope with the elements in such a pragmatic way. They seem to be different to most normal people, and are seldom slowed by rain or even blinding sunshine. There is one thing they can't cope with, though: FOG! Some drivers are, of course, better than others in foggy conditions, and a navigator reading the bends on the map for the driver quickly learns how good or bad they are. Only one driver I've ever met has actually told me they enjoy foggy driving, and furthermore I have seen proof of it. I was on a night rally in mid-Wales in the early sixties, co-driving one of the regular *Motoring News* championship brigade, driving over the twisty moorland roads before going down the Bwlch-y-Groes valley and on into Dinas Mawddwy – places known well to rally drivers. We were making good progress – well, as good as any of our usual rivals – when suddenly a blaze of lights appeared in our mirrors.

The lights came closer and started flashing. We could not believe it, but as 'baulking' is the most heinous crime in rallying, we pulled over to let the obvious maniac pass. We were astonished. We were even more flabbergasted to arrive at the next control and find that the driver was a fifty-something year old! It was, in fact, Sydney Allard the famous winner of the 1952 Monte Carlo Rally. He was driving an Allardette: a Ford Anglia modified by his own company, which had formerly built Allard sports cars, including his Monte-winning example. I met him at breakfast in Llandrindod Wells after the rally, and said, probably somewhat sycophantically, how impressed we had been (not to say humiliated!). "Oh, I like foggy conditions," replied this boyhood hero of mine. After Sydney died in 1966, I learnt that he had been blind in one eye since childhood, but obviously kept very quiet about it until he stopped competing. I hope you find that as amazing as I do.

I don't want to keep mentioning the sixties, but everything was happening for me then, and it was a pretty exciting time in many ways. It may be difficult for you to realise the significance of the RAC Rally of Great Britain, but, for anyone interested in rallying, this was the pinnacle: up to 200 cars would charge round

Britain, day and night, for nearly a week. For most of the time they would be scrabbling through the rough tracks in huge forests of Britain, which few people then knew anything about. Other than a few forest workers, no-one even went in a forest. There were no leisure trails for walkers, cyclists, joggers or doggy folk. The general public were banned from driving on the forest roads. But it all changed when the marvellous Jack Kemsley, consultant to the Royal Automobile Club, which controlled all motorsport, decided the old RAC Rally which had toddled around Britain since the 1930s visiting various airfields and car parks for driving tests, then a few mountain passes and a bit of intricate map reading thrown in, was a thing of the past. I got to know Jack well a decade later and I always regret not asking him about the actual moment he came up with the brilliant idea of going into the forests. Did he wake up one morning, go down to breakfast, and halfway through his boiled egg shout "Eureka!"? Anyway, it changed the face of Britain's most important rally, and put the event firmly on the world stage, where it stays to this day. Mind you, like all the other world rallies, it is now a pale shadow of its former glorious self, being shorter, more clinical, more spectator and environmentally friendly, and, would you believe, nicer for the drivers, who all go to bed each night at 10 o'clock with their cups of cocoa, ready for another day. We oldsters scornfully call it 'office hours rallying.' Don't get me started on this hobbyhorse of mine, please!

In fact, at this stage, I should say that the current top rally crews are quite brilliant, and surprisingly, thanks to my various recent trips to world rallies with Rallytravel Ltd, I have got to know most of the young stars like Sébastien Loeb, Jari-Matti Latvala, Mikko Hirvonen, Petter Solberg and Ott Tänak, among others. Their speed and precision is utterly amazing, and they all seem like good chaps, young enough to be my children if not my grandchildren! Anyway, that's got rid of that subject, so I may keep a few more readers.

Having shot off on one of my tangents (don't worry, I am taking the tablets for it!) I must return to the topic in hand – the RAC Rally – and my first minor involvement in it. In 1961 the rally started from Blackpool, before travelling through the lanes of north Lancashire and Yorkshire, and up to the then new and much-feared forests, which would make up most of the event. Happily for me there would be several control points along the lanes near Lancaster and Kendal, so several car club members applied to marshal. I can still remember the precise location of the control point we were allocated (it was at map reference 89/582822, near Kirkby Lonsdale, if you must know, but this is now getting a bit nerdy). The control opened early in the evening and a small group of us set forth with torches and pens at the ready. I can't remember too many details (you will be pleased to know), but various officials' cars appeared and gave us signs and clocks and things, telling us that the first cars would be along shortly. That was the understatement of the century, for three minutes later there was a loud popping, screaming sound, and a red Saab shot around the bend and skidded to a halt one foot from our carefully sited control table. A huge man sitting in the left-hand driving seat glowered at us, whilst a gawky, callow youth in a peaked cap ran round the front of the car to insert his timecard into the printing clock, push the plunger, and receive an official signature. It was all over in a few seconds, and amid much wheel-spinning, tyre smoke, and oily smells the screaming Saab departed. That was my first meeting (if you can call it such) with Erik Carlsson and John Brown.

After our marshalling duties had finished we all fled to the little pub in nearby Lupton and had a pint or two, and chatted about all the cars and drivers we had seen. However, my mind was wandering, and I remember sitting there with glazed eyes (no, I hadn't had one-too-many). It was like those childhood dreams mentioned in earlier chapters. I must compete in the RAC Rally, come hell or high water. I had a new ambition.

The RAC Rally would have to wait, however, as I had to get on with my work in advertising, and, of course, rallying. Both went from strength to strength, I am happy to say. Although I was still navigating on local rallies for many of the drivers mentioned earlier, I continued to branch out by accompanying many better-known drivers on the national stage, so to speak.

My endeavours in this direction were helped considerably when I was approached by a splendid, if slightly eccentric, rally navigator by the name of John Hopwood. He asked if Bob Lamb and I would like to be made members of Ecurie Cod Fillet. Now, I realise that when you read this (if you've got this far) you will probably sit up and say, "What the hell is that?"

John Hopwood was a successful navigator in the fifties and early sixties, usually for one of the quickest drivers in the country, Roy Fidler. This pair were well known as competitors in cars as diverse as a Buckler, a Triumph Herald and a Ford Anglia. Based in north Cheshire, they were enthusiastic members of the Stockport Motor Club, and organised the successful Regent Rally each year in Derbyshire. Fidler was a fishmonger by profession, which does have some bearing on all of this, as you will find out.

Team awards were an important part of rallying when two or three cars would link together on an ad hoc basis for different events. On bigger rallies manufacturers also had team entries, but we won't go into that here. Many teams had exotic sounding names like Ecurie Ecosse, Ecurie Squadra Corsa, and others. One night in 1955 when John and Roy entered a team on a restricted rally they decided to call it 'Ecurie Cod Fillet' as a bit of a joke, reflecting Roy's fishy connections. The team won the award and it grew from there, with numerous northern crews being admitted to the unofficial club that all started as something of a piss-take, if you'll pardon the expression. Gradually competitors from other parts of Britain joined the no-fee-required organisation, and eventually competitors from overseas were heard to ask "What is this Ecurie Cod Fillet?" Some were invited to join and now, some 55 years later, the club, if that's what you can call it, has 300 members, most of whom were former successful competitors or officials. Legendary names like Erik Carlsson, Paddy Hopkirk, Hannu Mikkola, Björn Waldegård, Timo Mäkinen , Rauno Aaltonen, Simo Lampinen, Sir Stirling Moss, Ari Vatanen, Vic Elford, Peter Procter, and John Sprinzel are members and regularly attend reunions and other functions. Even more recent rally stars like Jari-Matti Latvala, Mikko Hirvonen, Petter Solberg, and Mark Higgins are among the membership.

You'll notice I've only mentioned drivers here, but as navigators can get a bit peeved if they are relegated to being a forgotten breed, I'll throw in a few past and present international members of the brains department of a rally car: Stuart Turner, Paul Easter, Mike Wood, Claes Billstam, Jim Porter, John Davenport, Mike Broad, Don Barrow, John Brown, Graham Robson, Ron Crellin, David Stone, Paul White, Phil Mills, and Nicky Grist are all great supporters.

Ecurie Cod Fillet helped me enormously in meeting other drivers and becoming accepted, so to speak, and I am proud to now be a member of the small 'committee' that runs ECF. Roy Fidler, affectionately known as King Cod, is still at the helm, while Mike Broad, Alan Jolley, John Clegg, and I keep things going. John Hopwood died after a short illness in 2006, and is much missed.

Among my various outings was a completely new event in the calendar – the Manx Rally. This has a link with Ecurie Cod Fillet, as Roy and John actually thought the whole thing up. They went over to the Isle of Man with Graham Robson and plotted a tight road rally route through all the lanes which they thought they could organise to take place over one night. Before leaving the island the trio made a courtesy call to some senior bod in the IoM Tourist Office who, just as they were due to leave his office, casually asked, "Do you think it would help at all if we closed the roads?" The boys were flabbergasted, of course, and an amazing event consisting of a night navigation section through the lanes followed by a day's racing over closed major and minor roads was born. The first event in 1963 had a big entry of leading British names, and was won by Reg McBride and Don Barrow in a Ford Anglia. I was asked to navigate in an ex-works Austin-Healey 3000 for top driver Don Grimshaw, which was a great step up for me. I was most impressed by this powerful monster of a car, but regrettably we had an early retirement when we flew across a tramline halfway between Douglas and Ramsey, landing heavily and busting the big Healey's radiator. Not many rally people can say they retired from a rally by hitting a tramline!

I competed in numerous Manx Rallies over the years, in various cars with various drivers bringing various results. I co-drove again for Don Grimshaw, this time in a Triumph TR4, which he parked flat against a huge stone house at the bottom of Tholt-y-Will hill after a 100+mph slide over the finish line. The side of the TR became as flat as a pancake. Apparently, ornaments were knocked off the window sill in the house and a picture fell off the wall. I broke my wrist. I also competed in the Isle of Man with David Cowan, Frank Grange, Bobby Parkes, Roy Mapple, and Peter Clarke, finishing second, and with my old Morecambe driver Bob Lamb in his Mini-Coopers S. We had an engine fault on the first day, so were pushed onto the Isle of Man Steam Packet Company ferry boat in the evening for a night sail to Liverpool.

At some point late in the evening we went to an almost-empty bar at the front of the ship to enjoy a few beers and drown our sorrows after our early retirement. After an hour or so there was a bit of a commotion when a man, drinking by himself, fell over at the other end of the bar (not an unusual occurrence in such places, you might think). The barman tried to attend to the man but there was no response, so a nurse was summoned who also failed to get any response. She scurried off and returned with a doctor and the captain of the ship, no less. The bar had emptied by now, and red and white security tapes were wrapped around the deck near the bar to prevent other passengers entering. Bob and I were left alone in the far corner whilst all this was happening, but we couldn't help hearing that the poor man was pronounced dead. We saw him being covered by a huge grey Isle of Man Steam Packet Company blanket to await collection when the boat docked in Liverpool. In the midst of all this, the barman poured us another couple of pints and said we could enjoy them quietly round the corner as no-one else would be entering the bar. He then turned and gave us more beer, free of charge. What we didn't realise was that when needed to pop out to visit the gents, it necessitated us stepping over the blanketed corpse on the way.

Eleven

Getting (slightly) more serious

There is a unique rally in Scotland that was first organised in 1969 and takes place on the Isle of Mull. It runs over closed public roads, and also had a few forestry sections in the early days. A splendidly humorous gent called David Tomlinson invited me to navigate on this event in his Mini-Cooper S. It was my first trip with this likeable man, who was, let me think how to put this ... extremely overweight. In fact, he could have modelled for the Outsize Mans Shop, although I imagine his clothes were made by a sail maker or tent manufacturer! After a minor incident on the rally, we slid into one of Mull's many ditches and the car fell onto its side. Unfortunately, and as usual, it was onto my side. After much huffing and puffing my large driver undid his seatbelt and promptly fell on top of me, squashing me against my door, through which cold muddy water was now seeping. I felt as though I had been hit by an avalanche, and could hardly breathe as this great, shaking, lump of flesh started to chortle uncontrollably. It really was a problem, as David could not manipulate himself up to open the driver's door and I certainly couldn't escape through mine Eventually, after a lot more huffing and puffing I managed to slither up and over David towards his door, which was now being opened by some friendly spectators who had seen the incident. We righted the car and Mr Tomlinson emerged, none the worse and still chuckling.

We used to rally in all weathers, of course, and frequently had to cope with snow and ice, which most of the regular crews took in their stride, many of the top crews fitting the then new studded tyres. For smaller club events, like the Morecambe Bay championship rallies, the use of such tyres would be somewhat extravagant and beyond the reach of most drivers. I was navigating Bob Lamb's Sunbeam Rapier on one such rally, and we had filled the large boot with bags of sand and shovels in preparation for the hills ahead of us. At one point we lost grip going up a moorland road, so I ran round to the boot and started to throw sand under the spinning rear wheels. The Rapier was not making much progress, so I decided to sit in the open boot and bounce up and down to get extra grip. A little more progress was made, and my bouncing became more ferocious as the car rocked up and down. Suddenly, with no warning, the great boot lid decided to slam itself shut and lock me inside. The car stopped moving and I could hear Bob outside shouting, "Tony, where the bloody hell are you?"

The *Motoring News* championship was in full swing in the sixties, with entries of 120 cars on virtually every event. There was a strong core of regular competitors, mainly from the north, Wales, or the Midlands. It was a powerful group of competitors, and referred to by many as 'the circus.' There was a particularly strong group from the Manchester/Cheshire area who I mentioned earlier, if I remember rightly. They would set off late on a Saturday afternoon, often in convoy, but would always gather at a large fish and chip shop in Leominster for a meal, before heading into Wales for the start of the rally. It became a real tradition. We would all be joined by Bill Bengry, a top class driver who had been British and *Motoring News* champion in a VW Beetle. Bill owned the big garage across the road from the chippy, and would wander across when we arrived, often still in his greasy overalls. He was an amazing character, and was actually the Mayor of Leominster, no less, at the time! He had a splendid Herefordshire accent and a squeaky-ish voice, and entertained us with his tales of various running repairs during rallies, including one when he found a very large, long snake wrapped around the back axle of his works Rover 3-litre P5 on the East African Safari Rally.

On one occasion I was on my way to the Welsh Marches Rally, navigating for Bobby Parkes. Now I haven't told you this, but Bobby (real name George Herbert Farrer Parkes) was part of an important dynasty in Manchester, and had a very good upbringing involving chauffeurs and domestic staff, in a very *Upstairs, Downstairs* kind of way. He was very well educated, and a gentleman of the old school. What he was doing asking a scruff like me to co-drive with him I don't know. His father ran a huge company called Small and Parkes, manufacturers of Don brake linings. It went on to become Mintex, and is now part of the gigantic BBA Friction Group. On one of our trips down from the north-west in the Cortina, we offered a lift to Bob Redhead, who was meeting his driver, Frank Davies, at the start in Brecon or wherever. Bobby Parkes was smoking an expensive cigar as we travelled down the A49, and I always remember Bob Redhead leaning forward to offer him a soggy sandwich from his rally bag, despite the fact that we were going to stop and eat in Leominster. "No thank you Bob," he said to his back seat passenger. "It might spoil my cigar!" When we arrived in Leominster we walked through the large fish and chip shop, with huge glistening ranges and illuminated cabinets full of sizzling fish. We reached the seating area at the back of the shop, and sat down among all the 'Macclesfield Mafia' and others as a young waitress appeared at our table for our order. I will never forget the following conversation, starting with Bobby's immortal question "Do you have fish?"

"Yes, this is a fish shop," the somewhat incredulous girl answered.

"Oh good, I'd like smoked salmon please," said Bobby.

"No, sorry, we don't have things like that," the waitress replied.

Those that had heard this conversation creased themselves laughing (in the nicest possible way), and realised that George Herbert Farrer Parkes had never been into a fish and chip shop in his life.

Before leaving the topic of Mr Parkes, I should explain that he was a much respected ex-works Jaguar, Aston Martin, and Reliant driver, and had many successes, notably with Arthur Senior, with the exception of the 1964 Monte Carlo Rally when they dropped the Reliant Sabre off the edge of the road on the Turini pass. It fell 30 feet down to the road below and finished up as a load of plastic bits, put into a skip.

I moved forward quite a lot in 1964, and had a good go at the *Motoring News* championship, thanks to an invitation from one of the illustrious Cavendish Car Club mob in Macclesfield. Frank Grange was a young motor engineer and rally enthusiast who worked in the family garage in Styal, Cheshire (now nearly swallowed up by Manchester Airport, and better known as the location of one of Britain's biggest women's prisons – I hope you're enjoying some of the geographical tit-bits I keep throwing in here and there). Frank had a Ford Anglia, then a Cortina GT, both prepared and tuned to match the similar cars of Reg McBride and Phil Simister, who were all-conquering at the time. Frank had previously invited me to navigate his Anglia on the 1963 Regent Rally, and we were doing very well until we conked out. I realise such terms shouldn't appear in sophisticated motorsport books, but I can't for the life of me remember why we retired. I can, however, remember that the car was undriveable, and that we hitched a lift to the halfway halt at a garage in the middle of Derbyshire. A very, very strange man gave us a lift in a tatty Vauxhall (there, I've mentioned the brand again, in disparaging terms). I'm not sure if he was just gay (a term unknown in those days), or whether he was a psychopath or mass-murderer in the making, but he wouldn't drop us off where we wanted to be, instead insisting on driving somewhere else. As he stopped at some traffic lights, Frank and I escaped from the car and left him to go on to his next victims! Despite all this, Frank asked me to navigate for him in his pale, 'puke' green Cortina GT, and compete in as many of the twenty rounds of the 1964 *Motoring News* championship as possible. Few people would compete in every event, and there may have been a maximum number that counted for points.

The first round of the championship was a new rally to the series, and held in East Anglia – not the best-known rally territory in Britain. It was a rapid and rough event by the name of the Filldyke Rally, and was notable for having a massive 116 control points, all of which had to be plotted by navigators before and during the event. For us, it was one of those good nights that rally crews experience from time to time. The Cortina was 'on song,' Frank was fast and neat, and I was reading the maps well, as if my life depended on it. There were lots of unfenced ditches (presumably these were the 'dykes' mentioned in the title of the event) and grass tracks down the sides of fields. I remember driving along one such field and noting that our two team-mates, McBride/Barrow and Simister/Robson, were on the other side of the hedge. You can imagine how this put doubt into my mind, but I persevered and we emerged from the field to join a nice tarmac lane, whilst they had to drive halfway round the field again before joining the road. I was right and they were wrong! It gave me a great deal of confidence in my own ability and as we entered uncharted tracks in Thetford Forest I felt very confident. Thankfully neither Frank nor I put a foot wrong and were fairly confident when we returned to the Angel Hotel, Bury St Edmonds for breakfast and the results. There was some kerfuffle over them, as Toney Cox and John Davenport had missed a control in Thetford Forest that they said had an inaccurate map reference (do you realise how intricate all this navigation lark is?), but it was decided we were winners, and we duly collected our silverware and enjoyed a jubilant but long journey across half of Britain to get home. I must have been on good form that weekend, for my first *Motoring News* win inspired me to perform half of my cabaret act and tell jokes on the way back, using the navigators' flexi-light as a 'microphone.' When Frank met Don Barrow on Sunday evening for a drink, Frank said he was still aching from laughing so much. I didn't know I was that good, but it passed the time I suppose. Sorry if I sound a bit of a clever arse here!

It was a great season, but extremely demanding, and Frank and I kept our lead in the championship for the first part of the year until a concoction of broken exhausts, faulty brakes, and navigational errors dropped us to fifth in the championship.

Morecambe Car Club was going from strength to strength, and I was by now running a Mini-Cooper S (on a shoestring, I may add). I competed in auto-tests on tarmac and on the 'quarry trials,' which had more-or-less been invented by Morecambe Car Club.

These were fast events on the loose gravel tracks through various quarries and waste land in the Lancaster/Morecambe/Kendal area. They were very competitive, but I tempered my enthusiasm and tried to be as neat as possible. See, I had been learning from sitting next to all these better drivers! Anyway, I won a lot of these events or placed well, but I can still kick myself for throwing away the local championship one year when I entered a full-blooded sideways drift only thirty yards before the finish line of a stage in a disused brickworks. The surface was loose and dusty, and, most significantly, featured a number of half-buried bricks standing on end, protruding by an inch or so. I hit them, pitched the car into the air and did a 360 degree roll back onto my wheels (without scraping the roof, I hasten to add)! I pressed on to cross the finish line four seconds adrift, losing the championship to Tony Payne, Eric Clare, Dave Rayner, Peter Marshall, or one of my other club rivals. I don't care who – I just know I lost it by only a few seconds!

Twelve

Going clubbing

Whatever rallying I was doing, I still spent a lot of time on Morecambe Car Club matters as we had a strong committee comprising mostly local businessmen and professionals, and we organised a very wide programme of events. The club had 350 members, and was well and truly on the map as one of Britain's best motor clubs. It is a pity that car clubs are not as strong nowadays, as they offered great social and sporting opportunities, and, in my opinion, gave a better understanding of driving and motorsport than spending evenings gazing at YouTube, watching people crash cars.

The sixties saw the beginning of the Autocross events for which Morecambe became very famous. These events were held at various venues in north Lancashire and Westmorland, and again, huge crowds attended. The events were qualifiers for the Players No. 6 national championship, and we attracted top works rally drivers. Equally impressive were the show business celebrities who attended. A fellow member, Lister Baldwin (an occasional former driver with whom I rallied in a big Healey and whose Sprite I borrowed for Autotests) and I had the job of finding celebrities who were appearing in Morecambe or Blackpool summer season shows. I remember going to the ABC Theatre in Blackpool and waiting at the stage door for hours before being ushered into Mary Hopkin's dressing room. Mary was top of the hit parade at the time, and was blonde, petite and very affable. I instantly fell in love with her, of course! Whilst rooting about among old paperwork and other paraphernalia for this book I actually found a signed photograph of Mary which I must have kept. What did you say, 'soppy git'?

One notable occasion was at the very end of the decade when Stuart Turner brought along a huge Ford rally show, held on the Central Pier and featuring Roger Clark, Paddy Hopkirk and John Surtees. The pier, which no longer exists, was starting to crumble, and looked a bit secondhand as some of the wooden boards were loose. Stuart was somewhat concerned that the Ford GT40 he had brought along might fall into the sea below. Thankfully it didn't.

I had big involvement in the autocrosses, working with Edye Wiseman, Mike Griffiths, Mike Preston, and others. Not only was I on the organising committee, but I was also learning the ropes with commentary work. One member, David Alderson, worked for local timber merchants and waste disposal contractors Thomas Graveson and Sons. He persuaded his boss, Peter Graveson, to give the Morecambe Car Club a caravan to be used for commentaries, and it was in this that I practised the art that would eventually lead to my first assignment with BBC some twenty years later. Gravesons, needless to say, made the most of the publicity opportunity by painting its advertising slogan all over the van: unfortunately the wording was 'WE SPECIALISE IN TALKING RUBBISH,' which many of you might find very appropriate for my performances!

I've mentioned that top rally stars attended our autocrosses, but without showing any favouritism, I must admit that our greatest achievement was attracting Hannu Mikkola to our event. The then young Finn had just won the 1000 Lakes Rally in Finland in a Ford Escort twin-cam, and was on the verge of becoming a fully-fledged works driver for Ford. In order to broaden his experience it was decided that he should gain some tarmac experience by coming over to England to compete in some races and hill-climbs. One such event was cancelled, so Morecambe committee member Mike Preston quickly made contact with well-known rally co-driver Mike Wood in Burnley who was in charge of Hannu for a few weeks. He asked Mike if there was any chance of bringing his charge up to Kendal, where a car would be found for him. The young Finn duly appeared and borrowed Ian Harwood's Ford Escort. After a couple of practice laps Hannu went straight out and promptly made fastest time of day! I was commentator of the event, and it was arranged that I should sit in with Hannu and give a live commentary, which went out on the public address system. You can, no doubt, imagine my excited burbling and screaming into the microphone – an art I would perfect in later years when accompanying many motorsport stars for the benefit of TV cameras.

I pounced on the poor, unsuspecting Hannu after our little trip and invited him to be our guest at the next Morecambe Car Club meeting. I always did have big ideas! Although his English was then very limited, he agreed to attend so we organised a 'special' meeting at the local Skipper of Kendal Ford dealer. It was Hannu's first ever public appearance outside his native Finland, and he still remembers it well. Thankfully he understood my questions and it became quite a fun evening. Mike Preston prepared a Dinky model Ford Escort with stickers and numbers reflecting his 1000 Lakes win and it was mounted on a Lakeland stone plinth. It was presented to Hannu and he obviously treasured it, for when I stayed with Hannu and his family in their magnificent house in Helsinki recently, I spotted it among the very few trophies he has on display there. I mustn't jump ahead here, but these brief meetings in Kendal were the beginning of a great friendship that has continued to this day, and we have seen a lot of each other over the years in various parts of the world.

Shortly after Hannu Mikkola's Morecambe Car Club activities he went on to slightly greater things, like winning the 16,000-mile 1970 London–Mexico World Cup Rally in a Ford Escort. This was a magnificent achievement, and brought Ford tremendous publicity. Needless to say I was immediately onto this, and with the agreement of the committee I enquired if there was any possibility of Hannu's winning car appearing as a display at our next autocross. Incredibly, Stuart Turner, who Mike Preston and I had met briefly when we marshalled on the World Cup Rally, said yes. The car duly appeared, and was a great attraction indeed.

I seemed to have boundless energy back then, and seldom kept still. I was always darting about visiting other club members and checking things, and my Mini-Cooper became a familiar sight, known to many (including the police). I received one or two speeding tickets, but was also let off by young police patrol riders, many of whom had an interest in motorsport and seemed to know me.

My pièce de résistance, however, occurred early one sunny evening when I overtook a large, but slow, black Jaguar tootling along Morecambe promenade. It was doing 30mph. My Mini-Cooper was doing more than twice or three times that! As I overtook, I noticed a uniformed police officer was driving the innocent looking Jaguar, so I gently slotted in front of the car when it suddenly started flashing blue lights, forcing me to stop. The rear passenger door of the Jaguar opened and a large man in a highly decorated uniform and 'scrambled egg'-covered cap strolled slowly towards me. He leaned over and gave me the biggest bollocking I've ever had in my life.

The mystery man then strode off to continue his journey along the promenade. This was the Chief Constable of Lancashire Constabulary, one Mr William Palfrey, one of the best known Chief Constables in the country, who was in charge of one of the biggest policing areas as it included Liverpool and Manchester in those days. When I relayed my tale to a friendly policemen at the car club meeting (to which I had been heading), he said the reason I was not booked was because the Chief Constable wouldn't have had the paperwork on board, or possibly couldn't complete it even if he had.

I was a occasionally a bit irresponsible, there is no doubt. Another one of my little wheezes came about thanks to a friend who worked for the gas board, who had some splendid smoke bombs used to trace gas leaks. One club member was known for taking things very seriously, and got in quite a panic at an auto-test when his parked car was suddenly enveloped in smoke from one of my little 'bombs,' placed under the rear of the vehicle. Another good wheeze was to take a handful of these little wonders and light them at the roadside at a confusing junction, just prior to an evening rally arriving. The rallies selected were not Morecambe Car Club ones, of course, but those of neighbouring 'unregistered' clubs who, we felt, were encroaching on our sacred rally territory. You can imagine the pandemonium at the junction and the enjoyment it gave us!

Another incident I remember concerned a different sort of horsepower. One Sunday morning Bob Redhead and I were planning a rally route that included the old Warton slag-heaps on the edge of Morecambe Bay, which is notorious for having dangerous, uncharted quicksands. We suddenly noticed a bit of a commotion and saw a man running about in a demented sort of way, waving his arms about, so we drove out to see what was happening. We found a horrific scene before our eyes – a horse was half submerged in the quicksand, making a terrible noise, and of course the rider was in quite a state of panic. After racing to the nearest house to phone 999, we returned to the scene. Following a great amount of struggling by firemen the horse was miraculously released, a little the worse for wear. The rider was obviously relieved, but he flabbergasted Bob and me when he exclaimed; "What about the saddle? It cost a fortune. I'm going to try and dig it out." We left him arguing with the firemen.

∽ **Thirteen** ∽

Into the forests

You can probably imagine my delight and excitement when Bob Lamb, with whom I had done so much club rallying, decided that he wanted to compete in the RAC Rally of Great Britain in 1962. It would be Bob's first RAC, and (obviously) mine, and we would be taking his Sunbeam Rapier. I thought this was another big step forward in my rallying career, and another of my dreams coming true.

The rally would start in Blackpool in early November, traversing 50 British counties and covering 2200 miles, including 300 miles over forest tracks. There were 165 entries, with a good number of overseas drivers, and we were allocated number 104. I would be in charge of navigating, but also have to take the wheel occasionally on some of the longer road sections. I had to buy a load of Ordnance Survey maps stretching from the north of Scotland to Hampshire, which doubled the size of my collection. They were then priced at four shillings and sixpence each, which is now half the price of a packet of crisps, but was quite a lot of money in those days. Still, I felt very important as I collected the maps from W H Smith in Lancaster, and informed the manager that I was about to compete in the RAC Rally of Great Britain. I'm not sure he'd ever heard of it, and probably wondered what I was burbling about.

When the time came we went to Blackpool, where we reported to the rally headquarters in the famous Imperial Hotel. It was a great moment for me, as we were rubbing shoulders with all the greats such as Erik Carlsson, Eugen Böhringer, Pat Moss and Paddy Hopkirk, none of whom were speaking to me, of course. One little problem to be overcome concerned a small matter of weighing the crew. I don't know why, but in the early sixties the organisers decided that there should be a minimum weight for each crew member. We were seriously worried that I might be underweight (I wish I had that problem now, by the way!). We had considered putting lead weights in my pockets but were frightened of being excluded for cheating. I put a heavy jacket under my brand-new Les Leston rally jacket and I think I wore some heavy boots. It was a bit pathetic, but the weighing machine was an ordinary set of bathroom scales and the small gauge was so difficult to read that I'm not sure anyone knew what weight I came in at! Anyway, I passed.

The Sunbeam was scrutineered in the nearby Talbot Road bus garage with buses coming and going among the rally cars. We were lined up behind the Pat Moss Big Healey, which I peered into when Pat had gone off to deal with paperwork. On the dashboard in front of the steering wheel was a large notice saying 'handbag,' which fascinated me. It was thirty or so years before I asked Pat about that sign, and she told me she had once left her handbag in a hotel at a breakfast halt and was determined never to do it again.

After all this excitement, it was down to work for Bob and me, so late afternoon we went to our cheap Blackpool B&B. I had a huge set of road books for the whole event, consisting of many hundred pages and lots and lots of 'tulip' arrows with distances between, but no map references to where the forest stages started and finished. I set about marking the route on the Ordnance Survey 1in maps, finding it very difficult to measure the potential route with an opisometer (a small map measurer to you!). No-one else was in our B&B, so there were no other competitors to consult. We hadn't a clue where forest stages started and finished, but we laboured on. Bob went to bed at about midnight, but I slogged on until four in the morning – not the ideal way to kick off a six-day rally. I still had put only the first half of the route on the map, so when the rally returned to Blackpool for the overnight halt two days later, I would have to plot the second bit.

Eventually we were flagged off from Blackpool promenade late next afternoon, nearly an hour and three-quarters after the Mercedes Benz of European championship leader Eugen Böhringer. The route took us to the first forest near Slaidburn, and we put on the crash helmets we had borrowed for the event. Mine belonged to a friend who had a small motor scooter, and it was far too big for me: I later found that on bumpy sections the front would come down so I couldn't see anything.

At this point, you may be interested to know the way the Rapier was prepared for this great adventure. Well, it had been serviced at the local Rootes Group dealer, Pye Motors of Lancaster, and then extra titivations were added by Peter Wood at the Scotch Filling Station, in my home village of Bolton-le-Sands. It was fitted with a set of Dunlop SP3 tyres (not even knobbly ones), it had better seat belts installed, three spotlights, a big reversing light (just like the works Rapiers), and the number plate VFV 993 painted on the front bumper (again, just like the works cars). That was about it as far as I can remember, but I do know that it retained its shiny wooden dashboard and the leopard-skin seat covers, which had been fitted as an extra when new! Not a lot of people can say they competed in a major international rally in a car with leopard-skin seat covers.

The forests were frighteningly rough, with very poor arrowing, and we were worried about getting lost. After one five-mile stage we had been shaken to bits, and couldn't believe the car would last the trip. In fact, the good old Rapier took it all in its stride and nothing broke, which was a good thing as Bob and I did not have a service crew, and neither of us were good mechanics. After the first few stages we were beginning to wonder what we had let ourselves in for, as various earlier numbers were strewn about in the forest. Böhringer had crashed into the trees, and the Morley brothers' big Healey had somersaulted out. Previous winner Peter Harper, in a works Sunbeam Rapier, had also crashed.

We passed through the giant Kielder Forest (the biggest man-made forest in Europe, we were told, which frightened us to death!) and on up into Scotland with all its rough forests, getting as far as Inverness before returning via the Lake District and its fast, frightening and steep tracks. After two days and nights of non-stop rallying, we returned to north Lancashire, and around tea-time arrived at our home town of Lancaster, where Pye Motors had kept the workshop open to check over the Rapier. As we drove into the large empty workshops we were met by 'big boss' Jim Pye and the workshop manager, who waved us onto a ramp. I really felt I had made it, and felt like a real professional as I stood there in my pale blue overalls. Oh, yes! I forgot to mention that we had purchased some pale blue overalls, not unlike the ones Stirling Moss wore. There were two or three mechanics, all working at speed, and within twenty minutes we reversed out of the garage and drove on to Blackpool. We really were in the big time now!

After an overnight stop in rainy Blackpool (where I spent half the night plotting map references again) we set forth, and en route to Wales visited Oulton Park race circuit, where navigators were asked to leave the car. The drivers would then have to drive six laps before leaving the circuit to be given a time. As most navigators will tell you, drivers should not be left alone at any time, but this was forced upon us by the organisers. It has been known for drivers to do one lap too little or too many, so various clever schemes were devised by enterprising crews to ensure this didn't happen. Bob's bright idea was to put six little pieces of masking tape on the top of the dashboard, one of which he would remove every time he passed the pits. This was a good idea in theory, but in the event he found the little bits of sticky tape attached themselves to the fingers of his new string-backed driving gloves, and very nearly did one lap too many.

Wales passed without incident, but was long, tiring, and tricky to navigate. We traversed many stages with funny names that would eventually become very familiar to me. I imagine we also took in the Epynt ranges, but I know we were mightily relieved to get out of Wales after a full night and half a day, especially as there had been snow and ice. During this part of the trip I turned 21, but actually missed my birthday altogether as I forgot all about it.

After some amazingly rough and muddy stages on the military land in Hampshire and Dorset, we staggered into Bournemouth and found our suitcases, which had been carried on the Dunlop baggage van. We donned our dinner jackets and bow ties (quite a new experience for me), and made our way to the great dinner and prize-giving, where we enjoyed a drink or two to celebrate our 38th place overall, and, belatedly, my 21st birthday.

Next morning we drove north, expecting a nice, quiet run after all our excitement, but as we rounded a bend on the main road in the middle of Worcester there was a large crack and bang, and the car ground to a halt with a broken driveshaft. How about that for timing? We could so easily have retired on one of the last stages of the rally which would have been really disappointing, so the Worcester calamity was more of a nuisance than anything. Various phone calls were made, of course, but a new driveshaft had to be sent down from Lancaster by rail, so we stayed the night in yet another grotty B&B and went to the cinema to see the very first James Bond film, *Dr No*.

The advent of forest rallying certainly gave me a new perspective, and the early sixties were a time of great excitement for rallyists. It really opened up a whole new world. It also kept me pretty busy as the road rallying scene was in full swing. Nevertheless, I was determined to compete on as many stage rallies in forests as possible.

Two big rallies that very quickly leapt upon the forest bandwagon were the Royal Scottish Automobile Club's Scottish Rally and the South Wales Automobile Club's Welsh Rally, both long established events. The Scottish took to the forests in 1962 and the Welsh in 1963, although the latter had to be cancelled at the last minute because of heavy snow, and was eventually run in 1964. I competed in numerous Scottish and Welsh rallies in the sixties and early seventies, and became very familiar with the forests. Wales specialised in big drops while

Scotland's stages were much rougher, in general. I never had much success in the Welsh, competing with Frank Grange, David Cowan, and Peter Clarke among others. In Scotland I fared better, and did several with Bob Lamb in Cortinas and Escorts. I'm leaping into fast-forward mode here, as I later enjoyed good results on the Scottish with Peter Clarke in his Silentnight sponsored Escort TC in 1970, '71 and '72.

In 1972 I found myself hitching a lift back from Scotland with the winner of that year's Scottish, Hannu Mikkola. We were in Hannu's Mercedes with John Davenport as another passenger, and I was given the first stint as driver. It was a quick car, and I was enjoying my very rapid progress down the then empty motorway when we spotted a police car parked in a space at the side of the road. Hannu saw the police car leave its 'perch,' presumably to catch us. At that point I felt a tap on my shoulder and, from the back seat, was presented with Hannu's driving licence, issued in Finland. "This is where you now learn to speak Finnish!" he said. Thankfully I didn't need to, as the police car stayed behind us before leaving at the next junction.

Now that I'm dealing with this great era of rallying, I have to mention the 'Emerald Isle,' although I know it is not strongly associated with forest rallying. Ireland is, in fact, one of the greatest rallying countries in the world and the sport has a huge following there and always produces great drivers. I am lucky to have had a long association with Irish rallying, and have made many good friends at rallies and Guinness-fuelled social functions. I first competed there in 1965 on what every enthusiast knew as 'The Circuit.' The Circuit of Ireland Rally was a long thrash over the wonderful closed roads of Northern and Republic of Ireland, with particularly spectacular roads down into County Kerry, overlooking the Atlantic Ocean. The rally would usually be based in Killarney for two nights, as was the case in 1965 when I navigated Tom Beaumont in a Volvo PV544 that spent the entire rally going sideways! What a beast – the car, that is, not Tom! One incident on this event that I considered hilarious concerned the works Triumph 2000 of Roy Fidler and Don Barrow. The car had previously competed on long events in mainland Europe, and its huge boot had been fitted with an extra petrol tank to give the thirsty car more range. The tank had been removed for the Circuit of Ireland, and the filler cap on the top rear wing replaced by a rubber grommet. At a tiny, old-fashioned petrol station on the west coast near Galway, the ancient pump attendant was told to fill up the car using the filler on the right wing. Now, you may be ahead of me here for, needless to say, the pump was inserted into the hole on the left wing, the pump man having removed the rubber grommet. Roy and Don disappeared into the petrol station shop, ready to pay for the fuel but were somewhat puzzled when the Triumph was still being filled after several minutes! You've guessed it! Triumph AHP 427B was now the proud possessor of many, many gallons of best 'super,' all sloshing around in the boot. You can well imagine the panic that ensued as the precious but dangerous cargo had to be removed from the boot by a gaggle of young Irish motor mechanics armed with buckets and hosepipes.

There was further great excitement among the forest rallying fraternity when the long-established London Motor Club announced that it, too, would be taking to the British forests with the Gulf London International Rally. The London Motor Club had been running night rallies as part of the national championship for many years, the first one in the fifties, and surprised everyone by announcing that it had persuaded Gulf Oil to sponsor the event, which would take place in the summer of 1965. It would be a full-blown international rally and would attract a big entry, as free petrol was to be supplied to all competitors thanks to Gulf tankers positioned throughout the route. Can you imagine that happening today?

The Gulf London would cover 1400 miles, taking in 36 special stages totalling 400 miles. It would visit Wales, the Scottish borders, and Yorkshire, with some stages 30 to 40 miles in length. This non-stop charge would be very tough, for sure. Needless to say, I was keen to compete, and thrilled when Chris Knowles-Fitton asked me to co-drive his Mini-Cooper S as part of the Appleyards team from Yorkshire. The other driver was Appleyards' car salesman and very fast Mini driver Tony Fall, who was on the verge of a works drive with BMC. I believe both our cars had some works bits from the BMC team in Abingdon. One thing was for sure: here were two immensely fast drivers who were expected to do well.

Chris Knowles-Fitton is a splendid, eloquent chap, and well remembers our first and only outing together, which started from a London Airport hotel before heading along the old A40 to the Forest of Dean and Wales. Chris has a great sense of humour and also a certain eccentricity, which I much enjoyed and still do. I was most impressed by the speeds we were achieving over the stages during the night, as Chris slid the Cooper S through the fast and dusty tracks in the forests of mid-Wales. I remember that the car had a moveable spotlight mounted in the centre of the roof, which I operated with my right hand, whilst using my left to clutch my map and road book and hang on for dear life. It was three o'clock in the morning, it was dusty and foggy, my arm was aching, and the beam of the light was waving about madly, as I really couldn't see the twists and turns of the track that the light was meant to be picking up. My slightly demented driver was still going flat-out, driving like a man possessed.

"Chris," I shouted through the intercom. "I'm going to switch the light off; it's not doing much good, is it?"

"No, no" came the reply. "Wherever you point it, I'm following it ... Splendid!"

All the above antics were proving very useful, and by dawn we were in a very high position, as was our team-mate Tony Fall, with David Fawcett in the hot seat. In fact, we were neck-and-neck with the works Mini-Cooper S of none other than Paddy Hopkirk, the most famous rally driver in Britain after his Monte Carlo rally victory the previous year. "Could this last?" I wondered.

I soon had my answer, for all hell broke loose as we entered the infamous Dovey forest complex near Dolgellau. On the second of the stages there, a 30-mile charge, only two cars managed to beat the maximum time allowance. This was a very fast rally, to be sure. There was a huge number of retirements on the stage, including the big names like Vic Elford and Paddy Hopkirk. In fact, Paddy was very nearly our undoing, for his Mini-Cooper had electrical and overheating problems not far into the long stage, and instead of crawling to the end, he turned round and decided to return to the start. Chris, of course, was in full flight by now, and we met Paddy head-on – Chris says that to this day he does not know how he avoided wiping him out. Curiously enough, Paddy and Chris 'made up' over a number of Irish whiskeys at a recent Ecurie Cod Fillet reunion. They both remembered the incident. So did I, but they didn't invite me to join them for a drink!

Mason's Motoring Mayhem!

Back in Dovey forest, after the Paddy incident, we spotted David Pollard's Hillman Imp stuffed into the trees and, a few hundred yards later, saw a dejected-looking Roy Fidler and Graham Robson standing next to their stationary works Triumph 2000.

Rather stupidly, in my opinion, Mr Knowles-Fitton decided to give them a friendly wave. Not a wise move, for he lost concentration and we sailed off the road into the scenery at a very imminent hard-right bend. There was a steep drop and our Mini slid backwards, teetering over another drop, parked at about 10 degrees from vertical. We undid our belts and extricated ourselves immediately, realising the car could easily plummet further into the valley below. We crawled and scrambled up to the track, popping our heads above the roadside, when who should be approaching at breakneck speed but our team-mates, Tony Fall and David Fawcett. Fall couldn't believe his eyes, and I remember to this day his reaction. His mouth opened and he took one hand (if not both) off the steering wheel and pointed at us! Unfortunately, his car then understeered off the road, just as ours had, and gracefully spun round and slid down the steep bank to position itself just two or three feet away from the side of ours. Talk about precision parking!

Pandemonium then ensued whilst Knowles-Fitton and Fall screamed at each other, before deciding to winch our cars back onto the track by fastening a device to a tree on the inside of said track. Some minor progress was made by cranking the winch, but the project was abandoned when a Swedish Mini-Cooper appeared round the bend and sliced off its roof-light as it passed under the winch cable! Fall had had enough of this and decided to drive down a 1-in-2 hill through trees for a quarter of a mile before emerging in the garden of a forester's cottage, scattering cabbages in his wake. He regained the road, cutting out a good mile of stage, and was still in the rally for a short while.

We were there for over an hour before we were extricated from our predicament, thanks to a Forestry Commission tractor that appeared after the last rally car had passed. Our Mini was perfectly driveable, despite its little excursion, and Chris and I headed up to Yorkshire to assume the roles of spectator. There had been a lot of retirements, so the cars were no longer coming thick and fast. In fact, only 19 of the original 92 starters were still running. Of these, Roger Clark and Jim Porter were leading the rally in Roger's own Cortina GT, with which they had very recently won the Scottish Rally. They would go on to win this event, too, on their way to a works drive for Ford, where they would stay until 1981.

The 1965 Gulf London had been a great success, and the organising team enthusiastically set about planning further similarly gruelling events. They duly appeared in the summers of 1966, '67, and '68, and, of course, I was on parade with my maps at the ready. Another Gulf started and finished at Heathrow Airport, then two at the Excelsior Hotel at Manchester's Ringway Airport. All three were exhausting rallies with a mere three-hour break in three days or so. I competed with Bob Lamb in a 1300cc Escort GT, in which we won our class one year.

Fourteen

Further into the forests

The RAC Rally went from strength to strength in the early sixties, and I was lucky enough to be invited to compete a great deal, taking a week's holiday from wherever I was working at the time. On these outings I accompanied seven different drivers (which, you may think, indicates that no-one would have me more than once) in their privately owned cars. I enjoyed every trip, but the old memory isn't what it once was, and I certainly can't give you a blow-by-blow account, you will be relieved to know! I do have memories of relatively spectacular incidents that befell me, of course.

In 1963 Bob Lamb decided to enter the RAC again, and asked me if I wanted to come along to enjoy the 400 miles of forest tracks over a Blackpool-Bournemouth route not dissimilar to our maiden voyage the previous year. We were starting to think we were old hands at the game! Bob had recently acquired a Humber Sceptre, supposedly a sporty saloon in the Humber range from the Rootes Group in Coventry. Until then, Humbers had been best known for supplying limousines to Prime Ministers and a staff car to Field Marshal Montgomery in North Africa during World War II. In fairness, I should mention that well-known broadcaster-cum-rally driver Raymond Baxter actually achieved a class win and high position driving a Humber Super Snipe in the 1961 RAC Rally. The red Sceptre that Bob and I would take on the RAC was very comfortable, fairly luxurious and reasonably powerful, but it was a bit of a lumbering machine by today's standards. However, starting at number 125, we had a good run with no mechanical problems and not even a puncture, finishing in the twenties.

I was back with Bob Lamb a couple of years later when the RAC Rally started and finished at a London airport hotel. Bob had, by now, purchased a Ford Cortina GT, and we hoped for great things. However, our plans went somewhat awry when the northern part of Britain became blanketed in snow. Cars were slithering about on main roads, let alone in the forests. In fact one such main road, the steep Sutton Bank on the A170 east of Thirsk, became virtually impassable, and the rally almost ground to a halt. We got up the hill eventually by fitting snow chains to the rear wheels. However, we were having to go pretty quickly to avoid running out of time. After a few Yorkshire stages there was a cacophony in the rear of the car as the snow chains started to break. The noise was unbearable, but we pushed on merrily until the noises became even more peculiar. The flailing chains had torn holes in the inside of the rear wheel arches, would you believe? How we struggled to take off the broken chains and how frozen our hands became. It was a nightmare.

In the intervening year of 1964 the weather in Britain was much kinder, thankfully, and I enjoyed a trouble-free run with top British rallyist (and former

TT rider) Phil Simister in his red Cortina GT. For the first time the start and finish would be in the centre of London, at the Duke of York's barracks, to be precise. It seemed a bit bizarre walking through busy streets between the rally headquarters and our hotel, carrying crash helmets and other rally paraphernalia. Being a bit of a hoarder, I found the brochure of our hotel not long ago. We stayed at the Prince of Wales Hotel in DeVere Gardens in Kensington, where the price of a room was 45 shillings a night – that's £2.25 to you! Phil Simister had a very strong finishing record, and had been competing in the RAC since the late fifties. I hoped my navigation would be up to it. Thankfully it was, and we finished 21st out of the 158 starters.

Phil, who owned a Ford main dealership in Macclesfield, was a gentle, peaceful, man and far from the image of a very rapid driver. I remember he wore a woollen cardigan with a packet of cigarettes in one pocket and a lighter in the other. You don't really expect cardiganny sorts of people to drive at breakneck speeds through forests. You probably also don't expect rally drivers to smoke cigarettes during events, but Phil and many others did, sometimes even on stages. The brilliant Pat Moss was a heavy smoker, and in his eulogy at Pat's funeral in 2008 Stuart Turner recalled that rally drivers could always tell if they were on the right route by following her trail of cigarette ends!

I suppose I should let you know the co-driver's navigational duties on road sections of the rally. The road book had to be read constantly, noting all mileages – one could obviously be penalised for lateness, but other penalties could be applied if you exceeded an average of 40mph over more than 20 miles of public road. On the stages, it was a matter of looking for arrows provided by the organisers and keeping the timecard safe. Later on in my career, when I became more proficient, I would read the tracks from the Ordnance Survey maps during stages. I would also take the wheel occasionally, if there were long sections between stages. So you'll see, it was a busy little life.

I remember staying in Perth for the overnight stop in 1964, and the freezing cold hotel that most teams were patronising. Don Barrow, who was co-driving the great Finn Timo Mäkinen in a works Healey remembers the cold night and his icy bedroom. Next morning he asked Timo how he had managed. "No problem, Don," Timo replied. "It very cold so I turn on all hot taps in bathroom and leave on all night!" At that moment Paddy Hopkirk appeared in his dressing gown, complaining that there was no hot water for a shower anywhere in the hotel! After a long trek back south, via East Anglia, the final hurdle the following evening was the rush hour traffic in London, as the route passed by the Tower, Parliament Square and Knightsbridge. What a strange place to start and finish a rally.

As expected, my trip on the RAC Rally of 1966 with Roy Mapple brought a lot of laughs. Roy had won his class in his 998cc Mini-Cooper on the 1965 event. We were, and still are, great friends, and I knew we would enjoy our trip, which again started and finished at one of the big hotels at London Heathrow airport but took in 63 special stages, totalling over 400 miles. Roy had the somewhat unique habit of chuckling and giggling out loud at times of drama and excitement. I wouldn't say I found it disconcerting, more slightly surprising – no more so than in the dreaded Kielder forest, which was so rough and rocky that stones were pushing their way inside the car, beneath my feet. He found this very funny.

Before that, the route had taken us up as far as Aviemore in Scotland, with all the usual Scottish classic stages including the fast ones in south-west Scotland.

Continued page 113

The Tour of Britain was a 'race-cum-rally.' Roger Clark and I were entered by Ford in a Capri 3-litre.

A new experience for Vic Preston Jnr from Kenya, driving in Scotland in 1973.

A new car for Roger and me for the 1973
RAC – and seeded number one.

Sue and I were married in 1973
– the day I met my match!

Sideways, as usual.

The 1974 RAC was a bad year for us, as we finished seventh.

The *Daily Mirror* sign above the number is missing, as a new door had been fitted after a shunt in 1974.

The things you have to do for sponsors. Roger and I selling tins of hairspray in Boots chemists before the 1975 RAC.

The biggest rally show ever staged was Pirelli 'Star-talk' at Wembley in 1977. We had 19 guests, including Timo Mäkinen, Hannu Mikkola, and Erik Carlsson, seen here at rehearsals while I pontificate!

One of the many Clark and Mason performances.

Top billing in Oldham!

1975, and another second place on the RAC Rally.

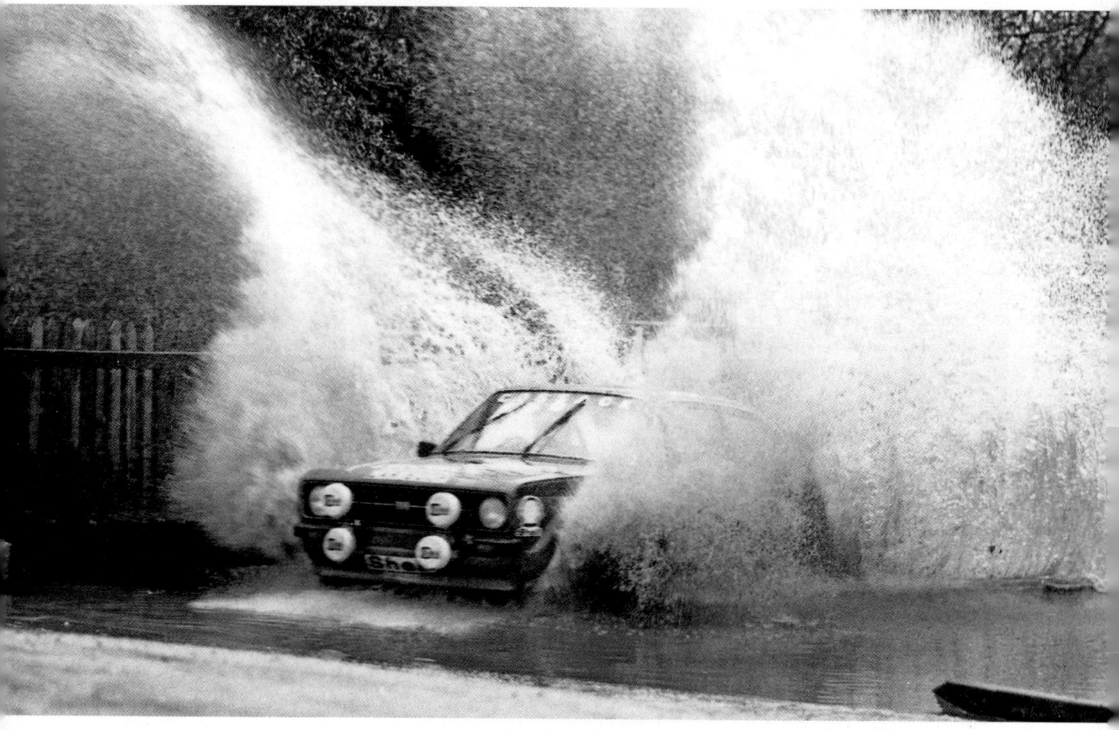

More water. We were trying!

In full flight at Scarborough's Olivers Mount.

Timo Mäkinen and Henry Liddon (centre) got their hat-trick in 1975. We were second. The baby on the left is my tiny daughter, Emma, in Sue's arms.

What's your name? Autograph signing at the *Autosport* Racing Car Show was a regular assignment.

A little more sedate! A get-together of Segrave Trophy winners. Here, I'm next to my boyhood hero, test pilot Peter Twiss. Also, left to right, pilots John 'Cats Eyes' Cunningham and Bill Beaumont, Peter Ashcroft of Ford, and world land speed record holder Richard Noble.

Our home from 1975, on the border of Northamptonshire and Oxfordshire.

In 1987 I was brought into the full BBC team for the RAC Rally coverage with William Woollard, Sue Baker, and Barrie Gill.

Sand racing at Weston-Super-Mare.

Stirling Moss always saw the funny side of me losing my hair (and catching up with him!).

Back in action! With Louise Aitken-Walker in a works Peugeot 309 on the
Cumbrian Rally for *Top Gear* in 1988.

We made it!

More *Top Gear* adventures. Trialling
with champion Julian Fack.

The Reliant Robin world
championship. I still finished fifth!

With Carol Vorderman filming an
Antiques Roadshow spin-off for BBC.

Every boy's ambition: to be an Eddie Stobart driver.

Another boyhood dream. Meeting (and driving) John Cooper of Mini-Cooper fame.

The 'Mason pounce.' Well, it certainly frightened four-time World Rally Champion Tommi Mäkinen.

Ready for the off. The Pirelli Classic Marathon started at Tower Bridge, London in 1989.

With Roger Clark, navigating my way through the Italian Dolomites.

We got there!

Ove Andersson, Timo Mäkinen, you-know-who, Roger Clark, Paddy Hopkirk and Stirling Moss after the final hill-climb.

Of course, I had to 'sing for my supper.' At least Paddy Hopkirk and Alec Poole enjoyed it.

The propeller-driven Helicar was the weirdest thing I ever drove on *Top Gear*.

Mind you, I was dressed for the occasion!

The Alpine Trial for vintage Rolls-Royces made a one-hour *Top Gear* special programme.

From the sublime to the ridiculous: the last of the Russian-built Ladas.

The centre of our little empire.

My former rally partner, HRH Prince Michael of Kent, visited our stand at a Frankfurt trade show. Lord knows what we were looking at!

The dreaded anti-static strip, which brought me to court with a lot of publicity.

TV presenting in the Isle of Man with legendary TT rider Geoff Duke. I know nothing about bikes!

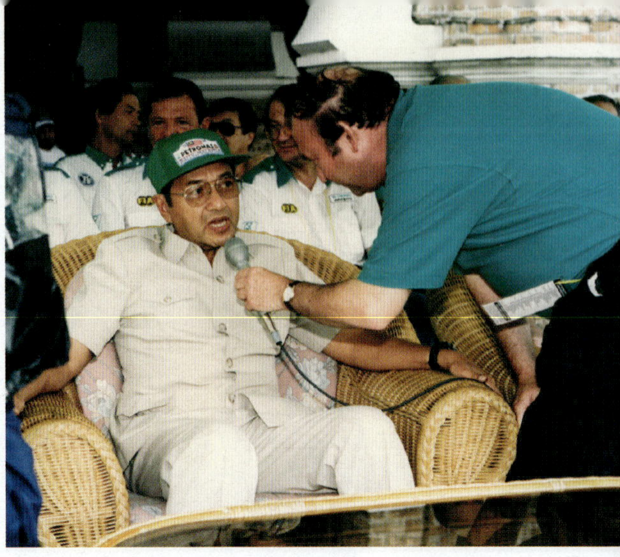

Not long after interviewing the Prime Minister of Malaysia, I was hauled off towards jail.

When seat belts were made compulsory in 1983, this product became a great success.

The Asian Automotive and Accessories Exhibition in Singapore in 1984 saw Sue and me in selling mode.

The rally attracted more than its fair share of publicity in 1966, because two Grand Prix stars, Jim Clark and Graham Hill, were competing. Clark was in a works Lotus Cortina, and Hill in a works Mini-Cooper S.

Graham Hill's assault was unspectacular, and he never really came to terms with the tiny front-wheel drive car. He retired on the second evening in Grizedale Forest in the Lake District. Jim Clark, however, was a different kettle of fish. He had been tutored by Roger Clark at Ford's testing sessions, and really took to the idea of driving flat out on rough surfaces. He was partnered by Brian Melia, a Ford works co-driver, former British champion navigator, and successful driver in his own right. Jim Clark had, in fact, started his motorsport career rallying as a member of the Berwick and District Motor Club near his home village of Chirnside in the Scottish borders, when he drove a Sunbeam Talbot 90 and had a reputation of either winning or crashing.

On the 1966 RAC Rally, Jim Clark astonished everyone by getting up to sixth place overall, mixing it with all the Scandinavians and actually taking the fastest time on one stage in the snow. He was phenomenal, and I was lucky enough to talk to him at various times during the rally. Although Jim had had one or two brushes with the countryside, it was in one of the fast stages in Dumfries and Galloway that he 'came a cropper.' The track featured a very fast crest followed by a left-hand bend, which caught out the great man. The Lotus Cortina left the road and rolled among the rocks two or three times. It was the end of a brave and brilliant drive. Jim and Brian Melia joined us at a dinner halt at the Station Hotel, Dumfries shortly after the incident. I shall always remember this. Jim said "I analysed it and knew what I had done wrong when I was halfway through the second roll. I wouldn't do it again."

My memorable trip with Mapple continued throughout the five-day event, and we really enjoyed our journey, which had included the famous Hardknott pass with which we were both so familiar. On the route back from Scotland to London there were more stages, including Sherwood Forest in Nottinghamshire and Silverstone race track. Now nearing the end of the event and positioned in the top twenty, there was a great happening – another memorable Mason incident. In the first Sherwood stage Roy indulged in a bit of 'ditch-hooking,' and hit a large tree trunk lying in the gutter. The Mini's tie-bar broke, and we emerged from the ditch with one front wheel hanging off. We realized that our service crew, consisting of Roy's father and 'Uncle George' from the family garage near Blackpool, would be at the exit of the forest stage a few miles away, and would have a spare tie-bar, of course. By this time we had been surrounded by spectators, so I asked if anyone could get me out of the forest, avoiding the rally stage route, so I could get a replacement. There were several volunteers and one young man offered to take me there. We set off in his Mini-Cooper like a bat out of hell, and I noticed we had two or three other Minis behind us. This was exciting stuff for them. It was quite exciting for me, too, as this enthusiastic spectator was driving me on the forest tracks between the trees faster than Mapple had ever gone! I was petrified, and as I feared, one quarter of a mile later we slid wide on a bend and fell on our side in a ditch. The driver of number two Mini-Cooper in the procession then offered to transfer me to his car to complete our journey to Uncle George. You probably won't believe it, but this driver then set off like another bat out of hell, and after a mile or so of extremely hairy driving and within sight of the forest exit we were aiming for, went off the track into another ditch! I must be the only person ever to go off the road in one special stage with three different drivers! I did take the new tie-bar back with yet another lunatic driving me and we happily finished the event, albeit out of the top twenty, in 34th place.

The following year's RAC was a disaster, as it had to be cancelled at the last minute. All the competitors were assembled at the Excelsior Hotel, ready for the off the next morning, when a severe outbreak of foot and mouth disease hit the headlines. It was affecting various parts of the country, and obviously, the last thing anyone wanted were rally cars charging through forests and over farm tracks, spreading the disease. I remember a special meeting of all competitors being called late in the evening, and a tearful Jack Kemsley announcing that the rally would not take place. I was due to compete with Graham John from Chester in his Austin 1800, and looking forward to a comfortable trip. I seem to remember we all drowned our sorrows, some people getting to bed around the time that they should have been setting off on the 1967 RAC Rally the next morning.

I enjoyed a surprise visit to Spain in 1970, after being contacted by Cal Withers, whose high-profile company, Withers of Winsford, dealt in rally cars and parts. It also sponsored and supplied rally cars to drivers of the calibre of Roy Fidler and Chris Sclater, among others. Cal wanted me to go to the Sherry Rally in Southern Spain to accompany Ian Harwood, who was servicing Chris Sclater's Escort TC. Ian and I were in a hired SEAT saloon, and chased Chris round three-quarters of the route before he retired with a cracked cylinder block whilst lying in third place. After this, we embarked on a 600-mile tow to Bilbao for a ferry back to England. Needless to say, mayhem was never far away! In the middle of Madrid, during evening rush-hour, we stopped at a set of traffic-lights and a policeman waved a huge crowd of pedestrians across the road. Unfortunately for them, owing to the darkness, they didn't quite see the black, greasy tow rope stretched between our two cars. I am sure you can now guess the rest of this story ... yes, you're right, there were, literally, dozens of Spaniards floundering about on the road with briefcases and shopping bags all over the place! The police constable (or whatever they call them in these parts) was not too happy, and didn't really like me taking photographs of the melée. Suffice to say, we were all carted off to the police station for a short stay.

More chaos was to come, however, when we arrived at a very steep descent from the mountains above Bilbao. I was driving, and heard (and felt) a 'clunk' as the SEAT lurched forward, not far from a sheer drop. Thankfully, Chris kept his foot on the brake pedal of the Escort as Ian and I scrambled about at the front of the car and discovered that a brake pad had fallen out. In the middle of these shenanigans, as we flapped and panicked, we observed a British coach coming down the pass. "Bloody hell! I don't believe it!" exclaimed Ian, who hailed from the border area between England and North Wales. "It's a Waggs of Oswestry coach. They run our local school bus service!" It's certainly a small world. Back to the matter in hand, we used a pair of mole grips to close the rubber pipe to the brake calliper, then continued to Bilbao docks, very gingerly, with three wheel braking. The hire-car office was closed, as you might expect, so we removed the mole grips and I consulted my Spanish phrase-book and left a note on the steering-wheel saying 'los frenos non funciona.' I do hope they understood my brilliant translation.

Also in 1970, I had a slight diversion from my co-driving activities as one of the greatest rallies in the world was about to take place. This was the 16,000 mile

London–Mexico World Cup Rally, which would start on the 19th of April from Wembley. It would be the longest, toughest, and most ambitious rally that the world had ever known, linking London to Mexico by way of Europe, South and Central America. It would take six weeks to complete this mighty event between two World Cup venues: London's Wembley and Mexico City's Aztec stadium. I'm not a great football fan (once, many years ago at a party in Manchester, I asked Bobby Charlton what he did for a living!), but I knew that England had won the World Cup in 1966 in London, and that this was a unique way of conceiving a rally. I then faced a dilemma. The event would be very long, and the immense preparation would take much time, so how could I compete? I could not take two months off work at K Shoes; if I did, there would be no job on my return. Although two or three drivers asked me to compete as part of a three-man crew, I really felt my career would suffer. Therefore I decided that although I'd have to be part of this great extravaganza, it would not be in the capacity of a competitor. Very cheekily, I telephoned John Sprinzel (whom I really didn't know from Adam in those days), as I gathered he was the inspiration behind much of the event and virtually in charge. I said I would be available to marshal for part of the event, and roped in my good friend Mike Preston from Morecambe Car Club, who was always up for such ventures. Mike and I had enjoyed a few trips here and there, including a trip to watch the Targa Florio road race in Sicily. We had also once ventured to Woburn in Bedfordshire (I think I may have mentioned that venue before, at the very beginning of this book!)

Mike and I went to Woburn because the final of the British Autocross championship was taking place in the grounds of Woburn Abbey. We were mere spectators, but had an enjoyable two days. On returning from a pub late one evening we passed Whipsnade Zoo, and to our utter amazement saw an escaped wallaby hopping down the road towards us. I am not sure what possessed me, but I told Mike to stop the car and leave the headlights on to mesmerise the wallaby, which I would then catch and put in the back of the car, so we could return it to the zoo and maybe get a reward. I may have been watching too many David Attenborough TV programmes, but I approached the beast and leapt upon it, and actually manoeuvred it to the back door of Mike's car. Its legs were flailing about, and in hindsight probably could have injured me. However, the wallaby had had enough, and didn't seem to want to get into the car – it kicked me in a most sensitive part of my body and scurried off into the bushes! I suppose this is a bit of a diversion, but you might like to know how I spent some of my days and nights when not rallying!

Mike Preston and I were duly enrolled as marshals for the World Cup Rally, and if I remember rightly, he went to the RAC motorsport headquarters in Belgrave Square, London to collect all the paraphernalia connected with marshalling. Flags, banners, control boards, armbands, and goodness knows what else. It was a very impressive package. We were allocated two major marshalling points, one in the French Alps and another in Lisbon, before the cars departed for South America. We would have liked to go to South America, but it was better than nothing, and we were still on the reserve list for possible jobs there.

We performed our duties and met a lot of important rally names, like the Morley brothers and Val Domleo, with whom we shared a hotel in Nice. They were also travelling marshals. Our control was in the tiny village of Sigale, which we pretty much took over. We put banners everywhere, commandeered the pub in the town square, and generally felt very important. Several hours after setting up we were ready for action, and waited for the cars to arrive. It was hectic, as we were on a very tight 'prime' section of the rally, but we enjoyed every minute. I am not sure how the rally was seeded, but the start list seemed a bit of a hotch-potch so we were never quite sure who was going to arrive next. I briefly remember speaking to former European champion Sobieslaw Zasada from Poland (we didn't have a lot to say, as my Polish isn't too good) and Hannu Mikkola. I remember speaking to Bill Bengry, driving a Rolls-Royce Silver Shadow, and the man with the marvellous name of Emanouil Lifchits, driving his Russian state-entered Moskvich 412. I don't think Major Lifchits had much to say, but I will always remember his name, printed as 'Lift-Shit' in the local newspaper and various magazines.

Back safely from our travels, it was time to think about the RAC Rally again. For the 1970 event I was asked to partner George Beever from Yorkshire, with whom I had done one or two smaller events. We were having a good run until George blotted his copy book on a stage on the old toll-road at Porlock in Somerset. Our Escort TC was flying up the hill, which had several tight bends all covered in wet leaves. In fact, 'flying' is an appropriate word, as halfway up the mile-long stage George lost it and we sailed over the edge. There was a very steep drop, and as we fell between the many trees I noticed, to my horror, that below us and coming up very quickly was the Bristol Channel. This had all the makings of an horrific accident, and I was convinced that it was the end of our rally, if not the end of the car and us! Thankfully, a sturdy tree halted our progress down the steep hillside. When we alighted, we discovered that the car was not too badly damaged, so we affixed a tow rope to the back and I persuaded dozens of spectators to heave the car back onto the road, despite the marshals' protestations that it should stay down the bank. We lost ten or more minutes with this little manoeuvre but made it to the finish of the rally some days later in 33rd place. Another Mason moment!

Assuming you've read the first chapter, I think you've read all you need to know about my 1971 RAC Rally with Peter Clarke. The Woburn Lake incident says it all; apart from the fact we managed to get out of the lake, thanks to the RAC Land Rover. We were almost an hour late, but stayed in the rally and finished 23rd back in Harrogate, still sitting on very damp seats. I'm not sure if you can get rheumatism in the bum but if you can, I'm sure I got it.

Later in 1971, I received a surprise telephone call from the Ford competitions department at Boreham to say that Roger Clark was contesting the British Rally championship in a works Escort. He and Jim Porter had won the championship back in 1965 in a Cortina, and would be competing as a full works entry in 1972. Unfortunately the first event, the Mintex Seven Dales, almost clashed with the Hong Kong Rally, which Ford was also entering with cars for Roger Clark and Timo Mäkinen. Roger could enter the Mintex Seven Dales, but would have to leave immediately after the finish on Sunday morning to fly to Hong Kong, where Jim Porter would be waiting for him, having prepared all the maps and pace notes. With this phone call, I could see another life-changing and amazing moment heaving onto the horizon: Stuart Turner wanted me to co-drive Roger. I've never been a great telephone person (probably as a result of never having one in the home when I was young), and surprisingly, I still don't enjoy telephone conversations, so I suppose I spluttered and said all the wrong things to whomever it was that called me. Nevertheless, I was duly signed.

The Seven Dales Rally, which had had various names and sponsors over the years, has always been the top rally in the north of England, as it included special stages in forests and elsewhere as well as being a night navigation rally. The 1972 event would be no different. Starting on the morning of Saturday the 26th February, the 450-mile route took in 14 forest stages, tarmac stages like Scarborough's Oliver's Mount, fast airfields, and an eight-hour night navigation section all over the tightest lanes in the northern counties, finishing at Selby in North Yorkshire on Sunday morning. There was mist and fog all over the notorious Stainmore, with its fast roads and blind crests, and there were muddy sections across the moors using difficult-to-read white roads. There was a closed gate, I remember, and I had to rush out to open and close it, but obviously someone behind us rammed into it, head on. The sturdy wooden gate was lying across the track and was practically invisible in the mist. One Mini-Cooper driver hit it at speed, and recalled the incident to us at the petrol stop in Kirkby Lonsdale. "That was a bloody rough cattle grid up on the moors," he said!

No-one at Ford ever said why I had been selected to partner Roger Clark on this event, but the fact that the rally had a difficult map reading section may have influenced their choice, as I certainly had good knowledge of the roads. My first works ride had been a daunting prospect, made all the more difficult by the fact it was in a left-hand drive car, the ex-Jean-François Piot Ford Escort RS. A rally with hundreds of time controls in narrow lanes is not the ideal place for a full-works left-hand drive car. At every point I had to hand the timecard, attached to a clipboard, across to Roger to give to the marshal, who then handed it back to me when we had checked that the correct time had been written in the appropriate place. It was a hell of a rigmarole, to be sure. A lot of marshals were somewhat flustered when we screamed into the control, with the driver sitting on the wrong side and it being Roger Clark to boot. I had never been so fast in my rallying career; we were charging through the narrow lanes at unbelievable speed. One section – down from Firbank Fell near Kendal – was well-known to me and all other local rallyists. No-one had ever been able to get between the two points where controls were always sited in under ten minutes. We did it in 8 minutes 49 seconds, can you believe?

I am pleased to say I never made a single map-reading error, gave Roger the severity of bends and instructions at junctions accurately, and seemed to have adjusted to his remarkable speed and car control. At the finish control at the Selby Fork Motel on Sunday morning we had a lead over the previous year's winners Eric Jackson and Ken Joseph of 12 minutes, 48 seconds. To this day, this margin between first and second places remains a record, and has never been equalled on a national British championship event.

Motoring News reported the rally in detail, and was very complimentary about our efforts, saying "Obviously, the combination of Roger Clark's driving ability and Tony Mason's superb navigation paid dividends and, for a change, on an RAC Rally championship event it could be honestly said that the skills of both driver and co-driver contributed to the success." And, just in case you thought I wrote this glowing report, as a regular contributor to the newspaper, I can tell you it was written by regular competitor and rallies editor Mike Greasley. The 1972 Mintex Seven Dales was the last rally in the RAC national championship to feature a map-reading road section, so I was unable to show my prowess in the future.

Fifteen

The RAC Rally – the big one

A s I write this, it is exactly 40 years since I experienced what is known as a life-changing moment. Those of you who have ploughed through the previous pages of ramblings will have gathered that I had enjoyed life, had a modicum of success, a lot of fun, and caused a bit of mayhem along the way. On the 5th December 1972, it all happened. I achieved the ambition of every rallyist in the British Isles by winning Britain's biggest, most famous, and toughest rally – the RAC.

I've already mentioned the RAC Rally quite a lot, and you probably don't need me to explain much more about the event that, over the years, had established itself as Britain's toughest motoring challenge, Britain's biggest single spectator attraction, and one of the world's greatest rallies.

It all started way back in 1932, when Colonel Loughborough in a Lanchester (not Colonel Lanchester in a Loughborough, as erroneously stated by my fellow presenter Tiff Needell on *Top Gear* once) won the 1000-mile RAC Rally, decided by a series of tests on Torquay promenade. The good Colonel's Lanchester had a fluid flywheel (whatever that is), which enabled him to drive slower than anyone else on one of the piffling promenade tests. He completed the 100-yard course at less than 1mph, so you could say he won the rally by being the slowest. I find that rather splendid.

The RAC Rally continued in a similar vein, with a number of starting points all over the country converging on a seaside town on the south coast of England, and more silly tests. Of course, all this so-called motorsport had to be suspended when World War II came along, but the RAC Rally resumed in 1951 with what was, effectively, another tour of Britain with a few slightly more competitive auto tests thrown in. It was won by two of the great names of rallying history, Ian and Pat Appleyard, in a Jaguar XK120. They came third the following year, and won again in 1953. Shortly after this, the event became tougher, with a considerable amount of map reading required, which, evidently, came as something of a shock to some competitors who arrived one year without the appropriate 1in Ordnance Survey maps.

The event improved bit by bit, but was still not popular with overseas drivers because of the night navigation sections between the tests. Something had to be done, so Jack Kemsley, a prominent member of the organising committee since the very first 'Colonel Loughborough' event, took charge and introduced the first special stages in 1960, as I've mentioned.

Fast forward to 1972. Things were a little different to those early rallies when Roger Clark and I won the event by nearly three-and-a-half minutes, beating 191 other cars into the bargain. My trip with Roger in a works Ford Escort was ten years after my first RAC Rally, and it was a storybook trip to be sure. There were 72 fast special stages to be attacked, and it was one of those few motorsport events where everything just 'clicked.' The car ran perfectly and hardly missed a beat, and Roger and I never put a foot wrong, thankfully.

So, how on earth did I come to be sitting on top of that marvellous Ford Escort on the finish ramp in York that Tuesday night in December 1972, facing a battery of television lights and being sprayed with champagne? This was certainly the greatest rallying moment for both Roger and me, and appeared to go down very well with the British public. I still remember virtually every inch of the 2500 mile route, so I'll start at the beginning, so to speak.

In the previous chapter I mentioned my ever-developing association with the Ford Motor Company, and, indeed, my successful trip with Roger Clark in a works Escort at the beginning of 1972, when we won the Mintex Seven Dales Rally. Stuart Turner, Ford's director of motorsport, has always had a keen interest in motor clubs, and after my Woburn Lake incident (see chapter one) he decided to rope me in to join various motorsport 'forums' he was running at clubs around the country. Stuart also ran rally schools at some venues, and I was asked to cover rally navigation along with two ultra-successful, internationally famous co-drivers, Henry Liddon and Tony Ambrose. Exalted company indeed. They probably thought 'Who is this berk?' One of the events took place in Cambridge, and Stuart thought it would be a good wheeze at this great seat of learning to provide legendary Finn Timo Mäkinen with a gown and mortar board for his lecture. Stuart always liked giving people challenges, and gave me about an hour's warning for this little task. I can't remember how I found these accoutrements, but I borrowed them from somewhere and we duly equipped Timo for his lecture. I heard very recently that this single example of initiative influenced Stuart in signing me to accompany Roger Clark on the RAC Rally.

In mid-1972 Stuart Turner invited me to attend a meeting at the Swan Revived Hotel in Newport Pagnell, which was to be attended by various motor club officials from around the country, and would help Ford to develop its interests at the grass roots of motorsport. The Ford Mexico rally challenge was on the go, and it was felt I could give my opinion on the series with regard to selection of events. I duly attended, but was disappointed to find that Stuart was not in attendance because another major Ford function had been organised at Ford's London office. It might even have been the time he went there to meet Henry Ford himself, which I know happened once, and I would imagine that would be a more important meeting than one with a load of hairy blokes in rally jackets in Newport Pagnell. Bill Barnett, Ford's much respected and long-serving rally manager, deputised. Although I didn't know Bill well, I had met him and had discussions with him over the telephone (including discussing my fee for co-driving Roger on the Mintex Seven Dales – the first time I had ever been paid anything to go rallying, not including the free sausages I sometimes got when I rallied with Bob Lamb, the butcher!). During one telephone call I recall Bill saying he and Stuart had been talking about the RAC Rally. He casually asked me what my plans were for the November event. I said I assumed I would be doing it with Peter Clarke, but nothing had been discussed. My little mind started ticking when he said "We may be able to use you on the RAC, as Jim Porter is not available because he's going to organise the RAC Rally." Nothing more was said, and Roger Clark's name was never mentioned. The phone call was suddenly terminated, as Bill had been told by his secretary that Hannu Mikkola was hanging on the phone in Helsinki. I gave a lot of thought to that phone call with Bill, but never mentioned it to anyone.

At the Newport Pagnell meeting I listened intently and commented when necessary, but didn't do too much pontificating as I wanted to keep in Bill's good books at all costs. At the end of the meeting Bill shuffled his papers, stuffed them into a brief case and said "Thank you very much gentlemen, I'm off." All evening I had been working out how and when to ask him about my possible involvement in the RAC Rally. Now, horror of horrors, he was gone. I leapt to my feet, ignoring everyone else, and scampered out of the door and down the stairs to catch up with Bill near the front of the hotel. "Bill," I spluttered, now gabbling in panic mode, "You once mentioned something about the RAC?" "Oh! Yes," he said "Could you co-drive for Roger Clark? I'll have to confirm it later." And with that he was gone. Eventually, I received a letter confirming my booking to co-drive Roger and, indeed, my fee for the week, which was nearly a third of my annual salary at K Shoes. He also invited me to visit the competitions department at Boreham in Essex to get to know everyone.

Next thing I knew, I received a phone call from someone at Boreham saying I should enrol at the Jim Russell Racing School at Mallory Park in Leicestershire. I suspect Stuart Turner had suggested this, as he had already sent me to lessons to polish up my French language skills. He liked sending people to places. I didn't quite understand this racing school bit, but now realise that they knew that Roger would want me to drive on some road sections of the RAC, and felt a course of eight lessons would be beneficial. I duly enrolled and toddled off to Mallory every Saturday morning to drive Formula Fords with a lot of budding racing drivers. On many of the Friday nights prior to my racing driving I would stay with Roger and Judith Clark at their home in Hinckley, and, inevitably, enjoy a few pints with Roger and his friends. I don't know if I was the star driver at the school (I doubt it), but no-one seemed too critical, and I received a splendid certificate, which amused Roger no end.

A few weeks before the date of the rally I received a nice letter from Bill Barnett's secretary, Pam Goater, welcoming me to the fold and enclosing a thick Ford service schedule that gave all the details of the forthcoming rally. I was asked to go to the Viking Hotel in York on Thursday 30th November in preparation for scrutineering the next morning, and the start on Saturday 2nd December. Details of every service point were shown in this schedule, together with a list of all six service crews, driving Ford Granada Estates, and, of course, the start number of all the works Escorts: Hannu Mikkola/John Davenport were number 10; Timo Mäkinen/Henry Liddon were at 15; Andrew Cowan/Brian Coyle at 22; and, hurrah, Roger and I were seeded at number 4. It was an ideal number, allowing the first three cars of Stig Blomqvist, Harry Källström, and Håkan Lindberg to 'sweep' the stages and indicate lines through bends (and discover any major hazards). An added advantage was that we would be first of the Fords into every service point, before the Finns could commandeer the mechanics! The star-studded entry list showed legendary names like Waldegård, Aaltonen, Lampinen, Eklund and Andersson, among others. Ove Andersson was, in fact, driving a Toyota Celica representing the very first Toyota factory entry in a rally outside the Far East; a sign of great things to come. In due course Toyota would win Britain's premier rally three times and the World Rally Championship itself, also three times. There were entries from 16 works and dealer teams with 199 cars on the entry list, 192 of which would start. When I saw the published entry list in the motoring magazines I could hardly believe it: major names in British rallying were down in the hundreds. Did I think we would lead this lot for four days and two nights? No! Much as I respected Roger's abilities, there were Finns and Swedes everywhere you looked and, remember, no Brit had ever won the tough forest event. Everyone, but everyone, considered it the prerogative of the Nordic races to win the RAC.

I thought we'd do well, as Roger had spent a full year driving in British forests in our own championship, and he looked very confident and rested after a two-week holiday in Kenya. But an outright win? I really didn't think we had a cat in hell's chance! And just in case you think I am being disloyal, I would mention that Stuart Turner himself had said during TV interviews for *Wheelbase* (the forerunner of *Top Gear)* that all the best rally drivers were from the frozen north of Europe. Stuart is astute enough never to say the wrong thing during interviews, but a lot of people thought he implied that Roger was not in the same class. In fact, Roger always thought that was what Stuart meant, and among the first words Roger said to me on arriving in York that wonderful evening in December 1972 were "That'll show Stuart!"

I suppose we had better get down to the technical bit now, as you'll want to know what was under the bonnet of our shiny, newly-repainted Esso Uniflo-sponsored car. Incidentally, the reason for it being shiny and newly-repainted was that it had received a new bodyshell after Roger rolled the car while filming a promotional film for Esso. In fact, there were two kinds of Escort in our four-car team. Ford had been working with engine-builder par excellence Brian Hart, who had designed and developed a 2-litre alloy cylinder block for the BDA engine, and, as this was homologated in 1972, the engines were fitted to Timo's and Roger's cars, while Hannu and Andrew had the old, heavier, iron block 1.8-litre engines producing 210bhp. For those really interested in such matters, our car was fitted with experimental Lucas fuel-injection, and boasted around 235bhp, whilst Timo's was normally-aspirated. As our car had the newly-supplied alloy engine and new fuel-injection, on paper we looked the most vulnerable of the four cars. Being new to the team and relatively ignorant of such mechanical matters, I didn't know a lot about any of this – otherwise I would have definitely thought we'd no chance of even finishing!

I haven't mentioned Peter Ashcroft yet, to whom we were to owe a great deal of thanks. Peter was Ford's brilliant engine man, and was instrumental in introducing Brian Hart's new alloy engine block, which we used on the RAC to give it its first big win. He had been appointed competition manager when Stuart Turner moved to another Ford location as director of motorsports, and I got to know Peter during the 1972 British championship in which Roger and Jim Porter were competing with great success. A fellow northerner – Peter was born in Preston – we got on really well, and I could not believe his amazing knowledge of engines. I remember once standing at the side of the road, waiting for Roger and the rest of the team's cars to appear. We could hear the screaming BDA engine of the first car even though we were quarter of a mile away. "That's Andrew Cowan," Peter said "and that's got a crank shaft problem." Peter was unique in diagnosing problems before the cars arrived at the service point. He was really in charge of the 1972 RAC Rally team, and his presence at the service point after Dalby Forest in Yorkshire certainly saved our bacon, as you will shortly read.

So, the big moment came as we lined up at York Racecourse alongside huge sheds that contained the serving counters used at horse racing meetings, and, much to Roger's delight, the 'longest bar in Britain.' Obviously, we were not going to imbibe there and then, but Roger enjoyed me giving him facts like that, and chatting about anything that came to mind during the road sections on rallies. Roger was a quiet man, but had a good sense of humour, and found it relaxing to talk about non-rally things. We got on well.

I suppose we should both have been pretty tense as we lined up behind the previous year's winning Saab 96, a Lancia Fulvia, and a Fiat 124 Spider, but in fact we both felt very relaxed and well-prepared for the task ahead. I remember feeling confident that I could do my job efficiently, but aware of the huge responsibility on my shoulders. I boosted my own confidence by telling myself that it was me, no-one else, that had been booked by Ford to sit in the car, and this somehow kept nerves away, even when other British competitors came up making flippant remarks about us, and asking me what I was doing sitting next to the 'maestro.' I told them to piss off!

I checked my clocks to see that they were exactly on Greenwich Mean Time, waited until the secondhand moved towards 9.04am precisely, then told Roger to move towards the starting ramp, which was surrounded by a huge crowd and bedecked with stickers for *The Daily Mirror*, Embassy cigarettes and Unipart. My timecard received its first signature, and various RAC and York civic dignitaries waved us on our way, leaving behind the strong smell of chocolate permeating the air from the huge Terry's factory adjacent to the racecourse.

The Halda twin trip meter started doing its bit as I checked my road book, containing its accurate Tulip arrows, which had been meticulously prepared by the man usually occupying my seat, Roger's long-time co-driver Jim Porter, who first sat alongside Roger in 1960. As we left the racecourse complex I pulled the little knob on the upper of the two Haldas (the lower one stayed on accumulating total mileage). "Turn left," I told Roger calmly, thinking that this would be the first of about 10,000 instructions I would give him before (if?) we returned to York. We then trundled through the streets of York, passing the station, York Minster and other historic attractions as good crowds cheered us on, despite the rain that had now appeared. I suddenly had a flash-back of getting totally confused in the streets of Glasgow at the start of the Highland Rally just ten years before. I shuddered at the memory, and double-checked the street map of York that was helpfully included in the road book.

Half an hour later we were at the first stage in Bramham Park, near Leeds. Crowds surrounded the road into the stage, and inside the park there were thousands of spectators lining the route, which dived in and out of the trees along an unbelievably muddy track. Wearing our orange helmets with sensitive intercoms, I was spotting the arrows and forthcoming obstacles, and giving Roger clear, calm instructions. Although a lot of drivers found the sea of mud unsuitable for a stage on a world event, Roger took it in his stride and drove neatly to clock 4 minutes 34 seconds for the three-minute stage. I checked the times of the cars before us, and informed Roger that Stig Blomqvist was one second quicker. I later discovered that Leif Asterhag (yet another Swede) had clocked fastest in his BMW, over 20 seconds quicker. However, I'm pleased to say he didn't last long.

At the next short two-minute stage at Harewood House, Roger drove tidily, but fast, and we equalled Hannu Mikkola's time, a second ahead of Blomqvist and Mäkinen. The fight was on. Drivers have always called these short spectator stages on RAC rallies 'Mickey Mouse' stages, regarding them as 'fiddly' and a bit of a nuisance: you cannot win a rally because of them, but could easily lose one.

More Mickey Mouse than most was the next in Bradford, where a two-minute stage traversed the fast tarmac tracks in the delightful Esholt sewerage works. When I advised Roger of this little excursion, he said "Blimey! If we go off in here we'll really be in it!" Nevertheless, Roger really got going, and we clocked another fastest time ahead of Tony Fall's powerful Datsun 240Z. As Fall was born and bred in Bradford, and still lived there, we assumed he knew every inch of this bizarre rally venue, and probably walked his dog there every morning.

After the three opening stages in Yorkshire there was a run of 170 miles across to North Wales, so, after driving competitively for all of ten minutes, the great man decided it was time for me to take the wheel. Now, I may have mentioned this earlier, but Roger Clark was a very 'lazy' driver. He only ever drove quickly enough to win, and could adjust his speed on stages quite miraculously in order to keep ahead of the next man. He liked his sleep, and took every advantage to have forty winks between stages. Even if he didn't want to close his eyes, he would change seats at the earliest opportunity, putting the driver's seat into my position before vacating it. In fact, the seat had a special handle that moved from Roger's setting to mine. If he didn't feel sleepy, he would happily sit in the passenger seat, reading the road book to me and flicking the Halda switch. In his best-selling autobiography *Sideways to Victory*, Roger was very complimentary about my driving and said he felt very safe. Well, he had plenty of time to observe me – like 50 per cent of the road section, if not more!

Nevertheless, there were times during my outings with him on RAC rallies when I drove, with some trepidation, sandwiched in convoy between Mikkola and Mäkinen, keeping up with them on twisty Welsh roads in appalling weather. It appears that these Finns preferred to drive themselves at all times. Any driver who hands over to a co-driver usually likes to get back behind the wheel a good few miles before a special stage start line. Roger couldn't care less, and asked me to drive up to the start area where he would disembark before stretching, sniffing the air like a fox about to go hunting for food, then strapping himself in, fastening his helmet, and plugging in the intercom. At the end of a fast stage I would be checking the clocks and times with the marshal and would look up to see him standing next to said marshal, ready to get into the passenger seat again.

By early afternoon we'd checked into a Pontins holiday camp in Prestatyn on the North Wales coast for a one-hour break, before another short stage through some gardens and part of a go-kart track, with the route defined by oil drums. For the third successive stage we were fastest. "I quite like these Mickey Mouse stages, you know," Roger casually announced as we drove along the A55 coast road to our next port of call, Llandudno, and a frighteningly fast stage around the Great Orme with its blood-curdling drops into the Irish sea.

There will be a little interlude here while I tell you that my future father and mother-in-law lived in Deganwy, near Llandudno, and on a visit there, instead of enjoying afternoon tea, I decided to drive over the Great Orme a few times, aware that it was to be a stage on the RAC Rally. I paid the attendant in his little box the five pence or so, and set off for a gentle drive to check the severity of the bends. The Great Orme road is about three-and-a-quarter miles long, so I had soon completed my little trip and decided to have another go. And then I had another one. And another one. By now the attendant selling the tickets was giving me some very funny looks, I must say. I had, in fact, done about twenty passes, committed to memory the severity of every bend, as well as the fact that some of the kerbs were very shallow and corners could be cut. Pace notes were banned on the 1972 RAC Rally, so I made a few notes on a large-scale map and went back to the tea party with the future in-laws.

It was just before five o'clock in the evening as we moved forward to the Great Orme start line. Roger unleashed the 235bhp, and we shot off into the dark and windy night. I had told Roger I would help by calling the route, and told him how fast it would be. We had racing tyres on the car, and as we sailed into the first tightening left-hand bend I really wondered if I was being a bit too clever with my plan. The Escort was handling beautifully, we were cutting corners across the low kerbs, and I could feel that we were within an inch of the granite stone wall, which was all there was between us and the sea below. It was a remarkable drive, and we were clocking not far off 100mph as we screamed down the long straight to the time control on the very edge of the town. Surprise surprise, we were clearly fastest, ahead of Källström. Our fellow Ford works drivers were far behind us and couldn't believe our time. Looking back, I remember it as my most memorable drive in a rally car, ever.

After another 'Mickey Mouse' at Colwyn Bay, it was into the proper rallying and Clocaenog forest, where there were three very quick stages, then on into darkest Wales with a group of famous and fearful forests. Penmachno and Coed-y-Brenin featured first; here, two of the Ford team faltered. Andrew Cowan spluttered to a halt with the Escort's ignition dead, and Timo Mäkinen went off the road, losing a wheel. Both were out of the rally. There was a long stage of 15 miles in the dreaded Dovey Forest, before a one-and-a-half hour supper halt at the Wynnstay Arms in Machynlleth, a familiar watering hole on rallies. I remember that Roger and I were ravenous and were tucking into a hot beef stew and chips. There were no motor-homes with chefs and dieticians in those days, you know.

Can we pull it off?

We were due to leave the Machynlleth supper halt at 11.30pm that Saturday night, and were bracing ourselves for the predicted snow and sleet when a marshal appeared in the dining room and chalked some results onto a blackboard. Everyone gathered around as he laboriously lettered the drivers' names and time penalties. Roger continued to finish off his supper while I pushed through the scrum that had gathered behind the man with the chalk. "My God, I don't believe it!" I shouted across to Roger. "We're in the lead by 20 seconds from Stig!" Tony Fall was sitting with Roger and thought it highly amusing that our names should be top of the list. "You'll both be able to tell your grandchildren that you were once actually leading the RAC Rally," he chortled.

The weather was horrible, with gales and a lot of rain as we splashed our way through the muddy stages. We were obviously still going extremely quickly, but we were taking no chances, aware that tens of thousands of spectators were now willing us to win. At control points it was bedlam, and we felt like The Beatles as spectators clamoured to speak to us or get our autographs on soggy bits of paper. I will always remember going into a time control at Prynnes Garage in the hamlet of Garth, near Builth Wells. This was another well-known fuel stop for rally folk, and was absolutely seething with spectators. It was all a bit of a shambles: chock-a-block with cars parked everywhere, and full of people in wet clothing. The small café was open, and fights nearly broke out when some well-meaning, new-found fans tried to barge through the melée as we were trying to get a cup of tea and a bun.

It was now 3 o'clock in the morning, and many of the drivers were somewhat apprehensive, as the next two stages were on the fast tarmac roads of the famous Epynt ranges in the military area near Brecon, which is frequently used on Welsh rallies. There are blind brows and bends, and it's a much-feared place for those who don't know it. To cap it all, freezing rain was falling and we all wondered whether there would be ice on the Epynt roads, and whether tarmac racing tyres should be fitted. Roger was in a dilemma and so were our service crew, consisting of the wonderful Norman Masters and Don Partington. Norman had built our car, LVX 942J, and he said it was the best car he'd ever built. He was Roger's personal mechanic, so to speak, and would do anything for him. Don was the top auto-electrician at Boreham, and was invaluable in a service area.

Eventually it was agreed we would fit wet racer tyres, but 'not do anything stupid.' I had been to Epynt several times on club rallies, but had a lot less knowledge of the twists, turns, and bumps than many other British crews. It's widely acknowledged that however good a professional driver is, he or she will be lucky to equal times put in by 'locals.' The crests are so numerous, and the open moor so featureless, that it really takes prior knowledge to put up competitive times. In the event this proved to be the case, with Epynt specialists Tony Fowkes, Frank Pierson, Russell Brookes, and Chris Sclater beating all the works teams. Thankfully, we had no calamities and were about fifth fastest behind the specialists, but knew they were no threat to our overall position. We were, however, still aware of the previous year's winning crew, Stig Blomqvist and Arne Hertz, snapping at our heels, as we were only half a minute ahead of them. Fortunately for us, but not for the poor animal, Stig hit a sheep, destroying two spotlights and the radiator and water pump of the Saab. That eased the pressure as we drove out of wet and windy Wales to Gloucestershire's Forest of Dean, where more bad news awaited the Ford team. At least we were out of Wales though, which had worried me immensely.

Hannu Mikkola's Escort had been having water problems on Epynt, the temperature rising alarmingly. He cautiously drove up to the first stage in the Forest of Dean, and actually queued up ahead of us at the control there. Roger looked at the exhaust pipe, and came out with one of his typically succinct comments: "That car is f----d," he said. The first of the stages in the Forest of Dean brought the final drama, as Hannu's engine finally boiled itself to a standstill in a cloud of steam – its cylinder head gasket had blown. The mighty Ford team was now down to just one car. And that was us.

We were relieved to get out of Wales unscathed and enjoyed our Sunday morning breakfast at the Severn Bridge service area, despite the thousands of supporters who all decided to come into the cafeteria for breakfast the very moment we entered. We were now being treated like stars, and some Ford PR men pushed to the head of the queue and collected our breakfasts, while a man from Esso found a table for us by moving someone off it. Nowadays, crews would be closeted in huge motorhomes with blacked-out windows, but Roger and I had to endure a mass of enthusiasts surrounding us, all watching every mouthful we ate. Thank God there were no mobile phones with which to take photographs in those days. As it was, there were hundreds of photographs being taken as Peter Ashcroft joined us, looking quite serious in light of Hannu's recent demise. He didn't say anything, but we knew he wanted to say 'be careful,' 'take care,' 'don't take any risks,' or some such inanity. Competition managers have to have total faith in their drivers, and Peter knew that his lone car was in good hands and said nothing. However, he knew, as we did, that Stig Blomqvist had been chipping away at our lead, and had actually taken 13 seconds off us on the three Dean stages, where he had been fastest on every one.

On our drive up through the Cotswolds I told Roger details of the day's stages ahead of us, including a very fast tarmac section through the grounds of Blenheim Palace in Oxfordshire, before which we visited the Dunlop van to fit racing tyres. In one fell swoop on the Blenheim stage we grabbed back the time Stig had taken off us before breakfast, and continued to keep him at bay as we started to move north. There were stages at Silverstone, Donington, and in the fast Sherwood Forest, but there was one stage that would bring great drama, and will be remembered by rally enthusiasts forever.

The stage in question is in an area not usually associated with rallying: Birmingham – or, to be precise, Sutton Coldfield. The large Sutton Park is completely surrounded by residential houses, but contains a network of smooth tarmac tracks that wind their way through the many bushes and trees. There are very fast bits, and a couple of tight hairpins through some rhododendron bushes. Needless to say, it attracted record crowds. Some say there were seventy thousand people in there. It certainly looked like it, and was a lot more than the nearby Birmingham City Football Club would get to its matches.

A few weeks before the rally, I happened to be staying in Birmingham on K Shoes business (having persuaded my boss that it was vital that I visit the Birmingham office for something or other), and planned a quick visit to Sutton Park. Pace notes were banned on this rally, as I have mentioned, but I thought a few marks on my maps might come in useful. I telephoned a good pal of mine, Mike Broad, one of the top navigators in the Midlands who went on to become British Rally champion in 1985 with Russell Brookes, and won the 1977 London–Sydney Marathon with Andrew Cowan, among other things. On this 1972 RAC Mike would be co-driving for Finnish champion Hannu Palin in an Opel Ascona, so I thought he wouldn't take much persuading to show me round Sutton Park, which was not far from his home. So, late one afternoon, Mike collected me from the Albany Hotel in the centre of the city and we set forth in his MG 1100 for an unofficial recce. No-one at great rivals Ford or General Motors knew about this, of course, but it proved very useful indeed for both of us. Also useful was the fact that Mike, as a Sutton Coldfield resident, had a little sticker on his car's windscreen that gave him free access to the park, otherwise I would have had to pay as I had at the Great Orme in Llandudno. Come to think of it, I never did get reimbursed by Ford for my expense going round and round the Great Orme.

Mike Broad knew the precise route that the rally would use around Sutton Park, covering just over four miles of tracks. He knew all the hazardous bits, and said he thought that the fastest car on the RAC would do the stage in just over five minutes. It was a worthwhile evening's work, and I was grateful to Mike; for his trouble, I think I bought him a pint afterwards at the Albany Hotel. I suppose I could have claimed for reimbursement from Ford for that, too. However, Stuart Turner would probably have said that I shouldn't have been recceing and refused to pay!

On the great day of the rally we arrived at Sutton Park early on the Sunday afternoon, and set off with great gusto. Roger was blisteringly quick on the smooth tarmac, and our Dunlop racing tyres were doing a fine job. When we got to the tight hairpin among the rhododendrons, Roger handbraked perfectly and we entered a narrow, dark 'tunnel' through the dense bushes. Roger flew through this like a rat up a drainpipe, before emerging onto a long, fast, left-hand bend. My little trip to the park with Mike Broad had proved very useful and we clocked the fastest time by far, at 5 minutes 18 seconds.

We had noticed some skid marks across the grass on a hard left-hand bend not far from the end of the stage, and learnt from the finish marshals that they belonged to Stig Blomqvist. He had understeered off, and sailed merrily over the grass to perch the car on top of a park bench. All four wheels were off the ground, the red Saab literally astride the bench, like some rampant wild animal in a safari park. It must have been a bizarre but splendid sight, and we all saw it in due course, as 'Stig's bench,' as it is now known, was filmed by all the TV and film crews. Stig lost a radiator and a minute or so in time as a result of this little incident, which gave us a better cushion as we led the rally back into York on Sunday evening.

We slept in York that night, and both had a couple of pints in the Viking Hotel bar, but had to refuse any more. There was even the unusual sight of journalists offering to buy us drinks. Amazingly, neither Roger nor I found it easy to get off to sleep that night, as I think we were both haunted by the fact that our lead of 1 minute 50 seconds could be wiped out by Stig if we had a puncture, or if either of us made a minor mistake during the 800 miles of motoring ahead of us. We knew that the following two days would be just as difficult as Wales had been, as the Yorkshire forests were notorious for being very fast and deceptive. Scotland was to be visited in this next leg on the Monday night, with severe weather warnings given, and, if that wasn't enough, the infamous 'Killer Kielder' – the biggest man-made forest in Europe – was to feature strongly. It had a reputation for 'eating' rally cars.

We both felt well at the restart area next morning, and were very impressed as all the mighty Ford team members fussed about us like mother hens. Nothing was too much trouble for them. Even the ebullient Mick Jones, the splendid foreman at Ford's competition department, showed us great respect. Andrew Cowan, who had retired from the rally on Saturday night in Wales, suddenly appeared, and told us that he had been told to trail us for the rest of the event. His car was there to donate any bits that we might need between service areas. Here was another 'mother hen,' and it certainly gave us a boost, with Roger responding by driving magnificently in the Yorkshire forests that followed next. I had been reading the tracks from the Ordnance Survey maps for all of the rally, and I knew having a good knowledge of the forest stages helped Roger, particularly on long, fast straights where I could advise him of any deceptive firebreaks. Also, I should mention that the 'dayglo' arrows, positioned at bends, do not signify the severity of the bends, so I could help him with these, too.

Only once on the entire rally did we slide into a ditch. It was on the long,

15-mile Dalby stage, where a hard right-hand bend developed a peculiar adverse camber halfway through. There was a wide ditch, about three feet deep, with smooth, sloping sides. The Escort slid the nearside two wheels into it (my side, of course!). We were still motoring quickly at an angle of 45 degrees. I could see the ditch levelled out, and instinctively shouted "Keep it going!" to Roger, to which I received the curt reply "What the hell do you think I'm doing?" I have to say, in all the rallies we did together, I think those were the nearest to any cross words or words of castigation I ever heard from Roger. Thankfully, there were no rocks or tree trunks lurking in the ditch like there usually are, and we emerged unscathed and still made fastest time, some 19 seconds ahead of the mighty Stig, who may well have been in the same ditch, as there were tracks there.

We were both enjoying our visit to Yorkshire, and we clocked the fastest time on eight of the ten stages there. Our man Clark was on form.

It was after the Dalby South stage that we noticed a change in the engine note: it sounded like croaking frogs to some observers, who all prophesied our imminent retirement. Thankfully, luck was on our side, for Peter Ashcroft, the engine guru who had allocated the alloy block 2-litre engine to our car, was at the major service point. His sensitive ears had heard us arriving, and he diagnosed fuel starvation immediately. There was mild panic as it was discovered that the main fuel-injection pump wasn't providing sufficient fuel, as there were air bubbles coming through the pipes. A spare pump was fitted alongside the one in use, and Peter had the bright idea of coupling up both in tandem. The coughing and spluttering ceased immediately and we were off again.

It was getting dark as we arrived at the Scotch Corner Hotel near Darlington, where we were met by massive crowds, photographers galore, and brilliant TV lights. The media had really cottoned on to the 'Brits leading' story, and joined in the growing euphoria. Our leading position was mentioned on most TV news programmes, and regular mentions were made hourly on BBC radio. This was a main control, where we had planned to eat a meal before the dreaded Kielder forest (on the basis that it might be our last meal ever!). The dining room at the Scotch Corner Hotel was pandemonium: it made our breakfast halt at the Severn Bridge service area, mentioned earlier, seem like a vicarage tea party. We got something to eat, but were interviewed incessantly throughout our meal. How we didn't get indigestion, I'll never know. Ford had booked us rooms at the hotel, but we only had fifteen minutes in them, enough time to have a wash and brush-up.

Without giving a blow-by-blow account of the nine Kielder special stages, I can safely say that they were as rough and frightening as they have ever been. There were the usual blind crests and firebreaks that have caught out so many over the years, and there was rain, with touches of fog as the icing on the cake. There were numerous retirements in this area, and no service cars anywhere in the forest. We felt very lonely. However, our 'mother hen,' Andrew Cowan, was hovering nearby, with his co-driver Brian Coyle doing a marvellous job of meeting us at the end of every stage. Thankfully, we did not need their help. In the middle of the Kielder complex there was a passage check and a small group of spectators, one of whom was my old Lakeland rallying mate Bob Redhead, who popped his head into the car and wished us good luck, saying what a marvellous job we were doing. We had also seen huge banners held by the hardy spectators in the forest. Most of these said "Good luck Roger and Tony," or something similar, and we felt that we were being swept along on a huge wave of patriotism. It was an amazing feeling, to be sure.

We had spent three hours in the dreaded Kielder complex, and although we were treating it with the respect it deserves, we had been fastest car on half of the stages and always in the top three. To say we were relieved to get out in one piece was the understatement of the year. What we didn't know was that worse was to come across the Scottish border, which we crossed at about midnight.

Scotland for the brave

We were greeted in Scotland by more and more rain, and, the further west we went, by gale force winds. It really was a bleak scene, and the previous day's feeling of excitement and glamour changed to one of slight fear. It was a pitch-black December night, and Roger and I were experienced enough to know that if things were to go wrong, it would be during the hours of darkness. We were now wanting to get the rally over and done with.

We kept up our pace through Craik, Castle O'er, and Twiglees forests, then on into the Forest of Ae where there were two stages. Although it was well past midnight, the stages in the Forest of Ae were packed with spectators, particularly at the well-known hairpin at Gubhill Farm, where they lined the route, many only inches from the rally cars.

At the unearthly hour of four o'clock in the morning, we entered the ground of the sumptuous Turnberry Hotel, on the west coast of Ayrshire. The hotel was a main control and, hurrah, there was a break of one hour or so. Again, Ford had reserved rooms for us, so we left the mechanics checking and double-checking everything on the car, despite the atrocious weather. We were handed the keys to our rooms by Boreham's delivery driver, a marvellous man by the name of Reg. He was very popular with everyone at Boreham and all the drivers. Among other things, he drove the big Ford transporter. Reg – actual name Horace Redgewell – had joined the rally in Scotland, bringing a van full of spare driveshafts and other bits that might be required to get us to the finish.

At Turnberry, Roger and I crashed out immediately and later agreed that the beds were the most comfortable we'd ever slept in. Mind you, any bed is pretty special when you've been driving for nearly twenty hours! Our faithful servant Reg had spare keys for both our rooms, and at the agreed time came in to wake us, fill the baths with warm water, and make us each a cup of tea. How's that for service? All this, plus a change of clothing, refreshed us but prior to that, on first awakening, I peered out of the window and saw the horrible weather outside. It was a wild storm, to say the least, and never before or since have I felt less like getting out of bed. Mind you, pity the many private crews who hadn't the luxury of a hotel room, and had been trying to sleep in their cars in the buffeting wind. I bet they thought we were being pampered like prima ballerinas.

Pampered or not, we were unprepared for the drama that would meet us at the infamous Cairn Edward stage in the Brennan Forest, near New Galloway. It was a complete nightmare from beginning to end. What was meant to be a straightforward, fast five-minute stage developed into a free-for-all, and many cars spent nearly ten minutes or more in the mêlée that followed. As we sat in the Escort on the start line, Roger and I hadn't a clue what was about to happen. We felt reasonably confident, as both of us had been through Cairn

Edward numerous times and couldn't remember anything too hazardous. We had recharged our batteries at the Turnberry rest halt, and the Escort was in very good nick thanks to the attention it was getting from Ford's hard-working mechanics. Since entering Scotland, our service crews were fitting new halfshafts and wheels at virtually every stage, no matter how short. Remember, one puncture could easily have lost Ford – and us – the rally.

We received the usual countdown of 10-5-4-3-2-1 from the Cairn Edward start marshal, Roger let in the clutch, and we blasted off the line into the wet and windy forest. The first half mile or so was no problem, but after a slight left-hand bend there was a Y junction. "Keep left," I called, assuming the slightly wider road would be the required route, whilst wondering to myself why there was no arrow. Another similar junction came up and we took the major road. My stomach starting churning slightly, and I glanced at Roger who was still driving furiously, looking his usual calm self. Should I say anything? At a third junction we had a similar situation. I had been glimpsing at my Ordnance Survey map but it was little help. "We've got a problem," I said, explaining that there were no arrows. I felt bewildered, angry and upset – all at once. Roger kept pedalling, but I could feel his vibes and knew that he had lost confidence. Horrifically, we came to a dead-end with a wide turning area.

"Handbrake, go back!" I called. We retraced our steps for half a mile to the last junction and took the track to the left as a set of headlights appeared and went along the route we had just left. After another mile we came to a crossroads in the woods. I realised the following car would be with us any time, so asked Roger to park the Escort across the track. I knew there was some major problem, so undid my belts and ran across to flag down the car, which happened to be our great rival Stig Blomqvist. I spoke to co-driver Arne Hertz, who was all for setting off down one of the three tracks that presented themselves to us. I was determined not to let Stig get ahead of us, so we slowly manoeuvred our car around in the track to keep Stig locked in. Just then, another two cars came past us, one completing a 360 degree turn. It was chaos, and I knew the stage would have to be cancelled. Very slowly we set off in convoy, and found cars heading towards us. To this day I cannot believe that there was no major accident, as there were rally cars going everywhere. Some cars drove inadvertently off the stage at a very high speed onto a main road. The poor stage finish marshal hadn't a clue what was going on as cars approached from different directions.

According to Jonathan Lord, the chief of Royal Scottish Automobile Club Motorsport, there still remains a mystery surrounding the whole affair. The wind and rain could have disposed of some arrows, but surely not all of them. In any case, arrows in neighbouring forests were unaffected. When the course-opening car went through Cairn Edward, they were all in position. All very odd! Jonathan remembers the whole incident, for he was then a 19-year-old University Student who had travelled over from St Andrews to act as a stop-line marshal.

Anyway, we knew the stage would be cancelled, and we put the whole thing behind us as we drove down through the last two stages in Scotland, where Blomqvist kept the pressure on us, nibbling away at our lead. With all the earlier shenanigans, it was clearly time for Mr Clark to have a rest, so muggins here took to the wheel for a pleasant run across the border to Carlisle. We clocked in at the Hilltop Hotel for another shortish break, with time for a wash and brush-up in our rooms. Here I was accosted by a reporter and photographer from the *Lancashire Evening Post*, who wanted to take a photograph of me in the bath. I declined on the grounds of good taste, and not wanting to frighten the newspaper's readers.

There were enormous crowds along the route through Carlisle city centre and into the hotel car park. Apparently, there had been hourly bulletins about us after the news on the main BBC radio channels and the media was out in force. It was noticeable that I was getting more interviews here than Roger (not that he was worried, of course, as he hated such things). I was now on the fringe of my home area so it was 'local boy makes good' syndrome. I must say I enjoyed it, but tried to dampen the euphoria by saying to everyone that there were thirty more miles of difficult stages to go. "I'm very superstitious," I told the ITV film crew. "I don't like to count my chickens until they're hatched, and I won't believe it until we get on the finish ramp in York." These were prophetic words, indeed.

I cannot deny that I much enjoyed the adulation, and it was an amazing feeling to see banners and cards with my name on them. In fact, as we travelled further south, towards the Lake District, my name was seen more than Roger's.

We drove in the morning sun down to the Greystoke Forest near Penrith. This was a rough, seven-mile stage through narrow tracks beneath overhanging branches, and it was like driving through a bumpy, dark tunnel. Despite our caution we were fastest at 7 minutes 21 seconds, ahead of Simo Lampinen, Rauno Aaltonen, Stig Blomqvist, and Harry Källström. Those are a few good names for you to remember.

Astonishingly, Roger was quickest again on the stage at Wythop in a small, hilly forest near Keswick, but discretion was the better part of valour at Dodd Wood, which twisted and turned through trees over a narrow track with very steep drops down towards Thirlmere Lake far below. I warned Roger of this, and told him how many people had gone over the edge on previous rallies. I may have exaggerated, but he obviously took notice, as we came only fifth there.

I was really on home ground now, as we drove through Ambleside to a time control at the Drunken Duck near Coniston. This pub was one of my haunts over the past few years, and, as it was early afternoon, there was a sizeable crowd outside the pub, most with glasses in their hands. Cries of "Want a pint, Tony?" were heard and there was much cheering and shouting. We obviously declined the offer of drinks, and travelled the short distance to the last stage of the rally, number 72 at Grizedale Forest. Here was a bit of a sting in the tail, as it was ten miles of fast and tricky forest going. Never, ever, have there been such huge crowds in the forest at Grizedale. They virtually lined the entire ten miles. Unbelievably, we could actually hear the cheers of the crowds from inside the Escort. They were certainly willing us to win. I will never forget that. Roger drove sensibly, but still very quickly by normal standards, as we knew that we were three minutes ahead of 1971 winner Stig Blomqvist, and all we had to do was finish the stage and tootle the 110 miles back to York. Or was it?

Before York we stopped at the Swan Hotel at Newby Bridge where there were very big crowds and 'Welcome' banners galore. Situated at the southern tip of Lake Windermere, the Swan had always been a favourite place of mine, and I had often attended Furness District Motor Club dinner-dances there. We clocked out of the time control at 2.30pm, and I took the wheel of the mud-covered 'Esso Blue.' I'm not sure if I've mentioned this before, but Esso Blue was a popular nickname for the car, much used by followers. The paintwork of the car featured a prominent blue stripe, and Esso Blue paraffin featured in a popular TV commercial of the day, complete with catchy jingle. I bet you didn't know all that!

I was very familiar with the route from Newby Bridge to York, and pointed the car towards the A590, then the A65 to Kirkby Lonsdale, Skipton, Harrogate, and York. Roger decided he didn't need to read the road book, and settled down for a good sleep before all the carousing that was bound to follow throughout the evening in York.

Not far from Skipton, on the moors near the splendidly named Blubberhouses, I felt the steering getting slightly more stiff, and, above the rattles and bangs acquired during the previous 1750 miles, thought there was another grinding sound. I woke Roger and pulled into a gateway. Roger took the wheel and after a quarter of a mile pulled into a lay-by. He had a look at the front wheels and discovered the front offside wheel bearing had seized. What did I say about not counting chickens?

Neither of us panicked, and I worked out how long we would have to get back to York within 'fail time.' It would be fairly tight, I estimated. First, however, we had to get in touch with the team. In 1972 there was no radio communication, no mobile phones, and not too many red telephone boxes on Blubberhouses moor. Within minutes, twenty or more rally followers steered into the lay-by, and at least five drivers of Escorts kindly offered spare parts from their own cars. Roger declined the offers, realising that a standard wheel bearing would not solve the problem. Time was marching on as we jacked up the car and Roger stripped the front hub. At that very moment, out of the blue, we heard the dulcet Scottish brogue of Andrew Cowan. Never have I been so happy to see anyone! He had been following us ever since York on Monday morning, but had fallen behind us by about ten minutes because of heavy tea-time traffic near Skipton. All the service cars were heading back to York, presumably using the direct route from the Lake District, as we were. However, they were yet to appear.

Roger and Andrew then calmly set about cannibalising Andrew's retired rally car, leaving it on three wheels in the lay-by while Andrew awaited rescue. I had been constantly calculating the time required to get back to York, and keeping a close eye on the clock. I wasn't frantically worried, but was admittedly very relieved when Andrew and Roger lowered the car off the jack. Roger quickly strapped himself in, and I told him to "go like hell."

We were lucky not to get caught by the police as we sped through built-up areas and overtook lines of traffic, flat-out in fifth gear. On the outskirts of York we did encounter flashing blue lights. "Oh, shit!" Roger muttered, and I must admit I thought that this was the bitter end of our great trip. We pulled up behind the blue lights in yet another lay-by, and suddenly realised from the beaming faces of the two police motorbike riders that they had been sent to wait for us and give us a police escort through the streets of York to the finish at the racecourse. "Where the bloody hell have you been, Roger?" one of the riders asked in a strong Yorkshire accent. We told them of our troubles, and I said we had only a few minutes in hand to get to the racecourse. With that, these two splendid men told us to follow them and accelerated off down the road. As we neared the centre of York they took us through traffic lights at red and down shortcuts off the official route, and we arrived with only five minutes to spare. It was a near thing, to be sure, and apparently we'd caused pandemonium at the rally headquarters in the Station Hotel and at the finish area. No-one, including Ford, knew where we were!

As long as I live, I shall never forget the glorious 'clunk' as we drove onto the wooden finish ramp. The spotlights and photographers' flashing light bulbs were blinding, the noise of cheering was deafening, and a loudspeaker was blaring out phrases like 'Britain's new motorsport heroes,' 'superstars,' 'history has been made,' 'brilliant performance,' and so on, ad infinitum.

I passed my timecard to the marshal, making sure he signed it and entered our correct time of arrival, as silly mistakes have been made among the euphoria of rally finishes. Then it hit me – we had won the RAC Rally of Great Britain, an ambition of both Roger's and mine! And we had beaten the great team of Stig Blomqvist and Arne Hertz by a splendid three minutes and twenty-five seconds, into the bargain.

We undid our seat belts, climbed out of our mud-spattered home of the last four-and-a-half days, and clambered onto the roof for the statutory photographs. And, boy, were there some photographers! We were shouted at to wave, hold hands high in the air, stand up, sit down, and then we were given a massive bottle of Moët et Chandon champagne (1966 vintage), which Roger opened before spraying the crowd, most of the officials, many photographers, and me. Mind you, he had a few quick swigs before that, and so did I. We dismounted from our now slippery perch by sliding off the front. In doing so, Roger contrived to rip a large hole in the seat of his overalls as he inadvertently caught the pin that secures the Escort's bonnet! Needless to say, we all thought that a highly amusing conclusion to proceedings.

In fact, it wasn't a conclusion as we were interviewed incessantly by dozens of TV, radio, and press reporters, and by well-known novelist Jilly Cooper, no less, who had been travelling for part of the rally as a guest of Ford. Jilly wrote a marvellous article for her column in *The Sunday Times*, and certainly captured the tension of the closing stages, which all rally folk will fully understand. Here's part of it:

"So we waited yet again in one of the tensest half-hours I can remember. Looking into the valley where the sunlight rusted the larches, the grey river choked over the stones down to Windermere. Fans lined the walls, stamping their gumbooted feet to keep warm. Their girlfriends slowly turned blue. Mechanics for once not talking much, chain-smoking, warming their blacknailed hands on cups of coffee.

"There was a familiar growl from the valley, everyone stiffened. A souped-up motorbike thundered by. Everyone groaned in disappointment. Then, suddenly, a howl of triumph went up as the dirty, mud-spattered little Ford drew up beside us. I was slightly ashamed how moved I felt. Roger Clark and his co-driver, Tony Mason, sat in the car, black rings under their eyes, their faces seamed with tiredness, charisma rising like steam from their hair – real Stupor-stars – it was like the end of an Alistair MacLean novel.

"Later, after they had clinched the victory in York, everyone drank too much champagne. I felt as though I had just won the pools."

The article later appeared in a book, I am pleased to say, and I often dine out on my appearance in a Jilly Cooper publication – regrettably, not in one of her bodice-ripping specialities!

Sixteen

Ford calls

The media coverage of our RAC Rally win was immense by any standards, and certainly in comparison with the current national exposure of world rallying. Ford placed full page advertisements in all the national and major regional newspapers in Britain, and all of them featured our success, mostly on the front pages. It was the second or third item on BBC and ITV main evening news. We were included in BBC's *Sports Personality of the Year*, and a longish film of the rally was shown on the sports programmes on both channels. I loved the TV bit with all the interviews, of course, but Roger hated it. Looking back, I never imagined that one day television would play an important part in my career.

So, if you thought 1972 was a fairly dramatic year for me, I can tell you that 1973 was just as momentous for a variety of reasons. Obviously, the big win was still being celebrated by Ford, and every dealer in Britain was displaying huge "We've won the RAC Rally!" posters in its showroom windows. Ford also produced small stickers saying the same thing, to be attached to the inside of cars' rear windows. It appeared that almost every Escort on the roads of Britain was sporting one of these! The winning Escort, Roger and I appeared at Ford dealers the length and breadth of Britain for special evenings, sometimes joined by other race and rally personalities as one of Stuart Turner's famous forums would take place. Every car club in the country wanted us to give them an evening for their members, and, if we could fit them in, Roger and I would tootle off to show a film of the rally and tell the audience all about our trip. We became quite polished as a double act, and gave everyone a good laugh before the obligatory autograph session. Some of those signed photographs are occasionally offered for sale on eBay, I understand – I wish I was getting something out of it! I always remember going to a sellout club evening in Shropshire, where there were healthy queues outside the front door of the hall in which we were to appear. All the club officials who would greet us were inside the hall, of course, so we made our way in among the paying customers. Sitting behind a table was an ancient gentleman who, I presume, had something to do with the club, but didn't really seem to know what was going on as he insisted that Roger and I show him our tickets before we were allowed in! He was adamant we should have tickets, and hadn't got a clue who we were. We very nearly had to pay to go into our own show!

I was still living and working in the north of England, but spending more and more time with Ford, and I was a regular visitor to Boreham where I became good friends with the competition manager, Peter Ashcroft. I was involved in various test sessions on Boreham Airfield, and on the fast gravel tracks there, sitting in with Timo Mäkinen and Hannu Mikkola, among others. Peter asked me if I saw my future as a works co-driver, and was prepared to bring me into the team. There was one possibility that excited me somewhat: being regular co-driver to Hannu Mikkola. I also saw quite a lot of Jim Porter, who was often at Boreham. We got on well, but I always had something of a feeling of guilt about him, as Jim had loyally worked alongside Roger Clark since 1961, but relinquished his co-driver's seat when he took over the organisation of the RAC Rally in 1972 – the year I sat in with Roger and got a lot of the limelight. Jim is a modest, quiet man, but to see another co-driver in his seat really must have been a bitter pill to swallow. However, Jim never, ever showed any sign of animosity or jealousy to me, and we remain good friends to this day. Jim co-drove with Roger for 21 years in total, winning 49 rallies and four British championships. He organised 14 RAC rallies, and improved the event enormously during his time at the helm.

I was enjoying my new-found fame, as you might imagine, and was much in demand as an after-dinner speaker, opener of fêtes, and presenter of awards here, there, and everywhere. I was interviewed on local TV sports programmes, and went to a great function in the town hall in Morecambe, where I was fed egg sandwiches and received the Freedom of Morecambe. I went to the finals of the *Daily Mail* 'Woman driver of the year' competition, and drove Cilla Black round a manoeuvrability test on Blackpool's promenade in a 3-litre Ford Capri that had appeared from somewhere. I remember Cilla screaming and squealing as I showed off with my handbrake turns. She did say she thought I "was so clever." Aren't I a bighead? Sorry! I suppose it would be non-PC or sex discrimination or something to have a 'Woman driver of the year' competition nowadays.

Another function I attended at Morecambe's outdoor super swimming pool might fall into the same category. It was a heat of the Miss Great Britain contest, where I was to appear as a judge, along with various other local worthies, sponsors, and the singer Matt Monro, who was appearing at the nearby Winter Gardens theatre at the time. I still have the red, white and blue rosette that was attached to me. More used to motorsport functions than beauty contests, I expected to be invited to 'scrutineering' the night before at the nearby Pontins Holiday Camp, where all the lovely contestants were staying. My offer was refused! Pontins was situated just outside Morecambe at Heysham Head, overlooking Morecambe Bay. This was also the location of a kart track built by the Hesketh family on the top of a steep cliff, where major kart races were held, including the finals of the world championship. An up-and-coming young kart driver by the name of Nigel Mansell once gave himself some nasty injuries when he crashed heavily, narrowly avoiding dropping over the cliff. He ended up in the Royal Lancaster Infirmary and very nearly died from his injuries. I have since met and talked to Nigel quite a lot, and discussed the Heysham Head kart track. He says it was the most dangerous race track he has ever raced on anywhere in the world. I wish I'd known that when I appeared there in 1973 in a full works Escort, on my way back from a national rally in Scotland. I was invited to entertain the crowds at the kart race by doing a few flamboyant laps. I believe I made the fastest time round the track ever recorded by a car. I know I frightened myself silly.

Among the prizes for winning the RAC Rally were return air tickets to Kenya for the Safari Rally, in which Ford was competing with a strong team. Bill Barnett, who was running the team, included me in all the Ford arrangements and allocated me a room at the famous Norfolk Hotel in Nairobi, which was the team hotel. It would be my first visit to a country outside Europe, and I was quite excited as I arranged all my injections for this great expedition to the tropics. Among the Ford crews were Roger Clark and Jim Porter, who I would accompany before the event whilst they were making route notes. I also had another job to do for Roger, which was quite unusual, to say the least. Roger had been in Africa for a couple of weeks' recceing with Jim when his second child was about to be born in his home city of Leicester. It was agreed that I should keep in touch with Roger's family, and if the baby was born before I left for Nairobi, I should take a Polaroid photograph of him or her and take it with me to give to Roger. Nowadays, with all the mobile phone cameras around, this is no big deal, but at the time it took a lot of organising. Roger's wife, Judith, gave birth to a little boy, a brother for two-year-old Matthew, the night before I was due to leave. I duly appeared at the maternity home, en route to Gatwick, and took a shot of baby Oliver. After an overnight flight, I arrived at the Norfolk Hotel and proudly presented my photograph of Roger's new son and heir. "Isn't he pink!" Roger exclaimed. We had a few jokes about it probably being my thumb over the lens, and then, along with Roger's close friend and Nairobi resident Bill Parkinson, began 'wetting the baby's head' and enjoy a few Tusker beers.

I thought Kenya was marvellous, of course, and was quickly introduced to all the great names associated with the Safari Rally. The Ford team had an arrangement with Kenya's greatest rallying family, the Prestons, who operated a major Shell garage in Nairobi. It was allegedly the biggest petrol station in the whole of Africa. Vic Preston won the first two 'proper' East African Safari rallies in the fifties, and was Kenya's 'Mr Motorsport,' having been East African motorcycle champion several times. Although acknowledged as East Africa's top driver (he also twice finished in second and third place on Safari rallies in the sixties), he was renowned for his careful planning and meticulous attention to detail. Having driven Zephyrs and Cortinas on the Safari throughout the fifties and sixties, Vic had long associations with Ford, and the Preston garage became the unofficial competition department for Ford at Safari time. Not only that, but Vic's only son, Vic Preston Junior, had followed in his father's footsteps, winning local motorsport events on two and four wheels, and, in fact, had finished third overall in a works Escort on the 1972 Safari Rally, which Ford had won with Hannu Mikkola – the first ever win in the world's toughest rally by an overseas driver. I got on with the entire Preston family really well, and all of us, including Vic's delightful wife June, had the same sense of humour. As time went on I would spend a lot of time with this rally mad family and would co-drive Junior Preston several times. Back to this first trip of mine, I thought this was 'heaven on earth.' I was working with Peter Ashcroft, along with the Prestons and Vic's partner in one of his businesses, Bill Parkinson. Formerly from Northern Ireland, Bill is one of the funniest men I have ever met. He had his own light plane, and this was used as part of the Ford service arrangements. He took Peter Ashcroft and me up in the plane several times, and we both flew it – completely illegally, of course. As one of Bill's many practical jokes, he introduced me to a friend at the Wilson Airfield Aero Club in Nairobi, and suggested I had a short flight with him. I did not know that this man was the East African aerobatics champion, or some such, and of course we looped the loop, fell backwards out of the sky with no engine running, and did the most frightening things. I am pleased to report that, surprisingly, I was not sick, which seemed to give me some sort of acceptance with Bill and his pals.

The Safari Rally used to be held in three countries around Lake Victoria – Kenya, Tanzania and Uganda – but in 1973 Uganda was dropped from the event as President Amin had begun his mad activities. Among my first jobs with Ford was to be sent down to Dar es Salaam in Tanzania to meet the local Ford dealer, Riddoch Motors, and set up service arrangements. I spent a pleasant evening having an alfresco drink with the local manager, and vividly remember a large fruit-bat diving into my full pint of beer and spraying it all over me! I know that's a bit trivial, but you don't want all sorts of rally facts non-stop, do you? I also remember visiting Arusha in Tanzania with Roger and Jim Porter before the rally. Now, here's another interesting fact: it is one of the only places in the world where a special rock called 'meerschaum' exists, which is used to make tobacco pipes. This white rock is amazing, being one of the few types in the world that float. We made a brief visit to the area where we met someone who was an expert on meerschaum. "Why is it called meerschaum?" I asked. Quick as a flash, Jim Porter interjected "It probably means bloody hell, it floats!" I was having a good time in East Africa with all my new-found friends, and really taking to the old colonial way of life. I was left by myself in Dar es Salaam until the rally arrived, early on the second day.

Huge crowds of locals had gathered by the main control at Dar's biggest hotel, and as the first cars arrived the crowds were going mad. There was much whistleblowing, and suddenly a van full of policemen arrived, complete with tear-gas guns, which they proceeded to fire all over the crowd and into the foyer of the hotel where the official control was sited! Everyone had to be evacuated.

The first car to arrive, in fact, was that of my mates Roger and Jim, who had a marvellous four-minute lead at that point. After various telephone calls to the Ford team back in Nairobi I was told to go and pick up one of the recce cars, which had been left broken in Dar but had now been repaired. 1969 Safari Rally winner Robin Hillyar then appeared and introduced himself, saying we would be together to take the Escort recce car back to Nairobi. Robin was part of the Ford brigade as an unofficial 'hanger-on,' a bit like me. He had won the Safari driving a German Ford Taunus 20M. By the time we got away from Dar es Salaam it was getting dusk so a ten hour night drive was called for. There are two things I remember about our trip: the first was around midnight, when I stopped the car I was driving whilst Robin was asleep. I needed to stretch myself and take the opportunity to have a pee in the bushes at the roadside. When I returned to the car and put the headlights on, I had the shock of my life. A huge lion had been standing a few feet away, but obviously didn't fancy any of my bits on his menu that night. The other incident took place when Robin was driving at about three o'clock in the morning, as we passed from Tanzania into Kenya. We stopped at the border control, and I went in with our two passports only to see the two guards completely flat-out on benches behind the counter. They had obviously been on the 'banana juice,' and had their eyes firmly closed. I couldn't wake them, so I decided to stamp our own passports as the rubber stamp and pad were within reach on the counter top. I was quite pleased with myself, but didn't really have time to tell Robin as I climbed into the passenger seat and we sped off. Suddenly there were floodlights, and, more worryingly, loads of loud gunshots in our direction as we sped off somewhat rapidly!

Back in Nairobi, I was asked to drive top Boreham engine man Terry Hoyle round, visiting various service points where his skills might be required. At the time I had been a regular autotest competitor, and as we approached the equator I couldn't resist a handbrake turn to stop astride the yellow line that crossed the tarmac road. Terry thought I was mad, but I thought it was a pretty unique achievement, and I'm proud of it!

Back home, I was becoming more used to various telephone calls from Ford folk, but still stood to attention if Stuart Turner was on the other end of the line! I knew he had a good opinion of me and my great enthusiasm, and he admired the way I ran Morecambe Car Club with a meticulous eye to detail. He used to give me little projects from time to time, like writing a monthly column for *Ford Sport* magazine, which he had introduced. I used to write quiz questions for him, and prepare tabletop rallies that he used as an initiative test for budding navigators. I was also asked to write to the 'opposition,' Chrysler, Vauxhall, Datsun, and British Leyland, asking for their help in suggesting my entry into motorsport with their make of car. I then sent the replies onto Stuart for him to analyse. I had to ring Ford dealers around the country asking them about their views on motorsport. In short, I was becoming a bit of a general dogsbody for Stuart, and felt quite privileged to be.

Stuart interviewed me for a possible job in the Ford press office on one occasion, and also wanted me to run the Fordsport club, so I was certainly getting my feet under the Ford table. However, I was completely unprepared for one telephone call. Now, I don't know if you've ever had a phone call from Mr Turner, but he doesn't go in for pleasantries like 'Hello, how are you?' 'Isn't the weather terrible?' or 'This is Stuart Turner here.' The phone call in early 1973 that really flabbergasted me went as follows: "This may be the most stupid thing I've ever done, and I may regret it, but I'm offering you the job of rally manager at Boreham. You can buy yourself a Guinness tonight and put it on your expenses, but only one! You'll get a letter tomorrow with all the details." Bang! The phone went dead at the other end, and I sat down, numb. When the letter arrived I noticed that the projected salary was four times what I was earning at K Shoes. I didn't need a lot of persuading, and accepted the job, which was retitled 'competitions co-ordinator,' as it would involve work with various racing projects. I would also look after the rallycross programmes for John Taylor and Rod Chapman, and organise all Ford forums, as well as the new Mexico Rally championship and all other motor club activities. Looking back, it was an amazing happening. Aged just 31, I would be replacing Bill Barnett, who was moving to a senior corporate post in Ford's Warley headquarters, and rally drivers like Timo Mäkinen, Hannu Mikkola, and Roger Clark would be taking orders from me. It was quite bizarre, in a way. Peter Ashcroft had been promoted to competitions manager, with Stuart as director of motorsport, operating from the Ford Advanced Vehicles Operation at South Ockenden. I was looking forward to working with Peter, who was an engineer at heart, so I knew he would be happy to let me get on with all the peripheral duties. It was certainly another daunting prospect for the Mason agenda, but I knew I could do the job, otherwise Stuart Turner would not have asked me. I then started to think of all the people he could have asked, and thought that they might all envy me. It was, of course, fairly big news in the motorsport press, as not one journalist had got a whiff of it before the official Ford press release landed on their desks.

Seventeen

Upping sticks

By early summer 1973, I was packing my bags to go down to Essex to take up my new position as Ford competitions co-ordinator. I continued to live in the north, but spent four nights every week at various hotels in and around Chelmsford, returning home each weekend. On arriving that first Monday morning, I suddenly realised what a gigantic operation Ford Motor Company was. The welcome pack on my desk was about three inches thick, and full of rules and regulations for everything. I was given a number that would have to be included on every letter or memo I issued, and, indeed, on any expense forms, which had to be signed by two people above my grade. Henry Ford himself had a number, I was told.

Peter Ashcroft spent a lot of time introducing me to everyone at Boreham and elsewhere, but I did have a shock on my first visit to the multistorey head office at Warley, near Brentwood. Obviously, everyone at Boreham knew who I was after the RAC win, but I felt like a complete stranger at Warley. Surprisingly few knew of my RAC success. I would eventually visit Warley a great deal, working with the press office and other departments, and very occasionally meeting my 'ultimate boss,' the great Walter Hayes, who was so important in establishing Ford's motorsporting pedigree. As has been reported many times, Walter was a man of great vision, and he and Stuart Turner were a magical team. I was honoured to be part of all this. One of the forms I had to complete and sign (not forgetting my Ford number) was for my means of transport. I applied for a 3-litre Capri, which became my 'management role' car. It was very welcome. Although I was sent to visit various Ford locations, like the huge Dagenham manufacturing plant, I obviously had to get my feet under the desk at Boreham Airfield where the competitions department was based. Pam Goater, who had worked with Bill Barnett for many years, became my secretary, and was really helpful in showing me the ropes. I knew most of the staff in the workshops as they doubled as rally mechanics during events, and of course I knew Mick Jones who was the workshop foreman and something of a well-known rally personality. Although I wasn't shown any animosity or unpleasantness I always felt that some of the staff there were a little wary of me, and couldn't understand why I had suddenly appeared out of the blue.

While my professional life was moving on quite dramatically, there were other major happenings in my private life – I was about to get married to a very attractive lady, Susan McBurnie. Sometime earlier her and her first husband had moved to the north-west of England, but had divorced. Sue had two lovely daughters: Jane was at boarding school, whilst Clare was at home. Sue and I married on 11th August, 1973.

We found a house in the village of Stock, but Essex is not as interesting as the Lake District or North Wales, where Sue had spent most of her life. It must have been difficult for her, as I was away at Boreham all day, and starting to travel away on Ford business. I owe Sue so much, and still do, for the world of motorsport is far removed from her own passions, which include fly-fishing, horse-riding, and gardening.

At the end of 1973, Sue and I had a belated honeymoon in Kenya. The Preston family were very helpful in recommending places to go, and booked us into a game lodge in the Tsavo Park, and at the famed Treetops hotel. We were loaned a Mercedes by Vic Junior and had a marvellous time, although Sue still remembers me dropping her off out in the bush and asking her to photograph me coming flat-out down a dusty road. She thought I was going to turn round and return after a few yards, but I actually disappeared over the horizon so I could get up good speed over a crest where she was standing. She was somewhat alarmed afterwards when we saw a pride of lions round the next bend! We also ran over a snake at one point, and I kneeled down to take a close-up photograph of the poor, dead reptile. Suddenly, the 'dead' snake shook its head and started to slowly squiggle away. When the photograph was developed back in Nairobi, I was told the snake was a deadly mamba, and, had it bitten us, we'd be 'gonners' in a matter of seconds! We did normal things, of course, like visiting the coast at Mombasa, and returned in time for a lovely family Christmas with Sue's sisters, Janet and Ruth, and their families.

I was very busy with work, but also still co-driving, and in 1973 and 1974 I continued to have outings with various Ford contracted drivers, as I had in 1972. I partnered Vic Preston Junior on part of his British rally programme, and won the Arkell Rally held in Cirencester Park. On the Red Hackle Rally we suddenly encountered snow, which 'Junior' had only even previously seen on the peak of Mount Kilimanjaro; he had certainly never driven in it, and slowed to a walking pace as we hit the snow-covered roads. I urged him to go faster and get the feel of it, which he did very gingerly. "Bloody hell!" he exclaimed after a few lurid slides, "This is just like murrum mud at home." With that, Junior accelerated and put up a very creditable performance, finishing not far behind none other than Roger Clark in a sister Escort RS1600.

Stuart Turner always wanted to find a female driver to emulate the great Pat Moss, and was impressed by Gillian Fortescue-Thomas from Dorset who, like Pat, had had great success on horses and was now racing Ford Escorts, beating the men at their own game. I was duly assigned to navigate her on various British rallies, and evaluate her performance driving a Ford Mexico. Gillian had great car control, as I would have expected, and we competed on a dozen or so night rallies together. We had moderate success, but I had the feeling Gillian was not too happy going quickly on narrow lanes between nasty stone walls. Stuart continued to search for a female rally star, and not long after joining Ford he instigated the 'Find a Lady Rally Driver' competition, in which the talents of 18-year-old Louise Aitken from Scotland were spotted. Louise, another former horse-rider, went on to win national rallies and have works drives for several manufacturers. After marriage to Graham Walker she became well known as Louise Aitken-Walker, and won the inaugural Ladies World Rally Championship in 1990, for which she was awarded the MBE. Louise hails from the amazing motorsport breeding ground of Berwickshire, along with Jim Clark and long-distance rally ace Andrew Cowan. Their local market town of Duns is well-known in rally circles, being the base for the Jim Clark Rally, which has run annually since the sixties and is one of the most popular events in the British championship. It is now the only event in mainland Britain to feature closed public roads. When I competed with Roger Clark in 1973, it was a mixture of stages in forests and on airfields, with some night navigation. I remember some very fast tarmac stages on the Otterburn military ranges, which featured blood-curdling crests. I also remember the Escort flying high in the air and landing so heavily that the magnesium alloy sumpguard hit the tarmac, and there were huge flashes that lit up the night sky all around us. After all those antics, Roger and I won easily ahead of Russell Brookes and John Brown, who were making their first outing in an Escort RS1600.

I was also asked to co-drive HRH Prince Michael of Kent, who had shown interest in rallying after successful seasons of bobsleighing. This was, of course, something of an honour, as I had not previously mixed in royal circles! It was agreed we would drive a Ford Mexico in the 1974 Seven Dales Rally, an event I had won two years earlier with Roger Clark when I first entered the Ford team. Prince Michael came over to Boreham to try the car and meet me (or, according to royal protocol, that should probably be 'I was presented to him'). He was aware of my RAC win, and when he telephoned me prior to the event would announce "This is your driver speaking!" He said he really liked saying that. We got on well, and were having a reasonably good run on the various airfield stages, although on one stage I noticed Prince Michael was leaning to the right and groping about with his right hand in the footwell. I couldn't imagine what he was doing but I soon found out! "I'm sorry about that, Tony," the Prince announced. "My tin of cigars became stuck under the accelerator!" I've heard a few excuses in my time, but that was a new one to me! We progressed through the night, putting in respectable times through the Yorkshire forests until dawn, when a deceptive junction on the tarmac bit of a forest stage caught out His Royal Highness. There was a Y junction, and I shouted "Left, left." The car went 'right, right,' then 'left, left,' and the next thing I knew … the car was on its roof! This was a new experience for Prince Michael, and I won't tell you the expletive he uttered, but you will be interested to know that royalty uses the same language as we peasants. Incidentally, climbing out of the tangle, I inadvertently stood on the Prince's head.

The RAC Rally came around very quickly, and it was agreed that I should again co-drive Roger Clark in the November 1973 event. As winners the previous year, we would have the honour of being seeded at number one on the 200-car event. The other works cars would be for Finns Hannu Mikkola and Timo Mäkinen. New cars had been built for all three of us, featuring consecutive '000' registration numbers. One of my jobs at Boreham was to organise registration numbers for new rally cars being built, and I was rather proud of this selection. The five-day rally would have a similar route to the previous year, and again be based in York. I don't propose to ramble on about stage times, but I would just like to mention that we clocked fastest time on three of the first four stages, and were beginning to wonder if history could repeat itself.

It's strange the little things that one remembers about a rally all those years ago. I don't remember the location of every incident we had, I don't remember much of the route, but I do remember driving every single road mile for the first half of the 1973 event, as Roger was not well and had contracted a virus. Individual teams did not have doctors in those days, but the RAC had appointed an event medical officer, and he was kindly attending to Roger at every control. Roger must have started to feel better towards the end of the first leg, as on our way up from the Barnby Moor control in Nottinghamshire he said he was hungry and didn't want to wait until late evening to eat in the hotel, back in York. In some small town near Doncaster we spotted a fish and chip shop, so I stopped outside it while Roger went in and joined the small queue. Clark in racing overalls queuing in a fish and chip shop was an incongruous sight, to say the least! Eventually, he emerged with two portions of cod and chips wrapped in newspaper and passed one to me. I opened my package and spread it out across my knees below the steering wheel while Roger started to tuck into his. We then set off up the road section en route to York, eating happily. Nowadays, could you possibly imagine the number one car on a world championship rally carrying on like this? Those were the days, my friend.

Despite Roger's ailment we put in some very good times, and had no trouble whatsoever. Things were looking good, but we had a wily Finn in our team, and despite carrying the unlucky number 13, Timo Mäkinen and Henry Liddon beat us into second place. It was a magnificent 1, 2, 3 for Ford, as virtually unknown Markku Alén, on only his second drive outside his native Finland, brought an Escort RS into third place. The car had been entered by David Sutton's private team with support from Motorcraft, and the drive by the lanky young man from Helsinki was the drive of the rally. A new star had arrived! On the fourth stage of the rally at Sutton Park near Birmingham, Alén flew off the road at a deceptive bend that had also caught out Mikkola. Hannu broke a bone in his hand and retired, but Alén got back in the rally, albeit having lost a lot of time. He set off after the incident languishing in 177th place, and, quite incredibly, climbed to finish third. Everyone was delighted when we returned to Boreham, and within days I was despatched to Finland to find the mysterious Markku Alén and sign him up for our team, if possible. There was only one little problem: Markku didn't speak a word of English. However, Ford Finland's press officer arranged for me to meet Markku and his mother and father, who did speak English, and have afternoon tea at the Hesperia Hotel in Helsinki. The result of this little tea party was that I offered Markku Alén a measly sum to drive a works Escort in the 1974 Welsh Rally in May. John Davenport was the brave soul selected to co-drive, which must have been an ordeal, as neither spoke more than six words of each other's language. Nevertheless, they won and Markku would become part of the team. I was also asked to find a very fast lady driver, Eeva Heinonen, and offer her a possible works drive. I did so, but a few weeks later received a note to say she was pregnant, so that was the end of that.

I made my first visit to the Arctic Circle in February to support our entries on the Marlboro Arctic Rally for Hannu Mikkola, Timo Mäkinen, and new boy Markku Alén, who had been given a car, but no money. The rally started in Roveniemi some 200 miles north of the Arctic Circle, and was held over snow-covered roads and ice-covered lakes, and on tracks between high snow banks. The temperature was as low as -40°C, and special additives had to be added to all the lubricants in the car to stop them freezing. When travelling through the night through tiny villages in Lapland, we could see buses and trucks parked for the night with their engines running so that they wouldn't freeze up. Equipped with fur-lined boots, thermal underwear, and a fur hat, I felt a bit like an Eskimo as I waited for the cars in a deserted village near the Russian border. My eyes were watering and I wiped them, only to find all my eyelashes had dropped off. I suppose it would have been worse if I had decided to have a pee ...

Prior to the rally, I was taken by Markku in the rally car to give it a shakedown, and I will remember that trip for the rest of my life. Daylight lasts for only a very few hours a day at that time of year, so it was pitch black outside as I sat, strapped in, whilst this 23-year-old madman drove me at breakneck speeds through the frozen wilderness. I believe Antarctic explorers can suffer from snow-blindness. Well, I think I got it staring ahead at the tunnel of snow we were passing through at 90mph. Markku's car control was remarkable, of course, thanks largely to the Hakkapelitta studded tyres that were made in Finland. It's no wonder Finns have won more world champion rally titles than any other race – everyone drives like that over there. I've seen post vans and old ladies on bicycles going round corners on 'opposite lock,' and during this trip I was driving sensibly on a wide, snow-covered road when I noticed a flash of lights in my mirror and a huge timber lorry and trailer overtook me.

Whilst all my gallivanting was going on, Sue was usually at home and struggling with the claggy clay, for which Essex is famous, using her immense skills to make a nice garden. One early evening in spring 1974, upon my return from work at Boreham, we sat on the bench in our garden having a cup of tea when Sue told me the marvellous news that she was expecting a baby, to be born at the end of the year. I was, of course, delirious, and could hardly contain my excitement. I didn't tell her what I had planned to discuss – that afternoon I had received a phone call from Junior Preston in Nairobi, asking me to co-drive in his works Escort on Easter's Safari Rally. Instead I made the instant decision to decline the Safari offer and stay at home.

Eighteen

Getting down to work

The morning after Sue had given me the news that she was expecting our first baby, I could think of nothing else as I drove my Capri through the lanes to my office at Boreham; I was going to be a dad for the first time. I still couldn't believe it. This was probably the greatest news I'd had since my marriage to Sue, and certainly put rally wins and other achievements into perspective. Sue was equally thrilled at the news, of course, but as a former state-registered nurse, and already the mother of two daughters, was a little more pragmatic about it.

I soon forgot my euphoria as I entered my office and saw the usual small pile of notes and memos that awaited me. Most were from Stuart Turner, who would have deposited them at some unearthly hour on his way to his office at South Ockenden. This happened frequently, and certainly kept me on my toes! 1974 was a busy year, with a wide variety of jobs and a lot of travelling, including trips to supervise the works cars on the Welsh and Scottish Rallies and the Tour of Britain, a race and rally event in which I had competed the previous year with Roger Clark in a 3-litre Capri. We had led the event until the halfway point, when we had electrical problems and handed the lead to eventual winner James Hunt. For 1974 it was decided that Ford would enter two Escort RS2000s: one would be for Roger Clark and Jim Porter, but who would drive the other one? I don't want to sound insufferably conceited, but what I like to consider a 'Mason masterstroke' occurred. Oh, alright, it is beginning to sound insufferably conceited! I had been attending a celebrity race meeting at Brands Hatch, where we had ten well-known names from show business and sport driving Escort Mexicos in a charity race for the Lords Taverners. At some point I bumped into Gerry Marshall, the ebullient, larger-than-life racing driver who was Vauxhall's top racer, and a regular winner of saloon races and championships. I asked him if he was entering the forthcoming Tour of Britain, and his reply astonished me: "No! The bastards are not giving me a run as it's not in my contract." Gerry explained that his contract with Vauxhall was for racing, and the company considered the Tour of Britain a rally. I was astonished by this, and asked him if he would like, or more importantly, would be allowed to drive an Escort. "Yes," he said "That'll show 'em." I then wondered what I'd let myself in for, but hotfooted it back to Boreham to check with Peter Ashcroft, who thought it was a brilliant idea. I put Paul White – a young Bristolian who had won the previous year's Mexico Rally championship as a navigator – with Gerry for the July event. The outcome was amazing, and the two Escorts were first and second on virtually every stage of the event. The large, cigar-chomping, beer-drinking Marshall took to the rally stages in various parks and stately homes like a duck to water. Roger Clark, no mean racing driver himself, was determined not to let Gerry get ahead on the tracks, and they finished every race within inches of each other. At the Snetterton night race they were neck and neck when Roger pulled a fantastic trick. Closely following Gerry, he put all his lights out, which confused Gerry who assumed Roger had gone off, and fractionally slowed. At that point Roger pulled alongside his team-mate, put his lights back on, and took the chequered flag.

It was planned that I should compete on a couple of events in 1974, one of which was the Scottish International in which we had entered Mäkinen, Mikkola, Clark, and Alén. I'm really not sure whose idea it was, but we put in an entry for 'new boy' Markku with me in the co-driving seat. I braced myself for a pretty scary ride, remembering that trip in the snowy Arctic waste in January. However, I needn't have worried unduly, as within days of the start the whole event was cancelled because of a strike by fuel tanker drivers in Scotland. Well, looking on the bright side, I suppose it saved me getting a few grey hairs! One rally in which I was entered did run, but with hindsight I wish it hadn't. Now, most people would be proud to be credited in the sporting record books with a 'world's first' achievement. Unfortunately, my one unique claim in this respect is that, as far as I know, I am the only competitor in motorsport history ever to have been run over by his own car during a major international event! This humiliating – and extremely painful – experience came as the last straw in a series of disasters during the Total Rally in South Africa, which turned out to be totally chaotic. I was co-driving Roger Clark in a Ford Escort RS that we sent out to be run by Ford in South Africa. Starting in Pretoria with a full day of daylight stages, followed by a second day, an overnight, and then a final day, the total event was mostly run through forests, but also featured one real 'Mickey Mouse' stage in the grounds of an open-air cinema in Pretoria, during which the cars virtually passed underneath the huge screen. As far as I can remember, no film was showing at the time! The stages were long and very dusty at first, with soft, dry, red soil everywhere that was easily stirred up into an impenetrable fog. The route instructions were 'tulip' diagram style, but difficult to read as there were many areas where two parallel tracks ran alongside each other, making it tricky to work out which one we should be on. To make matters worse, our car had a faulty mileage odometer device so that I ended up desperately looking for arrows while trying to calculate what the dreaded thing was meant to be telling me. We were nevertheless leading after the first day.

Darkness falls very rapidly in Africa, with very little twilight time. At the end of the second day it was suddenly pitch black, and when it then started raining very heavily, driving became a real struggle. With the added problem of the faulty odometer we had slipped to fifth or sixth place as the route climbed through the biggest forest in the world, and took us over the border in Swaziland. The early dust baths had had a harmful effect on the clutch, which first started slipping and then gave out altogether. A new one could be fitted by Ford South Africa mechanics at the next service point, but that was over an hour away, with difficult muddy tracks and great mountainous ranges to be negotiated. Roger had to resort to changing gear without using the clutch, but this presented a problem at the control points where we had to check in. We developed a system whereby Roger would slow down into first gear and crawl as slowly as possible on the approach to a control, allowing me to disembark from the left-hand drive vehicle and run to the control in the slippery mud, before running back to the still-moving Escort and jumping in again. My downfall came when, at one of these control points, I slipped in the mud as I was opening the door to get back in and slid under the car. Roger, thinking

I was half in and not wanting to waste any time, accelerated. The rear wheel ran over me, breaking bones in my foot and also injuring my leg and my wrist. Roger at first thought he'd simply run over a rock and accelerated even harder, leaving me lying in the mud. I never did forgive him! We managed to carry on through a few more controls, with me now hopping in and out of the car on one leg like Long John Silver, as torrential rain continued to bucket down, but the pain in my foot and ankle soon became so intense that we had to retire, and Roger drove me to the nearest hospital in a small Swaziland town. It was a rather primitive establishment in among a lot of strange tropical plants and trees. It had very basic facilities, and I worried that the local 'witch doctor' might chop my leg off! In fact, the doctor carried out temporary repairs and strapped up my ankle and leg. We then drove on to Johannesburg where I received further treatment and crutches for the long journey back to England. Not one of my more glorious homecomings, I can tell you.

Throughout the year I was appearing at Ford Rally Schools, forums and 'star evenings' with all Ford-contracted race and rally drivers, including Jackie Stewart, Graham Hill, James Hunt, Jody Scheckter, and of course, all the Finns. These were big affairs, and I recall one major event in the Guildhall in Preston with Timo Mäkinen, Hannu Mikkola, Markku Alén, and myself. Markku still didn't speak English, but the other two acted as translators.

I know that the golden era of rallying is reckoned to be the fifties and sixties; well, this was definitely the golden era for Ford Motorsport. Running rally and racing teams has always been an expensive job and, despite Ford's budget, which was much higher than most other car manufacturers', there was a need for extra sponsorship. Working with Peter Ashcroft, it was another of my jobs to try to obtain this. I had, of course, worked in advertising agencies for six years or so, and I was used to giving presentations and coming up with ideas. There were some successes and some failures on my part. Among the failures was my approach to Mars, who very nearly sponsored our RAC Rally entry in 1974, linking the sponsorship to a competition for customers to win ten Ford Escorts. It would have been an enormous on-pack promotion on Mars' major brands of chocolate bars, but the company withdrew when someone there suggested that the rally might be cancelled or one of our drivers might be killed. I also failed with a major record company with whom popular radio presenter Noel Edmonds put me in touch. Noel was a keen racing driver, and visited me at Boreham a lot. He appeared on Ford forums, at one of which, in a Ford dealer in Surrey, we managed to squash an audience of 750 into the showroom. Noel also competed in the Tour of Britain in 1974, and there was some talk of me co-driving. However, he decided to take his wife Gill instead, and possibly regrets it as they crashed heavily on the dreaded Epynt ranges in Wales. I was successful in getting the Milk Marketing Board to sponsor Mäkinen and Mikkola's cars in the RAC Rally of 1973, but was struggling until the last minute in 1974, when I came upon a man at a Round Table meeting where I was an after-dinner speaker. He worked for Colibri cigarette lighters, and was interested in sponsorship. We had a lot of hurried meetings. Colibri did not have a big budget, but offered Ford a huge amount of lighters for use as promotional gifts or whatever. As we had nothing else on the table, Stuart Turner consulted others on the upper floors at Warley and it was agreed to take the offer. There is probably a room at Ford's head office in Warley today that is still half-full of Colibri lighters, despite their being dished out at all sorts of dealer functions and other activities year after year. The motorsport press was very critical of the singularly unflattering brown colour scheme, but Colibri was happy because Timo Mäkinen's car won for the second year running.

Ford won the 1974 1000 Lakes Rally in Finland with Hannu Mikkola and John Davenport in first place, ahead of Timo Mäkinen and Henry Liddon in Escort RS1600s. However, the cars were a little unusual, as they were running on 15-inch wheels instead of the usual 13-inch. Timo was renowned for his obsession with technical changes, and had been impressed by the large-wheeled Volvos and Saabs that floated over the loose roads so easily. He therefore demanded a testing session in Finland, and found that the bigger tyres were up to two seconds per kilometre quicker. After the 1000 Lakes, which Peter Ashcroft and I supervised, we returned to Boreham and a barrage of telephone calls from Timo, who said he wanted 15-inch wheels for the RAC Rally in November. Hannu Mikkola, who had gone along with Timo's choice for the 1000 Lakes, wasn't sure they would suit the RAC, so we organised a big testing session at the Bagshot test ground in Surrey, often used by Ford and other teams. We spent several days there with Timo, Roger, and Hannu all umming and ahhing about the suitability of the tyre. I was sitting in with all three of them, with stopwatches whirring. I had driven quite a lot at Bagshot previously when component testing, and I was quite nifty on those tests – not a million miles off the times of the top guys – so sometimes I drove on these runs. The entire 13/15-inch testing was a bit of a palaver, quite frankly, and when I drove on the two sizes I couldn't tell the difference, which probably indicates that I'm a bit of a crap driver after all! It says in many motorsport books that Roger Clark did not like the 15-inch wheels, but the Finns did. This is not true, as Roger could see the advantage, but on the RAC this only presented itself on certain stages that were long, fast, and not too twisty. He knew that the handling of the Escort, which had been designed for 12-inch wheels, never mind 13-inch, was affected on tighter stages. He would be proved right on the Dovey Stage of the 1974 RAC, when we used the 15-inch wheels because it was such a long stage with many fast sections. They were our undoing, I must say, because we lost it on a tightening right-hand bend in mud and sailed over the edge into a bank. I had my door open as we ground to a halt, which wasn't particularly helpful as it broke the door hinges. Ever thought it wasn't your night? Roger and I scrabbled and scrambled about, and tried to right the car using a device consisting of a large rubber 'bouncing ball,' which was inflated by affixing it to the exhaust pipe. It *sort* of worked. but it was only when we had been in the ditch for 15 minutes that some splendid, trusty Welsh spectators appeared on the scene to extricate us.

We were down in 38th position after this little pantomime, and both of us a bit annoyed and depressed, but, true lion that he was, Roger kept up his attack on the following stages, and by the end of the rally we were in seventh place, which was in fact a truly remarkable drive. Having broken the door hinges during our little excursion, I should tell you that the remaining ten or so miles out of Dovey were 'interesting' to say the least. I was attempting to hold the door shut, but on any right-hand bend, which Roger was still attacking with great gusto, I was straining every muscle in my body to prevent it falling off. I succeeded, but only just.

It is widely thought that we never used 15-inch wheels again on the RAC after that incident, but this is not true. We selected them for the faster stages, and Roger and I would have a little confab in the service area before each stage to decide which size of wheel and Dunlop tyre to use. Because we had a much better knowledge of the British forests than the Finns, they listened in on our conversations and frequently made the same choice as us. On one occasion we naughtily decided to 'outfox' Timo Mäkinen. We loudly specified 15-inch wheels and had them fitted, then scurried off and reversed into a forest track just up the road. Once Timo had gone past on his 15-nch wheels, we returned quickly to the service area and fitted 'thirteens.' No one, to this day, ever knew that. Isn't it awful? Mind you, the whole 15/13-inch saga was a lot of trouble, and the great Timo actually competed on one stage with two odd-sized wheels on the car – and never noticed!

As I have recently mentioned, Roger and I did not cover ourselves in glory on the 1974 RAC Rally, partly due to going off the road in Wales. However, there was another intriguing story that slightly upset our progress back up the field. Late one evening, Roger was driving on a road section (for a change!) across a moorland road in the Scottish borders when we encountered a Hillman Minx driven by an elderly lady. We were not going quickly, but did have a slight collision. The lady was uninjured, very amicable, and indeed apologetic. She was hurrying home before the rally arrived, she told us. Her car was not badly damaged, but needed a bit of work at the front corner where the Hillman had attacked our offside door. We did a bit of work before a Ford service car appeared. The lady, thankfully, got on her way and was none the worse for wear. I cannot for the life of me remember who gave the instructions, but it was felt that Ford should keep this out of the newspapers, as the news of Britain's top rally driver bumping into an old lady on a road section of the RAC Rally would not be good publicity for the sport or Ford. During the night, a new white door was obtained from a Ford dealer somewhere, and a bit of paint and a number five affixed to it. Later on, a *Daily Mirror* sticker was added, having been removed from a retired car. It was an amazing bit of manipulating by Ford, but somehow the entire story kept out of all the specialist magazines and, more importantly, national newspapers. The whole thing was 'hushed up' very well, and the only thing I can remember is that the Scottish lady's old Hillman Minx was replaced by a new Ford Escort somewhere along the line. Now, you certainly didn't know any of that, did you?

There was another Ford entry on the RAC of 1974 that caused excitement for the Ford hierarchy, if not the spectators. It concerned car number 143. This Escort RS2000 was to be driven by Benson Ford Junior and Elliot Kaplan from the USA. The young Benson was, in fact, a nephew or some such of Henry Ford II, our beloved leader, and his involvement with the RAC Rally was instrumented by Walter Hayes, who had close contact with Henry Ford. Benson and his mate, Elliot, were great enthusiasts, but not too familiar with European rallying. They arrived a few days earlier than expected and made their way to Essex, where they found a hotel before turning up at Boreham. We welcomed them and showed them round, and at lunchtime I took them down to the Cock Inn in Boreham village for a pint and a sandwich. They spotted the dartboard, and next thing I knew, they were playing this 'quaint old English' game until about 3 o'clock in the afternoon. The same thing happened the next day, but our little trips were soon curtailed when someone at Ford HQ in Warley got wind of the fact they were here, and they were assigned a minder who ushered them off to a Park Lane hotel in London, providing them with a driver to get back to Boreham, if necessary. Having tested the car they started the RAC Rally, and were enjoying themselves until the much-feared Dovey forest in Wales, when they went off the road on both stage 15 and 16, then got held up in spectator traffic and arrived 'out of time' at the Machynlleth control, so retired. I never did get a letter from 'Uncle Henry,' thanking me for looking after his nephew.

This 1974 RAC Rally is going on a bit, you will be thinking, but it's not over yet! I also remember an amazing incident on the final leg of the rally on an icy, foggy Wednesday morning in the Yorkshire forests. We were still on our meteoric climb from 38th position, and now well into the top ten, but after the Cropton stage Roger announced that the clutch was slipping. It was, indeed, fortuitous that for the very first time on the RAC Rally the works cars had been equipped with two-way radio kits. I called to relay this information, using our call-sign 'Porky,' one of the many nicknames given to Roger by the ebullient Mick Jones. I'm not really into all this two-way radio speak, but if you say 'Roger' it means 'received and understood' which is a bit confusing for everyone. Hannu and Timo used their own names as call signs. Amid much crackling, the voice of Stuart Turner came over the airwaves, telling us to get ourselves to the Ford dealer in Pickering where a service crew would be stationed. Within seconds of this call, I overheard Henry Liddon's dulcet tones calling to say that Timo's clutch was also playing up. He, too, was told to make for Pickering. When both cars arrived simultaneously we found Stuart Turner had arranged for the garage to be cleared of customers' cars and two ramps were available for us. The place was swarming with Ford's own mechanics whilst they set about changing the triple-plate clutches in little more than 30 minutes for each car. Stuart, meanwhile, had organised bags of fish and chips for us. After all this excitement we set off like bats out of hell, and rejoined the fray running among all the low numbers. Apparently, many of these were astonished to be overtaken at speed on a stage by not one, but two works Escorts, and there were reports of some people stopping, thinking they were lost, having found their way onto another stage in the maze of tracks in these difficult forests. I know that we overtook three or four cars on the 18-mile Cropton stage, and 'helped' an East German Wartburg to get out of the way with a gentle (?) nudge. The last we saw of the Wartburg, it was gracefully sliding down a grassy bank.

I almost might not have been with Roger on the 1974 RAC Rally with all its dramas, as Stuart Turner toyed with the idea of entering triple world champion Formula 1 driver Jackie Stewart in the RAC Rally after his retirement from Grand Prix racing in October 1973. He knew of Jackie's immense skill, and thought he could emulate fellow Scot Jim Clark's RAC Rally outing, when he achieved so much publicity back in 1966. He also thought I might accompany Jackie in the co-driver's seat; it would be a good combination, as I was very familiar with all the stages and knew Jackie quite well, having been involved with him on several projects at Boreham. I had actually sat alongside him in a racing Capri at one point, and seen him in action as a brilliant, smooth driver. I had also had meetings with Jackie and Peter Ashcroft in his suite at the Dorchester Hotel a few times. Jackie is the only man I have ever met who can consume a large steak smothered in tomato ketchup, and never stop talking! He gave me quite a lot of advice in sponsorship-seeking and other matters, and I remember him telling me to make sure sponsors' names were high up on driver's collars, so that they would be seen in photographs and on TV. I am not sure quite how far Stuart Turner got with his negotiations with Jackie, but the RAC Rally project never materialised; possibly something to do with insurance matters, as Jackie had formally retired from competitive driving. I would like to have co-driven Jackie, but I expect it would have been very hard work.

Back at Boreham, after the RAC Rally, we were all in a happy mood as the rally

Mason's Motoring Mayhem!

cars were cleaned and stripped down and we celebrated Ford's third consecutive win in Britain's premier rally. Our celebrations were short-lived, however, for next morning a memo from our leader Stuart Turner arrived on Peter Ashcroft's and my desks. It soon brought us down to earth! This is it, word for word:

November 22, 1974

P Ashcroft
cc. T Mason

I always reckon that the time to be self-critical is when you're on top so, with that theory, here are one or two random notes I made on the R.A.C.

1. Our rally cars look immaculate but the service side looks scruffy. The mechanics' overalls tend to be a rag-tag collection, the service signs look as if they came out of the arc and we don't seem to be able to stop mechanics putting stickers all over their cars, e.g. Ford decals for no known reason on the back of Mick Jones's service car.

2. I think we were mildly out-fumbled by Saab on the service plot, particularly over tyres – they had snow tyres available several stages before us.

3. Some of our average speeds seemed dangerously optimistic.

I would hate to face a Police enquiry into an accident when our service schedule showed a high average.

4. In view of the help we got from Gilligans, Carlisle and the National Garage near Pickering, maybe we could have had known enthusiasts/garages on a more positive stand-by.

5. I wonder if we could simplify the catering we do on rallies perhaps by making more use of Thermos flasks? We do seem to spend a lot of time setting up Gypsy encampments whereas Saab seem to be up, up and away.

6. Even if it means losing the reclining seats we must put a protective cage behind the drivers in the service cars.

7. We must plan our events so that we have proper axles, etc. available.

8. I have got a scribbled note about Saab alloy wheels – I think it was Timo's point that their centres are carved away to save weight and reduce the risk of wheels coming loose because of too much paint surface meeting.

9. Studying the stage times it is clear we shall have to do a lot more development to get the power down if we are to stay ahead of Toyota and others in 1975 – but then motorsport is supposed to push development, isn't it?

Stuart Turner

As if that wasn't bad enough, we received another staff memorandum which announced that Ford would reduce its salaried staff workforce by 1750 employees within the next few weeks. There had been a sharp deterioration in the company's economic situation, and Ford had experienced one of the worst years in its history.

During 1974 we'd been making cutbacks, as the economic climate had changed for the worse and there were worries about petrol supplies. Rationing cards were even produced, but never used. There were strikes galore, three-day weeks, and one third of the light bulbs in use at Ford were removed. It was not a happy scene, and Boreham was told to make cutbacks. We reduced staff and motorsport programmes. I began to wonder about the future for my family and myself.

Nineteen

All change!

Whatever gloomy news there was about the British economy, together with announcements of possible cutbacks in motorsport programmes and staff at Ford, the beginning of 1975 was the most unimaginably marvellous time for me because, at 9.07am on the 28th January, I saw the birth of my darling baby daughter, Emma. Without going into too many details of Sue's labour, the baby was somewhat loath to make her entrance into the world, so was late arriving, obviously not having inherited her father's penchant for accurate time-keeping! Nothing will ever obliterate from my mind the beautiful memory of Emma's arrival, and the look of joy (and relief) on Sue's face. I think Sue thought I had hoped for a son to be born, but in fact I wanted a daughter, someone to be 'daddy's girl.' I was absolutely delirious, and when I left the Chelmsford St John's hospital to get into my car, got quite emotional when I heard the record being played on a BBC light programme on the car radio: it was Don McLean's hit *Wonderful Baby*. I always thought that if ever I was invited to appear on *Desert Island Discs*, this would be the first record I would choose. I returned to my office at Boreham that morning and told everyone my happy news, and invited all in the competition department to join me in the nearby Cock Inn for a celebratory drink at lunchtime. Peter Ashcroft was with Stuart Turner, elsewhere in Essex, but I did receive congratulatory telephone calls from both. The baby's arrival merited a mention in the weekly Fordsport news, produced by Harry Calton. He pointed out that all Ford's current co-drivers – Jim Porter, Henry Liddon, John Davenport, and now me, had produced girls. Maybe it's something in the genes but I know that all the Ford rally drivers of the time – Mikkola, Mäkinen, and Clark – only produced boys.

Back at my desk there was work to be done, but regrettably, much of it centred around cutbacks on rally programmes and staff. Peter Ashcroft had to make redundancies, and there was a definite feeling that motorsport's days were numbered. This had all started the year before, in fact, and we were lucky to be doing as much as we were, much of the motorsport being subsidised by the oil and tyre companies. Esso sponsored a series of Fordsport rally shows that I presented, and I was honoured to receive a letter from the then Ford chairman, Sam Toy, congratulating me on my efforts and saying what good feedback he had received from Ford dealers. We still planned to enter the Circuit of Ireland Rally with Roger Clark in a 'development' Escort, and Irish driver Billy Coleman in 000 96M. Billy, in fact, was and is something of a favourite of mine, and I first met him a couple of years before when I turned up at my office at Boreham and found this young, bedraggled person sitting in the small reception area. "Hello,"

I said, "Can I help you?" I wasn't sure who he was or what he wanted. "I'm Billy Coleman from County Cork" he said in his amazingly quiet and gentle brogue. "I was wondering if you have any works cars I could drive." I pushed him into the gents to dry off after his half mile walk from the place a taxi dropped him off and told him to join me in my office. I explained that works drives in Britain's top rally team were not doled out to anyone who turned up on the doorstep. I was, however, fascinated by this intelligent, quiet, young man who had some special charisma. He told me of his history and background (including the fact that his father, or grandfather, had designed and invented the power take-off system for Fordson tractors and still held the patent), and he told me what he had won as a rally driver. He also mentioned he had close contacts with Ford Ireland as Henry Ford (Cork) Ltd was just down the road from Millstreet where he farmed. When Peter Ashcroft arrived I made the introductions and asked Peter if he agreed to let Billy take me round the test track in one of the cars in the workshop. I sat in with Billy and was impressed. I'm rewinding and darting about here, but the Billy Coleman thing developed well and he won the 1974 British Rally championship, and the following year was leading it again. For the 1975 Circuit of Ireland we gave Billy a works car, but there was only money for the entries and hotels. Billy had always rallied with fellow countryman Dan O'Sullivan, but I think Dan was otherwise engaged or something, so Billy asked me to co-drive. Peter Ashcroft preferred me to accompany him in the management car, so I refused to go with Billy. We selected another Irish co-driver, Paul Phelan, who did a good job, and Billy won his first big rally – unfortunately without me in the passenger seat.

I know I keep darting off at tangents and burbling about things that most people would probably have forgotten, but I have a tendency to pick up on the bizarre and amusing things. Here's another one: when Ford entered the Scottish rally one year we were encamped in the Hilton Hotel in Glasgow, where the then top world superstar group The Osmonds were also staying. I probably don't need to explain that the hotel was heaving with security guards and there were huge, screaming crowds outside. The Osmond brigade were housed on the entire top floor of the hotel, and it had been sealed off. One of the lifts had been assigned to the Osmonds, and no-one else could use it as it had been programmed to avoid all floors except theirs. Billy Coleman was in our team, and, having telephoned him, arranged to meet in reception, near the lifts. The Osmond lift descended and arrived at the reception floor, and with all the other other 'rubber-neckers,' I watched as the great American Osmond family emerged. There, in the middle of them, was Billy Coleman! I'm not sure if he knew who they were or how on earth he got into the lift, but there he was. A magic moment for me, if not for Billy, or the Osmonds. There was another interesting happening for me at this hotel, as Peter Ashcroft and I had dinner with the fabulous fast rally driver, Michèle Mouton, who told us about her plans to run the Race of Champions in the future. She outlined her plans to invite every World Rally Champion to race against each other on a knockout basis. This would develop into a hugely successful annual event, and I was to have a close involvement with it in the future.

The Welsh Rally was next on the agenda in May, with works cars for Roger Clark and Jim Porter, Billy Coleman and John Davenport, Russell Brookes and John Brown, and Nigel Rockey and Ron Channon. The Welsh Rally was based on Barry in South Wales that particular year, and I was in charge as Peter Ashcroft was elsewhere. The day before it started I remember checking into the

International Hotel near Cardiff airport in Barry, and going up to my floor. I followed a young blond Finn called Ari Vatanen who was driving a privately entered Opel, but had already established himself as something of a young hotshot and possibly Finland's next star. I said "Hello," as he went into the room next to mine. Stuart Turner, Peter Ashcroft, and I had discussed Ari, and they had told me to keep an eye on him to see if he could be considered for a Ford drive at some point. You'll remember that Stuart Turner 'invented' Finnish rally drivers, discovering Rauno Aaltonen, Timo Mäkinen, Simo Lampinen et al. He changed the face of rallying, finding this lot! Back at the hotel in Barry, I was unpacking my bags when there was a knock on the door. It was my very good friend and rival Tony Fall, who was Opel's team manager. "I thought this was Ari Vatanen's room," he said. I told him it was next door. The cat was out of the bag! I instantly thought that the little meeting next door might mess up Ford's plans to get an involvement with young Ari, so I phoned my masters in Essex and alerted them to the happenings in beautiful Barry. A cunning plan evolved, and I was told to ring Timo Mäkinen at home in Helsinki, tell him the telephone number of the hotel we were in, together with Ari's room number, and ask him to speak to Ari immediately (in Finnish, of course, so Tony Fall couldn't understand), and tell him not to sign anything for Opel until he had spoken to me, as there could be an opportunity with Ford. The plan worked, and the rest is history. Ari won the British and World Rally Championships as a Ford driver, with David Richards as his co-driver.

Now, talking of David Richards, I have a long history of involvement there. In the very early seventies, when I had been appointed competitions co-ordinator at Ford, we were involved in what was then known as the Kléber/Wheelbase Rally championship – sponsored by the French tyre manufacturer and BBC TV programme of those names. One of the finalists was co-driver David Richards from North Wales, who partnered David 'Piggy' Thompson from Yorkshire. (David was a pig farmer in case you were wondering. His son James is now a championship-winning saloon car racing driver, by the way. With all this digressing, is there any wonder this is a long book?) After the presentation of trophies and other niceties I met David Richards (then known as Dave, incidentally, which is possibly not quite so sophisticated a name now that he is in the very top echelons of the motorsport industry). We had a couple of drinks, and I kid you not, he asked me for advice so he could emulate me and make a successful career in motorsport. I promptly advised him to do something or other and continue co-driving as much as possible. As I now read about the huge Prodrive empire he has created and see his name in various national rich lists, I feel happy that he took my advice! I now know David and Karen Richards well, and David kindly loaned me his helicopter for our daughter Clare's wedding in 1989, which was an amazing gesture. I do have enormous admiration for his abilities. Maybe I should go to him for advice on my diminishing career.

With all these cutbacks going on at Boreham I was getting slightly depressed, but following company guidelines, Ford loaned cars to all sorts of celebrities, particularly motorsport stars, and all of these were under my jurisdiction. I didn't decide who got them, but it was my job to be in contact on all matters. The cars were swapped regularly, so I had a lot of contact with the recipients of these loan vehicles. When the cutbacks appeared Ford had to reduce the number of loan cars, and I was given a list of names to contact and ask to give back the cars. No-one was too happy, of course, but accepted Ford's requirements. When I telephoned Graham Hill, I had the biggest surprise of my life. He exclaimed "What, the Ford Motor Company wants my cars back?" (He had two or three, by the way.) "You can't tell me that Ford are so poor they need my help." With that, the phone went click and the twice world champion Formula 1 driver had gone! Like everybody, I liked Graham Hill as he was a very humorous man, as well as being a brilliant record-breaking driver (who else won the F1 world championship, Le Mans, and Indianapolis?), but he had a sharp, cutting sense of humour. In early 1973, before I joined Ford, there was an amazing motorsport evening held at the Winter Gardens theatre in Blackpool. It was a sell-out as the guests were Graham Hill, Jackie Stewart, Roger Clark, and Stuart Turner, and, after my RAC win, I was brought in. The Winter Gardens theatre in Blackpool was, and still is, one of the greatest theatres in Britain, and every top show business star has appeared there. When I was treading the boards in wet Morecambe a few years before, I would have given anything to be on stage in this marvellous theatre. Here I was! After the show, I joined Graham and Jackie in a car that took us to our hotel. Graham did not want to stay, but hoped he could fly home in his private plane, which was parked at Blackpool airport. It was a damp, foggy night, and I remember Jackie saying "You'll never get off in this weather." Graham replied, "I'm bloody sure I can. If they can get a man to the moon, I reckon I can get out of Blackpool." He offered both Jackie and I a lift back, but we both declined. Just two years later, Graham Hill was killed when his light plane, which he was flying, crashed on landing in foggy conditions at Elstree, near his north London home.

I was meeting people on the world stage, and recalled arriving at my office early one misty morning to find Argentinean F1 driver Carlos Reutemann standing out of the rain in the front door area at Boreham. He introduced himself, and said he had been promised a loan car. It was hours before I got rid of him! I had phone calls from around the world, sometimes at home at very odd hours. I had received a telex message from Ugandan despot and madman President Idi Amin. He was annoyed at the organisers of the East African Safari Rally as they had now rerouted to avoid Uganda. He therefore planned to run his own major rally organised by the Uganda Motor Club. He wanted me to send two Ford cars. Amin was at the height of his mad, murderous activities, so I declined his kind invitation, as did all other western teams. I understand the rally did take place with seven or eight entries. President Amin himself drove a Citroën off the start ramp as car number one, but rapidly abandoned it and returned to his palace for the night. Next morning he emerged and drove the Citroën over the finish ramp to claim first prize! Now, you hadn't heard that one before, had you?

In midsummer, Sue, Jane, Clare, six-month-old Emma and I had a lovely holiday in the Isle of Wight, a place none of us had ever visited. When the children were asleep, Sue and I had walks in the evening and discussed the general situation of living in Essex, and the various problems that were appearing with my job. There was no real urgency, but we both felt we should consider a change for the future. I lay awake at night (which I still do, and have done all my life if anything worries me) and thought – "Could I give up one of the very best jobs in motorsport?" Would I miss all the amazing people I was meeting?

One evening, rally legend Paddy Hopkirk telephoned me and asked if I would be interested in designing a rally navigation 'romer' to be included in his successful range of car accessories. The new metric maps were being introduced by Ordnance Survey, and this scale would have to be included on this map reference plotting device. I met up with Paddy during a trip to London, and he discussed the design of the product, but also mentioned that his company, Mill Accessory Group, which he ran with fellow former rally drivers Peter Riley and Bobby Longmuir, was planning to expand its export side. He invited me to visit their office and factory near Dunstable for lunch. I thought the reason for my visit was to be introduced to staff as a fellow rally winner, but in fact Paddy, Peter, and Bobby asked me if I would be interested in joining them as export director. After the discussions Sue and I had been having, this was food for thought indeed. I returned home and we discussed the whole project, eventually deciding I should accept the new job.

Sue and I started to look at houses, preferably as far north of Dunstable as possible, as we still had so many connections in north-west England and felt we were maybe getting halfway home. We eventually settled on a nice old cottage on the Oxfordshire/Northamptonshire border. It would need some renovation, but Sue could see the potential and was attracted to the house because it had an adjoining two-acre field, which meant the girls could have ponies, eventually. The house was situated at the bottom of a narrow lane, along which a herd of cows passed twice daily to visit their farm for milking. When it turned up, the large removal van containing our goods and chattels blocked much of the lane, of course. Towards the end of the day we heard a kerfuffle in the lane, and discovered that the leading cows in the milking procession had walked up the ramp and into the removal van. The Masons had arrived!

We began the mammoth task of clearing up the grounds of our new abode, and making the house itself habitable. Sue has great vision, and soon started planning what would, after a great amount of work, become a superb garden. I helped with the heavy non-technical bits, and also started construction of a wall, to be built in the local stone that I cadged from friendly farmers, who did not then realise the value of old barns. I really enjoyed building this wall, and worked on it on summer evenings and at weekends. I eventually finished it, although it took longer than Hadrian took to complete his.

Before leaving Ford, during the summer I had agreed to compete on two more events with Roger Clark. One was an international caravan rally, would you believe, and the other the RAC again. It might surprise you to know that the Ford Motor Company competitions department would enter a caravan rally, but it did. In the glorious days before all those 4x4s and SUVs there were certain cars that led the field in towing caravans. Volvos and big Austins were popular, but Fords didn't seem to get in on the act. One of the sales divisions at Ford found a budget to compete in the International Caravan Rally in 1975, but somewhat surprisingly didn't specify a Cortina or Granada as the towing car, instead asking for a Capri to be used. They tied up with a major caravan manufacturer, found sponsorship from Dettol Cream, and Roger and I were booked. In preparation for the event, Roger and I met up and borrowed a trailer from a friend to practise reversing, then made our way to Silverstone where the event was based. We did all sorts of manoeuvrability tests, which Roger hated, and I calculated that some tests were taking so long that we would record less penalty by going flat-out and knocking all the cones flying. This was subsequently frowned upon in the caravan magazines as unsporting behaviour! After all this frivolity at

Silverstone, there was a full night section around the lanes and forests of mid-Wales, before returning to Silverstone. Roger really disliked this event, especially when we overshot a junction in a tight lane in Monmouthshire and he had to reverse. All the car reverse lights did was illuminate the front of the caravan, so he could see nothing. We then thought the best policy was to try and get rid of the caravan by going as fast as possible over hump-back bridges and through forest stages, letting the caravan drag behind with one wheel hanging over the edge. Regrettably the contraption held on like glue, and we emerged from Wales in second place overall! We had been supplied by Boreham with two works mechanics who didn't have a lot to do, but appeared to have eaten some of the provisions in the caravan, which had to be carried the entire route intact. We arrived back in Towcester, near Silverstone, with a chance of winning this great event, so the mechanics were given the job of repairing cupboard doors, some of which had splintered like matchwood, because of our antics. They also had to replenish the food stocks by visiting a local grocery store. We did finish second, incidentally, but in all my subsequent years of overtaking caravans, I never saw one being towed by a Ford Capri.

The 1975 RAC Rally was a different matter, however, and Ford was again entering in force, hoping for its fourth consecutive win. Newly prepared Mk2 Escorts were provided for Timo Mäkinen and Henry Liddon, and Roger and me, whilst Ari Vatanen joined the main team of three cars. Before I left Boreham, I had been involved in sorting out a good sponsorship deal with Cossack hairspray – a leading brand from the Reckitt Group. Hairspray for men was a completely new market, and we were working with a leading London advertising agency. They planned a heavy television advertising campaign, and these really helped Roger become a household name. I was in attendance when the TV commercial was filmed at Bagshot, and was actually sharing a hotel room with Roger when we had a rude awakening at 6.00am, when a fairly effeminate male hairdresser appeared to attend to Roger's flowing locks. It wasn't the sort of thing Roger liked, and he sat on the end of the bed with a very glum face while the hairdresser faffed about. The car Roger and I would drive would be in the bright red colours of Cossack, and we were both kitted out in red overalls and rally jackets. Before the start of the RAC Rally in York we had to appear in Boots chemists for half an hour, dressed in our overalls, signing photographs. I have often seen the funny side of all this, for soon after Roger's hair became prematurely white, and mine dropped out! I had better be careful here as the Cossack brand name is still used, although I understand it is now manufactured by a totally different company, with no association with the Reckitt group.

The RAC Rally itself was not the easiest rally we had ever done, and we really struggled a few times during the 1800-mile, four-day route. For the fourth year running the event was based in York, and at the halfway mark we were lying fifth overall despite a few calamities. On one of the Sherwood Forest stages we suffered a broken rear shock absorber, and at Cirencester Park were extremely lucky to escape another incident unscathed. At 100mph on a long fast straight, a front spring mounting collapsed and the front strut broke, shearing a brake pipe. Through the intercom, I heard a sudden change in Roger's breathing pattern and noticed his foot was pumping the brake pedal as if there was no tomorrow. In fact, there could well not have been a tomorrow for us, as we had lost our brakes completely at this great speed. "What's next?" Roger asked, surprisingly calmly.

"K left," I shouted, thinking we would have a hell of a smash in the trees. In an instant Roger saw a gateway into a field and went for it. We shattered the flimsy gate and flew into the field, where Roger handbraked the car to a stop. He then drove out of the gate, and completed about half a mile of the stage using the handbrake to slow us down. It was a near thing, and no mistake.

There were further dramas afoot. As we moved down to Devon we heard and felt severe engine vibration. Just before the Cricket St Thomas stage our service crew had a good poke about, and advised us that something had come loose from the crankshaft, which was very bad news. However, we persevered and managed to struggle out of the stage, but it was like driving a bag of nails as the engine vibrated frantically. The clutch was slipping, but it was a bigger problem than that. After crawling along for a few miles, we spoke over the radios and told the team we were retiring. We spotted a really nice roadside pub with welcoming early evening lights shining, so pulled into the car park and went in expecting to be eventually rescued, or at worst, stay the night. We had two beautiful foaming pints of bitter placed on the bar in front of us, and were literally taking the first sip when the door of the pub flew open and Mick Jones rushed in, saying they knew what was wrong, and it was something to do with the crankshaft, but that we should get ourselves up to Aust Services at the Severn Bridge where the service crew would change the clutch and generally fettle the problem. Having actually retired, we were now back in the rally and I remember thinking of that lovely foaming pint I had left in Devon. After the service at Severn Bridge I was driving the car along the old twisty A40 road through Raglan and past the Clytha Arms, which looked as brightly lit and welcoming as the pub in Devon. By an amazing quirk of fate, the 'Clytha' is now the nearest local pub and restaurant to my daughter, Emma, and her husband, Kevin, who live nearby. So I often visit it and relive my memories (no doubt boring everyone to death!).

Roger and I trundled on through Wales amazingly well with a healthy sounding car, and despite a few minor problems and clobbering a pile of logs in Kielder forest, two days later we finished second again. Timo and Henry had achieved their hat-trick – at the time, only the second ever after Erik Carlsson's. Sue and baby Emma came to the finish at York racecourse and stood alongside the finish ramp. My favourite rally photograph of all time is one of Timo, Roger, Henry, and I sitting on the roof of the car with Emma, in her mother's arms, peeping round the corner!

Writing this book – which is one of the most difficult things I have ever done, by the way – reminds me of a little publishing incident in which I was involved at Boreham. Stuart Turner has always been a prolific and amusing writer, and has published a number of books including *The Way to Win* in 1974. Stuart asked me to contribute my thoughts on co-driving, and give him a few illustrations to show map marking, pace notes, and other rally paperwork. I sent him a copy of a movement schedule for the Welsh Rally, which I had produced for Ford. At the time, a young rally nerd (his words, not mine) by the name of Fred Gallagher had been poring over the schedule details with a fine tooth comb, and discovered that if Roger Clark had arrived at the start of the event at the time detailed on the illustration, he would have been 24 hours late! Fred, who eventually became one of the top co-drivers in the world, with three Safari and two Ivory Coast wins to his credit, wrote to Stuart Turner, pointing out the mistake. Stuart explained that the page was purely for illustration purposes. Fred told me all this many years later, to which I replied "Ah! You were the clever bastard! I was called into Stuart Turner's office one morning for a bollocking and he was brandishing your letter, stating that some spotty university student had found the mistake, printed in his book!" Be sure your sins will find you out.

Around this time I did receive some astonishing news when I received a letter from the Royal Automobile Club stating that the prestigious Segrave Trophy was being awarded to Roger Clark in respect of the 1972 RAC Rally win. Roger's name was coupled with mine, Jim Porter, Stuart Turner, and the Ford team. The trophy is presented to the British subject who gives the most outstanding demonstration of transport by land, air or water and in doing so shows skill, courage and initiative. Having been awarded since 1930, after Sir Henry Segrave lost his life attempting the world water speed record on Lake Windermere, the list of previous recipients was very impressive indeed. Illustrious names included Amy Johnson, Malcolm and Donald Campbell, Stirling Moss, Jackie Stewart, and numerous test pilots including Peter Twiss and Brian Trubshaw, of Concorde fame. A lunch is held annually at the RAC club in London, and it was a great honour to go along and mingle with great names, past and present. It is, indeed, a unique 'club.'

Twenty

On the road

Moving from motorsport to a more normal business environment was something of a shock, although I was made very welcome at the Mill Accessory Group. I familiarised myself with the big product range for my first overseas selling trip, visiting existing customers in Europe, culminating in ten days at the Automechanika exhibition in Frankfurt. I have to say that I did not enjoy this last part of my trip, and found exhibiting rather tiring and often boring. I hated the requirement to stand around all day, warmly greeting existing customers, or even worse, introducing potential new customers to the range of products. I did not find it particularly challenging, and counted the hours to the end of the day when, with other British exhibitors, I would usually go for a meal and hear of their great sales success stories, which would depress me even more!

Exhibitions are, however, a necessary part of selling, and I would attend very many more in the years to come, both at home and abroad. I attended exhibitions in the United States, Singapore, and on one occasion Japan. Our appearances at the overseas shows were supported and subsidised by the Society of Motor Manufacturers and Traders, which wanted to encourage exports. I enjoyed my first visit to Tokyo, and was invited by the SMMT to join a group of businessmen visiting the Honda factory, which I found fascinating. The speed of the workers on the assembly line impressed me, particularly when a small man climbed into the boot of a finished car, clutching an infra-red light. Water was then sprayed onto the closed boot lid for a few minutes before the man emerged, still alive, and satisfied that there were no leaks! When our coach first arrived we were met by a gentleman in white overalls, before being handed over to several other people in white overalls to tour the production lines. We were then ushered into a meeting room for a question-and-answer session, where I got the surprise of my life – the man who had met us off the coach was sitting at the top table behind a name-board reading Mr Soichiro Honda. I couldn't believe it! This was Mr Honda himself, who had started the company thirty years before, in 1946. I asked him why Honda had pulled out of Formula 1 racing in the late sixties, and he said that racing was good for enjoyment, but not suitable for a commercial company. Next question!

Mr Honda wasn't the only surprise I had in Tokyo. The next day I was approached by a Japanese rally driver who knew of my RAC Rally success, and invited me to spend an evening with him in his country home halfway up Mount Fuji. Hiroki Uchiyama drove me for a couple of hours through open countryside, where I observed teams of Japanese women massaging the hides of cattle. Hiroki told me that this would produce the much-prized Kobe beef.

Mason's Motoring Mayhem!

My next surprise was to arrive at Hiroki's log cabin where the non-English speaking Mrs Uchiyama was already installed. I was given a conducted tour of the unfinished house, and noticed that there was only one bedroom; the second bedroom had a cement mixer in it. We three went out for a meal where I was provided with a very expensive portion of the aforementioned Kobe beef, and various other delicacies including goldfish that appeared to be still moving. Then it was back to the wooden house for a nightcap of Japanese Suntory whisky, then bed for my next surprise. Hiroki informed me that I would sleep with him in the large double bed, whilst his good lady would sleep elsewhere! In fact, she appeared with a bundle of blankets and slept on them on the floor at the end of our bed. I half-wondered if there was some ritual in Japan, not unlike some African states where one of several wives is offered to make male guests feel welcome. Thankfully, the whole incident was very innocent, you will be pleased to know.

After all this excitement, I moved further on in my tour of the Orient to visit the Philippines. I arrived early one Sunday morning and booked in at my hotel, where I noticed a number of guests already sunbathing around the swimming pool. It was hot and humid in Manilla, so I decided to occupy a sun bed in a shady part of the grounds near the pool. Not surprisingly, I fell fast asleep, and slept soundly for three or more hours. On waking, I had the shock of my life. There was not another body in sight; as the sun climbed in the sky, they had all moved to stay in the shade, leaving me sizzling in the midday sun. I was in absolute agony, and looked like a boiled lobster. I staggered off to my room where I remained for 24 hours, being visited by the hotel doctor who prescribed various pills and potions. It certainly taught me a lesson.

Being an export salesman was hard work, but I enjoyed my travels, and although I did not consider myself a particularly gifted salesman, I made good progress, and the Paddy Hopkirk range of accessories increased its overseas sales quite considerably. I can't have been too bad, for several competitors asked me to join their companies. However, whilst I was happy in my job, I knew that in order to make enough money to give my family a secure future, I would almost certainly need to own a business, and not merely be an employee.

Autoplas was a leading manufacturer of accessories run by Ken Harris, a jovial and genial man whom I had met at numerous exhibitions and trade functions. Ken suggested we should get together to start a company, and we should have an equal shareholding. He would introduce the limited finance necessary to get going and I would work from home, keeping all the overheads as low as possible. Sue and I had great discussions about this, and decided to give it a go. I started on the first of January 1979, working from a small card table in our bedroom. I bought a used Escort estate very cheaply, thanks to my links with Ford, and put together a simple range of accessories including mud flaps, door guards, and car mats (nothing very sophisticated, you'll notice). The products were sourced from other manufacturers, and Sue and I packed them, often being helped by our family at the kitchen table. Our brand name was 'Tonken,' and I produced a simple catalogue and allocated certain days to going selling, having to stay at home on other days when Sue was away; she had returned to her profession of nursing, which helped our meagre finances, but it was a great strain on her, one for which I will be eternally grateful. Life was a struggle, but we persevered and made slow progress. Even though I was now part-owner of the business I

Continued page 177

Mason down under, interviewing Australian rally legend and TV star Ross Dunkerton in Perth.

Back in Kenya for a Tusker beer!

May 1993 and *Top Gear* makes the front cover of the *Radio Times*.

Who's interviewing who? Murray Walker and I saw a lot of each other over the years.

My ambition was to be interviewed by the great Raymond Baxter. Here, I'm interviewing him with John Sprinzel looking on.

Strangers in the night! An evening encounter with comedian Rob Brydon.

The *Top Gear* team in the nineties: Jeremy Clarkson, Quentin Willson, Tiff Needell, Michele Newman, Steve Berry, and Chris Goffey, with yours truly hogging centre stage at a Silverstone TV special.

"Tony, you got me lost again!" With Stirling Moss in an Aston Martin DBR2 at Goodwood.

Five-time Le Mans winner Derek Bell took me on the Tour of Britain. We had a lot of laughs.

The flat-cap competition! Nigel Mansell giving me a lecture.

Who's your friend, Bernie?

A walk in the park with Lewis
Hamilton.

Lifting a wheel in New Zealand with Hannu Mikkola.

Hannu flew me around Rally Finland to spectate. We never missed a stage.

Another Segrave Trophy moment. The 'Generation Game' with Sir Stirling, Lewis, and yours truly.

Ten minutes after this picture was taken Carlos Sainz tried to kill me at the Race of Champions!

Racer/rallyman Kimi Räikönen.

Petter Solberg.

Nine-time World Rally Champion Sébastien Loeb.

Jari-Matti Latvala.

Mikko Hirvonen.

How tickled I am! Ken Dodd helped me a lot during my TV career.

The famous 'snowball incident,' shown on TV around the world and on YouTube.

Another *Top Gear* fan – Sir Norman Wisdom at his home in the Isle of Man.

I was honoured to be invited to Buckingham Palace for a celebration of Sport in the Life of the Nation in 1997.

Nick Mason of Pink Floyd fame is a great petrol-head. Many viewers thought
we were brothers.

A picture that says it all – "No problem, Tony!" Colin McRae had just won the
World Rally Championship in 1995. (© McKlein)

TV and radio presenter Chris Evans – another motoring fanatic.

Dressed as Chairman Mao at the Beijing start of the Peking–Paris Marathon.

General Roland Rueda and his cohorts looked after me well in Peru, but I was lucky to survive.

Filming 'Rhino Charge' in Kenya for *Top Gear Motorsport* with film crew Jim Knights and Gordon Nightingale, and one or two others.

All at sea ...

Sue and Emma showing their favourite sort of horsepower.

Like father, like daughter ... Emma holding forth. New husband Kevin keeps mum!

Wedding bells! A proud moment with Sue and Emma.

Sisters in the sun. Jane, Emma, and Clare.

did not have great enthusiasm for selling, and found it very degrading when visiting large customers. Some buyers would deliberately keep salesmen waiting so that they lost confidence before starting their sales pitch. Others would be quite rude, throwing some of my products down on their desks, saying that my products were 'me too,' and that other brands were better. I actually got quite despondent at times, but didn't want to worry Sue. Woolworths was one of the biggest names in the High Street in the eighties, and amazingly I obtained an appointment with a buyer in their headquarters in London. I had a good meeting, and the relatively pleasant man I visited showed interest in Tonken door guards. These were simple strips of extruded plastic which fitted on the door edge and were a very popular accessory in those days. I was promised an order would be put in the post to me, and drove home in a very elated mood, dreaming of a gigantic order. Life has its ups and downs, but you will imagine my disappointment when I opened an envelope with Woolworths' name on the postmark, only to find an order that must have been the smallest Woolworths had ever issued. It wanted just twelve packs of ten door guards, worth a total of £15! They were to be put in twelve different stores as a test. As part of this bizarre affair, I must tell you of one incident which, in hindsight, was very amusing. Woolworths sent one of their huge articulated trucks to collect the twelve small boxes. Arriving in our tiny village in those pre-satnav days, the driver became lost, and, in turning round, his truck became stuck in the mud on the village green in the early evening winter darkness. He was not too pleased, and nor were some of the villagers.

As I knew the location of the twelve selected Woolworth stores, I came up with a cunning plan – I would visit all the stores and buy most of my products back! It worked, as within weeks I received a whacking great order to be supplied to their main warehouse. The product would go into all of Woolworths' 1400 stores.

Bit by bit, Tonken expanded and eventually we moved to our own premises. Our range of products had grown considerably and, at one point, we were manufacturing some items and employing twenty people in total. Ken Harris was very much a sleeping partner and had his own business in Essex to occupy him, so after some fairly protracted negotiations between our respective accountants, it was agreed that I would buy Ken's share of the business and Sue and I would own it. After a short time we changed the name to Tony Mason Limited, and widened the range of products to include a number of items imported from Europe and the Far East.

One such product was nearly our undoing, however. We had been importing anti-static strips (those dangly bits of a rubbery material seen hanging from the backs of cars) from Italy. The strips were made of rubber containing a graphite substance that conducted static electricity from the car to the road. This could help to prevent travel sickness, it was alleged. We supplied a huge quantity of this product and it was available from Halfords, B&Q, Woolworths, many supermarkets, and most independent accessory shops. I've always disliked opening mail in case it contains bad news, and this certainly happened one morning when I received a letter from the Trading Standards Office. Evidently, some electrical boffin in London had purchased one of our anti-static strips as his daughter suffered from travel sickness. He fitted the strip, but there was no improvement. Being a boffin, he then decided to test the strip on a machine at his boffin-workshops, and discovered it was pure rubber and contained no material that could possibly conduct static. I was flabbergasted and felt sick. We had thousands of the things and more on the way from Italy and they were useless. What could I do? I consulted my solicitor who prepared a case as I would have to go to court. My defence was that we had never ever had a problem and this must have been a faulty batch where the manufacturers had omitted to include the graphite. Our company had a good honest record, and I had received a letter from Mrs Thatcher congratulating me on creating employment. I also stated that we had supplied a quantity of anti-static strips to the acknowledged experts in the field of static science – the Royal Air Force, who equipped all the fuel tankers at some of their bases including the Falkland Islands, where they were rebuilding the airport. We went to court, and I am sorry to say I was fined £1000. My appearance made the newspapers next morning, with *The Sun* headline "Maggie's boy gets a nasty shock." The other popular papers stated that "Tony Mason, who made a fortune from rallying, has made more money selling useless bits of rubber to the RAF." Amazingly, the RAF story was featured as the last item on ITV's national news. It was very embarrassing, but every cloud has a silver lining: sales of the product increased substantially, proving that no publicity is bad publicity.

I had continued to stay involved with motorsport, albeit at arm's length, but was not competing. I was therefore surprised to get a phone call from Jim Porter who was organising the Lombard RAC Rally from the RAC headquarters in London. He said they were looking for someone to handle the sales of Lombard RAC paraphernalia like scarves, bobble hats, rally jackets, and the like. I was obviously very interested and took on the project, which entailed mail order advertising in the motorsport press and selling from a stand at the rally start areas, of which Sue took charge. We widened the range, and looking back, it was the beginning of the rally clothing industry, which is now huge. The Lombard RAC Rally would soon play another significant part in my future career, one that I could never, ever have predicted. Read on.

On the box!

In the summer of 1986, I received a telephone call that was to start a new chapter in my life. It was from Nick Brittan, a well-known motorsport personality and rally organiser who was assisting Lombard, sponsor of the RAC Rally. He knew of my after-dinner performing and commentating activities, and suggested to the BBC that a 'rally expert' might assist Barrie Gill, doyen of the old *Wheelbase* television programme, in the commentary box for the live one-hour special stage in the grounds of Badminton. Nick asked me to meet John G Smith, the producer of the live coverage of the rally to be held in November, and I duly did at a nearby hotel in Towcester, where he was filming another programme. I had a nice meal with John and his team, but it was only at the very end of the meal that he discovered I had actually won the RAC Rally; he must have missed that bit of the conversation when we first met. I was asked to ring John at the BBC's Pebble Mill Studios in Birmingham a week later, and was told I should meet the rest of the production team at Pebble Mill one morning, later in the week.

I met executive producer Dennis Adams, among others, and also John Burkill, a VT editor who had special knowledge of rallying, and was an integral part of the RAC Rally coverage. Thankfully, John now knew all about my rally history, and I knew I had his support. We all went to the BBC bar where pints of beer were consumed, although I stuck to sparkling water, thinking I might have to go for a camera test or some other form of audition. After a good hour I gained the impression that our meeting was coming to an end, and was told I had the job, and there would be no further audition. Sometime later I was told I got the job because they all knew I wouldn't dry up during the live transmission!

When the rally came round, I reported to a hotel near the Bath starting point and met the rest of the crew, including presenters William Woollard, Sue Baker, and Barrie Gill. I was told I should go to scrutineering at nearby Colerne airfield next morning, the day prior to the rally. Nobody said what I would be doing, but I knew I could chat to rally drivers and polish up my notes for the live commentary, and in any case, my wife, Sue, would be present selling the Lombard rally gear from our company's stall. No-one had said anything about me doing any filming, as I had been booked for commentary purposes only for the whole event. It was, therefore, a bit of a surprise for me to be suddenly asked to go and do a couple of interviews as a "bit of an audition." This was a whole new world to me, and none of the camera or sound crews knew who I was or what I was doing there. One camera operator was, unusually, a pleasant young lady who suggested I keep my cap on for the interview. She said she thought it looked nice, obviously meaning that my hair looked not very nice.

My first 'victim' was one of Britain's top female rally drivers, Louise Aitken-Walker, who I later found out was considered not particularly easy to interview. I remember my very first words of introduction. Speaking to camera I said "There are only two lady drivers on the rally this year: Suzanne Kottulinsky from Sweden, and our own Louise Aitken-Walker. Louise, why are there not more women here? ..." I thought Louise answered my questions very well, and I was extremely relieved that the interview went without a hitch. I was then given further interviews to do including Tony Pond, Markku Alén, and Stig Blomqvist, all of whom I knew well, which probably helped the interviews.

My splendid camera lady, Karen Lamb, looked happy with the results, and I owe her a huge debt of gratitude for it was her idea I should wear my cap, which became my trademark on television throughout the next twenty years. Karen moved on to run Ventura Productions with her husband, Paul Colbert, and I subsequently appeared in their productions including a series on successful pubs and restaurants in Britain, a visit to Las Vegas for a short series of programmes, and the production of a sixty-minute video for Eddie Stobart, the famous haulage contractor.

The live stage transmitted on Sunday morning went without a problem, and Barrie Gill and I worked well together. Having a producer and director talking into my headset throughout the hour was slightly disconcerting, but I soon got used to it. So, the end of my first live television broadcast arrived without any dramas, and I was relieved to join a camera crew in their car to drive off to the Harrogate overnight halt, and then the next day to Edinburgh, with little to do until a night-time special stage at the Ingliston racing circuit.

I'm a big believer in being in the right place at the right time, and Ingliston was certainly one of these places. I didn't realise it, but I had entered bedlam! Nearly everything that could go wrong, did go wrong. The move of the technical facilities from Badminton to Harrogate did not go well, and tapes were slow reaching the mobile editing suites. The November weather was dreadful, and the helicopter that was due to bring the tapes of the Kielder forest stages could not fly. The heavy rain over Edinburgh caused gridlock, and to cap it all, the plans to cover the live stage at Ingliston showground were a shambles. It was pitch black and there was completely inadequate lighting. Now, just before the rally, the BBC had without warning decided to change the person in overall charge of *Top Gear* and its associated programmes. Tom Ross was the new executive producer who was thrown in at the deep-end; he discovered the plans for the live transmission were fatally flawed, and that if something was not done, rallying might be dead on television for a generation.

I was unaware of the politics and dramas, but Tom, whom I had only briefly met in Harrogate the night before, had to inform the BBC in London that because of a delay in starting the stage (not mentioning the fact that thirty minutes of car headlights in near pitch darkness would not be riveting television) he would not be able to produce a full 30-minute programme. London would have to fill in with a *Tom & Jerry* cartoon, and he'd supply a much shorter programme of the day's events. It was then decided to interview the early arrivals at Ingliston – but who could do it? Tom dragooned an exhausted film crew that had arrived from the forests, and took me to interview early leaders Juha Kankkunen, Mikael Ericsson, and Timo Salonen. Tom, being completely new to the programme, might have thought I had more experience of television than I actually had, and this could have been another disaster. In fact, my impromptu interviews went very well, and all was not lost. The programme escaped free of criticism, and, thankfully, I emerged without egg on my face. When the weekly *Top Gear* programme returned to the screens in spring 1987, Tom Ross announced that the programme would have a rally expert who would be expected to pounce on rally drivers and secure interviews, regardless of whatever else might be going on. Coverage of rallying was going to increase, and I would be able to play my part in it. As a television performer, I had arrived. It could be considered by mistake, actually.

True to his word, Tom Ross informed his two *Top Gear* producers, Jon Bentley and Ken Pollock, that rallying would be on the menu, and in May 1987 I was despatched to Northumberland with Jon Bentley to film my first ever item for *Top Gear*. I enjoyed being with Jon enormously, and particularly liked his sense of humour, as we pursued the cars competing on the Hadrian Centurion Rally, galloping around in the forests to interview the drivers at service halts. Jon had then scripted a piece to camera for me to perform, and this is where my career very nearly came to a premature end! TV viewers may not realise that a piece to camera is one of the most terrifying things imaginable for a performer. Firstly, you have to learn the words, then you have to sound as though you understand them, and then you have to appear completely at ease and very natural. And you have to repeat the performance time after time until the cameraman and producer are happy. Oh! I forgot. You will almost certainly have a group of bystanders (known as 'the great unwashed' in TV circles) who will rudely jeer if you get your words wrong. Leaning nonchalantly on a rally car I tried, time after time, to deliver the lines, but it was a pathetic performance, and must have looked so bad on the rushes back at the TV studios that the item was put together without a piece to camera. This was unheard of, and almost certainly one of the only times an item has been transmitted without the presenter being seen.

I was lucky to escape from my calamitous performance, and Tom and Jon never really mentioned my failing, but agreed that Jon should meet me in Pebble Mill car park one Saturday afternoon to practise further pieces to camera, and even 'drive and talk,' another thing that looks a lot easier than it is. Jon Bentley's help was invaluable, but he felt I had to struggle 'to sound like Tony Mason' at first. He was very patient, and I often think of that early tuition when I see Jon on television as a presenter on *The Gadget Show* and other programmes.

Although I was feeling a lot happier after another couple of items had been transmitted, I did not feel I was portraying the jollity and enthusiasm that was my trademark off-screen. However, another stroke of luck came my way when I met Ken Dodd after a show at the Opera House, Blackpool, where he had been starring. As I mentioned earlier, I had met Ken once or twice previously, but I was amazed when he said he had seen my early efforts on television and that he was very interested in cars. He then gave me the best advice I ever received. He said that before a recording or live transmission, I should think of someone I knew and liked, sitting on a settee and smiling and looking forward to seeing me. He then said that I should talk to that one person in a warm, friendly way and every other viewer would automatically think I was talking to them. From one of the greatest communicators in show business, this was advice I followed for the rest of my career. Doddy also said that *Top Gear* had quite a few 'smart alecs' on the programme, and I should develop a happy persona and always remember I was going, uninvited, into someone's house. I may have gone over the top occasionally, but it seemed to work. *The Daily Mirror* called me 'cheery', Anne Robinson on *Points of View* called me the friendliest of the *Top Gear* tribe, and national newspapers called me "ever-jovial." Ken Bruce, on his regular morning programme on Radio 2, said that I always reminded him of Wilfrid of the Bash Street Kids in the Beano comic! However, the *London Evening Standard* called me 'rumpled and bumbling' whilst Jeremy Clarkson referred to me, in one of his books, as having a relentlessly chirpy style which was a bit annoying. You can't win 'em all!

As the eighties went on I expanded my repertoire, so to speak, with a variety of items for *Top Gear*, including sand racing, banger racing, an old bus rally, the Land's End Trial, and various small rallies around Britain. Wherever possible, I would have a go at driving whatever vehicles we were featuring, and, over the years, handled trucks, buses, tanks, and fire engines. When we featured the centenary of the Leyland bus and truck company, I drove the actual Leyland PD3 double-decker on which I went to school. This really was one of the high spots of my career, I must say. I enjoyed the Leyland item enormously, and remember running up the steps to the top deck and sitting on the front seat, saying "See! I can prove it was this bus – my chewing gum is under the seat." When Pope John Paul visited Britain in 1982, Leyland built his 'Popemobile,' which is still on display at the Leyland museum. I climbed aboard and sat in the papal chair and gave a little wave, but director Chris Richards thought we had better not film this bit.

Another memorable item was a feature on two young racing stars of the future, David Coulthard and Allan McNish, who were emerging from successful kart racing. Both were predicted to do great things in Formula 1 and David certainly did, winning 13 Grands Prix. Allan also drove in Formula 1, but achieved his greatest success in sports car racing, twice winning the Le Mans 24 hour race twice. Prior to Formula 1, David drove for Paul Stewart Racing. I filmed with Paul and his father, Jackie, on several occasions along with David, who once asked me for advice on television interview techniques. At the time I was running courses on this very topic for budding rally drivers, on behalf of Shell, so I pompously lectured David on the dos and don'ts. Every time I see and hear him on the regular BBC Formula 1 coverage now, I think of those early days and wonder if any of it helped him. Probably not!

During the making of the *Top Gear* item about the 'young guns,' I interviewed Nigel Mansell about his views on the new talent. Ken Pollock was producing and directing the item, and told me to have a good chat with Nigel about other aspects of his career, which I did, with all the usual delays for changing camera positions, changing lights, and fiddling about with the microphones. After about half an hour of his valuable time we released Nigel and thanked him. Some weeks later, after the transmission of the McNish item, Nigel accosted me angrily at the Motor Show at the NEC. We had shown about half a minute of my interview with Nigel, which disappointed him somewhat, as he and his family had sat down to watch *Top Gear* thinking the entire programme would be devoted to him.

Although my forte was rallying, I seemed to be getting involved with racing drivers quite a lot. For the Tour of Britain in the summer of 1989, it was decided to put me in a Vauxhall Astra with five-time Le Mans winner Derek Bell, no less. I knew Derek quite well already, and it was an enjoyable trip. Derek had competed on the RAC Rally once or twice, so enjoyed the forest stages, although I must admit I was very careful to call every bend as accurately as possible to help him keep on the road! However, he came into his own on the race tracks and on other hard-surface tests, which included a very short Mickey Mouse autotest around a lot of bollards laid out on a supermarket car park in Norwich. We flew round very satisfactorily, and I have dined out on this little outing many times, for I must be the only person in the world to co-drive the five-time Le Mans winning driver on a race round a Tesco car park. Another racing driver with whom I was asked to share a car was fellow *Top Gear* presenter Tiff Needell, when we participated in a great scenic tour of Scotland called the Ecosse Tour. There was very little competition, if any, but there were lots of very interesting cars and crews, and our Jaguar XK120 was one of the best. Ken Pollock was directing and producing, again, and we fitted an 'in-car' camera so we could see all the wonderful roads over which we were travelling. The cameraman fitted the recorder under my passenger seat, and I thought he told me to press a switch down to record any nice views. I'm absolutely sure he said 'down,' but the long and the short of it is that I should have switched 'up' to film and 'down' for off. The result of this was that we obtained no road shots, but some lovely close-ups of walls and fences when we had parked the XK for an overnight halt in Oban. Ken was not too pleased! One person who thought it was hilarious was comedy actor Rowan Atkinson, who was competing with his wife, and whom we joined some evenings for dinner.

After my surprise debut in 1986, I became a firm fixture in the RAC Rally presenting team, and my 'pouncing' interviews were a regular feature. I knew all the teams and drivers, and had contact with them prior to the event, so they all knew I would be performing for the BBC. I had complete access to all the teams in the service areas; being a former competitor, I even had access to the motor homes, and could hoik a driver out for an interview. My interviewing on rallies continued for fifteen years, and I can honestly say I was never refused an interview or had an unfriendly reaction from a driver, even in the heat of battle or during any incident. The coverage of the annual RAC Rally was most impressive, with two programmes each night plus a full half-hour preview programme, and an extended version shown to peak audiences during Christmas holiday time.

I had my own producer and camera crew for all the RAC rallies, and we covered almost as many miles as the rally drivers. In-car cameras were in their early days, and involved huge, cumbersome recorders. The BBC arranged to fit them in one or two cars belonging to amateur drivers, but until 1987 they had never been fitted to a works car. All that changed when I wrote to Cesare Fiorio, the chief of the all-conquering Lancia team, asking if we could have a camera in one of his cars. Cesare agreed that a camera could be fitted to Markku Alén's, which thrilled all the producers, directors, and me, of course, as Markku was a spectacular driver and would surely give us plenty of action. It was a great disappointment, however, when the fiery Finn decided that the whole caboodle was too heavy, and after just a few special stages, he threw all the camera equipment out. That was a great pity, as Markku rolled the Lancia on the next stage at Chatsworth, and it would have provided a highly entertaining shot for our viewers. 'Sod's Law' is a regular feature in TV work!

Twenty-two

TV times

For the 1988 RAC Rally, we came up with a novel idea. We would feature a very popular British driver – Louise Aitken-Walker, who, you may remember, featured as a subject at my TV interview audition. As part of the buildup, it was decided we should film Louise driving a Peugeot 309 on a national rally some weeks before the RAC. Most appropriately, the Tour of Cumbria, which would take place in Kielder forest, became the selected rally, and surprise, surprise, I was to sit in the co-driver's seat. With the exception of a couple of short rallies entered by Peugeot's publicity department, Louise had never had a male co-driver, so this was seen as an added attraction by our producer, Tony Rayner. The rally started in Carlisle before entering Kielder forest with all its deceptive brows and bends, and there were no pace notes, so I would have to read the Ordnance Survey maps as well as I could; I hoped I would remember my old skills. I must say that I was most impressed when Louise set off on the first stage, but actually found that I was finding the map reading a bit difficult. I was with one heck of a fast lady here. Could I cope?

I had been briefed by Louise's regular co-driver, Ellen Morgan, who came with us on the rally to 'hold my hand,' so to speak, and she said that Louise liked to be given a lot of information. After a mile or two of slithering about on the fast gravel stages I felt more at home, and discovered we were actually doing quite well. Our team-mate was the then young, up-and-coming Colin McRae, and we were in fact beating his times. Colin crashed out of this one-day event, and we returned to Carlisle with a high place and collected a few trophies.

Meanwhile, I was beginning to feel at home with the *Top Gear* team and began to think of myself as a presenter. Motoring journalist Jeremy Clarkson was brought in by Tom Ross and Jon Bentley, and was soon followed by his pal Quentin Willson. Chris Goffey was still appearing a lot, as was Sue Baker. William Woollard was the 'anchorman,' and as a former presenter on *Tomorrow's World* and other popular BBC programmes of the day, was very professional and much respected. He took me under his wing, and when we were out on location would give me lots of tips. He realised I was a rallyman turned TV presenter, and knew how I worried about doing the wrong thing. He said he thought I had a good TV presence, and said that I mustn't just learn the words, but try to understand them. William also told me to start every question with 'how, what, or where?' As they became more established, Jeremy and Quentin developed a bigger influence on programme content, and I got the impression that they merely tolerated me with my unsophisticated items and northern accent, but I didn't ever fall out with them – as motorbike presenter Steve Berry certainly did. In fact, Quentin, who still had a secondhand car dealership in Leicestershire, supplied me with a

Ford Fiesta for my daughter, Emma, when she was made Head Girl at Lawnside School, Malvern. Quentin gave me a good deal, and personally delivered the car. Jeremy's wife, Francie, once told him that she thought I was the nicest presenter on *Top Gear*, which I don't suppose went down too well at home! So, all in all we were a happy team, but very much in competition with each other, being controlled by Tom Ross and also the very experienced Dennis Adams, who came in to oversee *Top Gear, Gardener's World* and several other top shows made in Pebble Mill. The big white chief, however, was John King, who had a huge list of major TV successes. When he arrived in Birmingham he asked for tapes of all *Top Gear* presenters' items, and arranged to see us all a week or so later.

I must admit that I was petrified as I went in to meet John King (incidentally, father of now top wildlife presenter Simon King, who shared our office in Birmingham). John looked a bit foreboding, so I cowered down in the seat in his office and waited for the worst. He put on his TV screen a tape of me doing a piece to camera during the RAC International Historic Rally in 1991. in which I competed with Roger Clark in David Sutton's Lotus Cortina. Our result was pretty pathetic, by the way, although we did win the team prize. Anyway, I'm digressing, as usual. John glowered at the TV screen and watched my ninety-second piece, filmed in the heat of battle as we entered a dark and wet Wales. Then there was silence, while I trembled, before the all-powerful man pronounced "That was the perfect piece to camera. It was good and really captured the situation. It was like hearing from a footballer in the middle of the match!" With that, I was ushered out of John's office and realised I'd kept my job. Phew!

Whilst on the subject of people and the *Top Gear* office, I should mention that I had to be wary of the many millions of people who would have liked my job. As far as the viewer was concerned, I gallivanted all over the place and found everything very jolly. In reality, I was worried that the BBC would find someone else. There was a lot of back-stabbing going on, and we all knew that the BBC TV centre in London wanted to control rallying as part of their sports output. Although I had a good relationship with Steve Rider, I knew he felt he should have more involvement with the RAC Rally each year. Inevitably, all the British rallying journalists envied me like mad, as they had greater knowledge of the sport (in their opinion), yet I was the 'face of rallying.'

From time to time there were little evening soirées of one sort or another organised at Pebble Mill. They tended to be held to celebrate the end of a run of programmes, or occasionally, we would be visited by BBC hierarchy from London where presenters of all the Pebble Mill programmes would be on parade. Jeremy Clarkson had recently moved to the Cotswolds, not far from my home, and kindly offered to give me a lift home in a Jaguar he was road-testing. Having left the M40, we followed a former B road to my house. It suddenly became very foggy so I instantly went into my co-driving mode telling Jeremy the severity of bends, twists and turns. Jeremy, who was never very keen on rallying in those days, was actually quite impressed. "Are these pace-notes?" he asked. "I'm quite enjoying this!" As we approached a hard right-hand bend which I clearly called "hard-right tightens," I wondered if we might be going a shade too quickly. Jeremy yanked on the steering wheel in typical Clarkson fashion, but we still put two wheels on the grass and the rear of the Jaguar sailed perilously close to a hawthorn hedge. He held it very well, in fact, and despite a bit of ditch–hooking regained the road safely. In a way, I'm sorry that we didn't stuff it in the ditch, as so many other motorists have done on this corner. The farmer whose land borders the notorious bend, and who is frequently called upon to haul cars out with his tractor, is John Penny, and he and his wife, Gloria, are good friends of my wife, Sue, and me. They were avid watchers of *Top Gear*, and I would really have loved to walked to their nearby farm house and seen their incredulous faces when they answered the door to see Jeremy Clarkson and me standing there in the fog. Could you imagine their shock and amazement?

Among the very good cameramen based at Pebble Mill was a vastly experienced Yorkshireman called John Couzens. It always helps if the presenter gets on well with the cameraman, and John and I hit it off immediately, although at first I was a little daunted by the list of major shows and stars he had worked with. He started his career filming the legendary *Dixon of Dock Green* then went on to shoot all the Saturday night variety and comedy shows on BBC television as well as *Steptoe and Son, The Good Life, Dad's Army, All Creatures Great and Small, Gardeners' World*, and all the Delia Smith cookery programmes. John and I worked together on most of my RAC Rallies, and there was an almost telepathic relationship between us. I remember standing at the end of a special stage in Kielder forest during an RAC Rally, waiting for the first car to arrive so I could interview the driver. It was a fairly dramatic arrival, to say the least, for the Toyota which emerged from the darkness was steaming and smoking, and the front nearside wheel was glowing red. Without any word from me, John focused on the wheel as the car skidded to a halt, then panned up to me as I opened the mud-covered door and pounced on my friend Carlos Sainz with my first question. John usually kept me in shot, particularly at the start of an interview, which was unusual, but really helped me to become established as television's face of rallying. John really knew how to put a presenter at ease, and while filming in glitzy Las Vegas many years later, prior to a close-up piece to camera, he came out with the bizarre news that he'd discovered a bar that sold Boddingtons beer! That tickled me. However, he could not put me at ease when shooting the Eddie Stobart story for *Top Gear*, directed by Richard Pearson, who wanted us to go up high in a Simon hoist/cherry-picker type thing so I could deliver a piece to camera with the huge Stobart fleet of trucks below in the background. I suffer from vertigo and felt very unhappy, and John said that it came across that I was petrified, so we abandoned the project and reshot the sequence with me sitting on a chair on terra firma with a green sheet behind me. This is known in the trade as a 'colour separation overlay,' I am told, and my bit was then overlaid on John's shots from on high. See! Never believe everything you see on television.

You can, however, believe an unscripted 'custard pie' moment with a difference that provided one of the most memorable – albeit unintentionally hilarious – highlights of my entire television career. It came during the 1994 Monte Carlo Rally when, as a presenter with the *Top Gear* team, I was sent to film a special feature on the legendary Col de Turini – the mountain pass 5000ft up in the French Alps, which has become famous over the years as the most difficult, dangerous, and exciting stage of the entire event. Twisting, tortuous, and yet at the same time very fast, despite almost always being covered in snow and ice, it attracts by far the most spectators, with crowds of more than 6000 making their way up the mountain to watch the cars slithering past at breakneck speeds through a barrage of photographers' flashlights. No other rally in the world can boast quite such a thrilling and atmospheric vantage point. The report I was there to present focused on Paddy Hopkirk, the genial Ulsterman who was once again competing in a Mini-Cooper, exactly thirty years after he had recorded one of the most celebrated rally victories of all time in the 1964 event, making a name worldwide for both himself and the Mini. Crowds of mostly French and Italian spectators started arriving on the mountain early in the morning, even though the rally wasn't due to arrive until after dark. There was a great carnival atmosphere, with vans selling all sorts of food and – naturally in that part of the world – wine and other alcoholic beverages. It had been snowing hard, and many people had lit bonfires in an effort to keep themselves warm. Our BBC film crew picked a location near the top of the pass, and set up the shot for my little piece to camera. I discussed what I planned to say with the director, cameraman, and sound recordist, and powerful spotlights were turned on in preparation for the first take. That did it! There was much shouting and jeering and heckling from the spectators nearby, many of whom had already been drinking for several hours by this time, and it wasn't long before some of them had the bright idea of livening up proceedings by throwing snowballs in our direction. When filming in public, one has to accept certain irritations such as people waving and pulling faces at the camera, but this was a completely new experience. As soon as the lights went on the snowballs started raining down. Although one or two of them found their target, most of them missed, and we all ploughed on as professionally as possible, with me trying hard to concentrate on getting my words right. After four or five takes with which the director wasn't 100 per cent happy for various reasons, we prepared to go through it one more time. I got as far as saying: "This is one of the most spectacular spectator spots in the world of rallying. I'm on the Turini Pass – it's 5000ft up in the French Alps and there are 6000 spectators …" And at that point the biggest snowball known to man arrived with pinpoint accuracy and exploded on my head. The timing was perfect, and the crew and thousands of spectators all fell about, thinking it was hilarious. At the time I couldn't see the funny side. I was cold and fed up with the whole thing. However, although I didn't realise it then, the incident was the best thing that ever happened in my twenty-year television career. Back in Birmingham various members of the *Top Gear* production team enjoyed looking at the rushes, and played my snowball moment over and over again for their own amusement. And they decided it warranted a wider audience. At the time the BBC was transmitting a series of programmes entitled *Auntie's Bloomers* and *Auntie's Sporting Bloomers*, featuring out-takes involving performers' mistakes and various other cock-ups, and needless to say, it wasn't long before I and my little misfortune became a star turn! I actually appeared on the programme with presenter Terry Wogan, who said it was the best thing he'd ever seen. He frequently mentioned it on his Radio 2 show, and the clip was shown time and again on BBC programmes, and repeatedly found its way onto screens all over the world. It topped the bill in *The Best of British Bloopers*, a hit show in Australia, and was apparently featured at the beginning of the Japanese version of *Top of the Pops* every week. After that people meeting me for the first time, including major stars, regularly exclaimed: "Ah, the snowball man!" What a way to earn a living.

In order to make a successful television item you really need a good team, and *Top Gear* had among the very best cameramen, sound recordists, editors, and producer/directors like Jon Bentley, Ken Pollock, Tony Rayner, Phil Thicket, Richard Pearson, Dennis Jarvis, David Leighton, Chris Richards, and Ian Thomas, with whom I worked the most. However, I had no such luxury when I embarked on a fairly hectic filming project in 1995. I was asked by the organisers of the last great city-to-city road race in the world, Peru's Caminos del Inca, to go out there and film it for BBC's *Top Gear Motorsport*, which had been launched in November 1994. Taking place on the spine of the Andes, most of it above 10,000 feet, it was a new experience for me. I had a local film crew, but there was a Peruvian TV presenter who floated about from time to time. He invited me to appear on his live TV chat show (with subtitles, I presume), but the programme was abandoned when there was an earthquake in Lima. All the TV lights started swinging about and everyone evacuated the studio mid-transmission! I had the interesting experience of being ferried 100 miles to one location with my Peruvian film crew (who spoke no English) inside a very rattly ambulance. On the whole, this was preferable to another form of transport employed when we reached Cuzco. It appears that General Roland Rueda was a great friend of the organisers. The General was a very important man, as he practically single-handedly killed off the terrorist leaders who had, until recently, caused havoc and misery in Peru. He was so important that he borrowed a helicopter from the President's own fleet so we could fly to our next port of call.

The General was accompanied by numerous other military men, and invited me to clamber aboard the helicopter. There were 18 of us, but only 12 seats. The extra passengers therefore stood up, strap-hanging, looking like London tube travellers. The General sat on an upturned beer crate by the open door. As we took off, several bottles of Pisco (their splendidly named local spirit) were dispensed very liberally. It was a very jolly flight, as the ancient Russian-built helicopter rattled its way between mountains. After one or two more glasses of the General's booze I began to resign myself to never seeing dear old Blighty again. It would be rather like the Titanic disaster, I felt. At least we'd all go down drinking! Whenever the pilot – who I assumed was not on the Pisco – saw a rally car, he would swoop down and land in a dusty field. We then jumped out and ran into villages to see the cars pass, cheering on the American star John Buffum, who was leading in his Audi.

I was looked after very well, enjoying various meals of roast guinea pig (Peru's speciality) and various drinks of Pisco, or whatever, at open-air bars in the various cities in the Andes that we visited. Several times, people came up to me for my autograph, which surprised me, as *Top Gear* was not shown in Peru to the best of my knowledge. Later on, flying on passenger planes from one city to another, I found people staring at me. It was all quite worrying. All was explained when I when I walked down a main street and noticed a newspaper stand. My face was on every newspaper. I was flabbergasted, but realised on closer inspection that it was not me, but Peru's obviously famous football manager. He was a dead ringer (poor chap), proving that everyone has a double somewhere in the world!

Twenty-three

Oh, and another thing ...

I've found it quite difficult to put everything in order in this book about my hectic and disorganised life, but I would have probably found it easier if I'd ever kept diaries, of course, in which case you'd now be reading lists of car registration numbers and dates of television transmissions. For those who like such things: hard luck! For those who don't, here are a few more details of my peripatetic life.

In the late eighties, when there were only four television channels, *Top Gear* was at its height, with regular weekly audiences of six-and-a-half million (that meant one out of every eight people in Britain were regularly watching the programme). *Top Gear* was also being shown in other parts of the world, and this gave me another 'right place, right time' moment. Whilst visiting Singapore, I was approached by Malaysian motorsport enthusiasts Yoong Yin Fah and Stephen Loh, who invited me to visit one of their club's rallies a few days later. Soon after that, I found myself acting as the European agent for the Rally of Malaysia, and visiting the lovely, friendly country on a regular basis. I made lots of friends there, and appeared at one of the ornate after-rally functions where I said a few words of thanks. Obviously, I slipped in a few of my one-liners during my speech, and suddenly found the place was erupting; apparently they didn't really have stand-up comedians in Malaysia. The next year I returned to find I was being billed as 'Malaysia's favourite comedian,' and made my entrance on stage down a sparkly staircase, accompanied by show girls. My stardom was short-lived, however, for the following year I attended the rally to make a TV programme and fell foul of the law. I interviewed the Prime Minister of Malaysia, who was there to flag away the cars on the big rally. I had been given permission to make the interview with Dr Mahathir, but I was suddenly grabbed by some security men who screamed at me, saying I had breached protocol. They demanded the tape from the camera (which they got, but didn't realise that cameraman Jim Knights had swapped it for a blank one!). I was then carted off and put in a police van, ready to be transferred to a Kuala Lumpur jail containing drug smugglers awaiting the death sentence. Thankfully, the son of the King was a Motor Club committee member, and organised my release. In my speech at the gala dinner after the event I was careful what I said, as Dr Mahathir himself was in the audience. I did, however, tell them that I thought rallying in the rubber plantations of Malaysia was easy, as if you 'went off' and hit a tree, you'd bounce back on to the track! Even the good Doctor Mahathir laughed. There, you didn't know I was big in Kuala Lumpur, did you?

My fame was obviously spreading around the Orient, as I was asked by the Indonesian Rally organisers to go to their event as an official. Their big rally was held annually in the tiger forests of Sumatra, and I was flabbergasted to attend the start in the city of Medan, where 50,000 people came to watch the start ceremony. There was little me (well, not that little!) flagging cars off the starting ramp with President Suharto, whose son Tommy was a rally driver for whom Dad used to purchase the latest world class rally cars in batches of three. When the cars were worn out or wrecked, another three would be provided. Still, I can't complain; my family and I enjoyed a nice holiday in Bali in a pretty good hotel where, only a short time before, American President Ronald Reagan had been staying. The Indonesian President's office organised this as part of my arrangement for getting their rally up to world championship level.

One of the very best things about these Oriental adventures was that I made friends with one of the funniest people I've ever met: five-time Australian rally champion Ross Dunkerton who, with his delightful wife Lisa, entertained and amused me, and who would in due course introduce me to the joys of their native Australia. Ross competed regularly in rallies in the Asia Pacific region, and won most of them driving a works Mitsubishi. This larger than life, Crocodile Dundee lookalike sees the lighter side of everything in typical Aussie style, and mixes practical jokes with seriously quick rally driving. He would turn up at the start line wearing a wizened old man face mask, or artificial oversized boots with false toes protruding! Among his memories, mentioned in his recently published autobiography *Dunko*, is one of rallying in Papua New Guinea. It was pitch-black, and whilst waiting to book into a control, Ross decided to have a pee at the side of the road. As he relieved himself in the darkness there was suddenly much shouting, screaming, and scurrying – unknown to him, there was a small silent group of local spectators sitting quietly on the side of the road where he was aiming!

Ross and Lisa were entirely responsible for getting me over to Perth, Western Australia for the first major Rally Australia. Garry Connelly, the organiser, was keen to get Rally Australia into the world championship, and asked me to do my BBC *Top Gear* role for Australia's Channel 7 in Perth in 1988. This was the start of my love affair with Australia, and the first of many, many visits. There! You didn't know I was also big down under did you? Although there may be some that dispute that! I went out to do interview and presenting bits for ten years, and remember working with a large, loud Australian sports commentator called Darryl Eastlake, who would stand next to me on camera and call me his "little Pommie mate," while tapping the top of my head with the flat of his hand. I was provided with a Channel 7 helicopter to get around, which enabled me to interview drivers at the start and at the finish of the dusty forest stages. When flying, the cameraman would sit in the doorway with his feet on the landing bars as we tracked the cars across sandy open country. I remember the helicopter flying really low, close behind Juha Kankkunen's Toyota, and on landing, the cameraman finding his bare legs were bleeding having been hit by the flying gravel from the Toyota. That's low flying! I was interested to see how popular Ross Dunkerton was in his native Australia, and impressed by his speed, but not by his practical jokes. One entailed driving me two hours north of Perth to catch some 'koonacks' that lived in the dams on a relative's farm. I was conned into squatting down at the water's edge, patting the water with my welding-gloved hands, ready to catch any that were attracted. 'Dunko' then appeared, holding a shotgun, which, he told me, was a precaution in case a big koonack tried to pull me in! Everyone enjoyed my gullibility, but I did feel a real twit when I discovered that koonacks are, in fact, small crayfish.

I had another unnerving experience in Perth when I had to do a live piece to camera at the start of the rally. My hair, which is now nonexistent, was thinning back in 1990, so I applied a special type of aerosol hair spray that had been given to me by a BBC make-up artist. It was magic, giving me a splendid head of dark hair! Fifteen seconds before I was due to embark on my live piece to camera the heavens opened and torrential rain fell. I ploughed on gallantly, but suddenly felt rivulets of liquid running down my face. How I kept going, I don't know. I was convinced my face would have black stripes running down it, seen by all of Australia. I felt ill at the thought, but at the end of the piece discovered that the colour had not run – it was just clear rainwater!

I was exceptionally busy as the nineties progressed. My *Top Gear* work was in full swing, as well as my PR activities working for Ford, Shell, Pirelli, Auto Windscreens, and other major motoring brands. Great *Top Gear* assignments included a long item on Britain's only works driver on the 1990 Monte Carlo Rally, Louise Aitken-Walker, who fulfilled all our requirements by storming through the long event to win the prestigious ladies award in her Vauxhall Astra. Female drivers featured strongly in my BBC schedules, as in 1993 director Richard Pearson selected me to cover a type of motorsport then unseen by TV viewers – off-road racing. We went to mid-Wales, where I discovered the rough-and-tumble world of the Welsh Hillrally. Specially built, powerful 'buggy' contraptions were driven flat-out over impossibly rough terrain, most of the time in deep mud. Quite incredibly we discovered that the previous year's Welsh Hillrally had not been won by one of the many burly, hairy mud-covered blokes that the sport attracts, but by two small and extremely attractive, young girls from Yorkshire. Richard realised they were great TV material so we went to meet off-road racing's 'first family' of David and Melanie Simmonite and their two daughters, Stephanie and Rachael, all of whom were competing. We made a great *Top Gear* item featuring Stephanie and Rachael prominently, including splendid shots from their in-car camera, although a number of 'bleeps' had to be inserted on the sound track to lose the odd swear-word! Having just missed out in the year we were filming (sod's law), Stephanie and Rachael went on to win the event again the following year, also winning the English and Scottish Hillrallies, and in 1999 they won the championship itself. This sport is very popular in France, so the girls started to compete there against fields of 100 off-road racers. Incredibly they won, first time out, before going on to win the French Tout Terrain championship the following year, becoming the first Brits to win it and the only ladies ever to do so. They received their trophies at an amazingly glitzy event I attended at Disneyland, Paris in early 2002, and were joined on stage by a shy young man called Sébastien Loeb, who had won the French Junior Rally championship. At the time of writing, Mr Loeb is nine times World Rally Champion, so he didn't do too badly for himself, did he? The story doesn't end there. The girls moved into the world of road rallying, and were often featured by our TV cameras on the Mobil 1 / *Top Gear* British Rally championship, and became British Ladies Rally champions three years running, having earned themselves a drive in the Ford works team.

It was the year 2000 when I first met Formula 1 racing's controversial billionaire supremo Bernie Ecclestone at a Pirelli calendar launch party in

London; I regularly attended these splendid functions, as I was involved in a lot of public relations work for Pirelli Tyres at the time. Bernie was accompanied by his tall statuesque Croatian wife Slavica, who towered well above and looked down on both of us as we discussed the recent inaugural Malaysian Grand Prix. I asked him who designed the circuit, to which he replied "I did," which may, or may not be true. I told Bernie of my connection with Malaysia, and daringly mentioned that the siting of the new Sepang Circuit had obliterated some of the best rallying stages in Malaysia. He showed little interest in this nugget of information, but in conversation he actually acknowledged my *Top Gear* TV presenting activities, and was, surprisingly, very complimentary about them.

Around that time Bernie Ecclestone had been granted television rights for the Paris-Dakar Rally Raid, Le Mans, and other events to add to his total monopoly of F1 Grand Prix racing. It was rumoured that the voracious Bernie had also set his eyes on world rallying, but I was, nevertheless, flabbergasted when he said to me "phone me some time. You'll know how to find me."

I could not believe it. Was I hearing right? Two or three days later I thought I had been dreaming. The memory plays tricks. Did Bernie Ecclestone really say that? I then wondered if I dare ring him and what he might want. I pondered this over the next few days, and speculated that he might want some information or advice about rallying, and I then thought he might want me to actually work for him. More worrying took place before I realised that, if this was the case, I couldn't possibly cope with curt telephone calls day and night from the famous megalomaniac, or adapt to his ruthless and frightening way of working. I knew that Bernie would eat me for breakfast! But then again, would I be missing the chance of a lifetime? I never plucked up the courage to ring Bernie, but did meet him a couple of years later at the Autosport International Racing Car Show in Birmingham, and asked him what he had wanted. He peered at me from beneath his famous grey donkey-fringe of hair and tersely replied "I don't remember," and walked off.

Twenty-four

No problem, Tony!

One of Britain's greatest-ever rally drivers, the late Colin McRae, played a major role in my television career. In fact, Colin's rallying and my television activities started around the same time in 1986. My first of very many interviews with him was for the preview programme for the 1987 RAC Rally. Colin's father, Jimmy, was then three-time British Rally champion, who would go on to win the championship a record five times. I had known that eighteen-year-old Colin was rallying a Vauxhall Nova, mostly on Scottish events, and had competed on the Swedish Rally earlier in the year. I thought it would be a super story for my RAC Rally report to have a father and son competing in different cars, and talked to Jimmy about it, but was told there might not be funds available. During the Manx Rally in September (where young Colin won his class), I suggested to General Motors' team boss Tony Fall that he should give Colin a few quid to get him on the rally. I am pleased to say that Tony came up with £4000, and Colin entered his first RAC Rally, an event he would go on to win three times. He never forgot that, which may explain why I had such easy access to him for so many years of television work.

Many people found Colin difficult to interview, and he really only 'tolerated' television crews, but he and I seemed to have some sort of special rapport and he never, ever gave me a problem. In fact, in confidence, at social occasions he would tell me what he thought of some of the other press and TV people. No names here, of course! I especially remember a *Top Gear* item we did prior to the 1995 RAC Rally, when the entire team of Colin, Richard Burns, and Carlos Sainz all went to the magnificent Butcher's Arms Restaurant at Priors Hardwick, near the Banbury base of Prodrive, which was running the world championship Subaru 555 rally team. Lino and Peter Pires, proprietors of this wonderful watering hole, closed half of the restaurant so we could film the item, including my interviews, during the meal. Not far from Silverstone, the restaurant has now established itself as something of a mecca for motorsport and television stars, as the amazing picture gallery in the coffee lounge will testify. During Colin's later assaults on the British Rally championship, I became known for popping up and interviewing Colin whenever and wherever he broke down or crashed. On one RAC Rally in the early nineties, he had to work frenziedly to rebuild the front offside suspension, after careering over rocks on the finish line of a stage in the Kielder Forest. We filmed the whole sequence and saw Colin complete the task before scurrying round to his driving seat. As he was fastening his seatbelt, I did the famous 'Mason pounce' and asked "Do you think you'll make it to the Penrith control on time?" Colin smiled wryly and said "No problem, Tony!" and a new rallying catchphrase was born. With some humour, he uttered this phrase time and time again over the years, and at one point 'No problem Tony' T-shirts were marketed. When Colin memorably won the world championship in 1995, and the RAC Rally the same year, I was on the finish ramp at Chester racecourse to interview him live on BBC television. My microphone was also linked into the main PA system at the racecourse stands, and when I asked him how hard had the rally been, the entire crowd of tens of thousands of Colin's fans shouted "No problem Tony!" Top rally photographer Colin McMaster of McKlein captured the moment brilliantly, as can see in this book. It was a memorable moment for me.

I went to my beloved Kenya for the last Safari Rally to be included in the World Rally Championship, in 2002, and at one point went up in the Ford helicopter with Phil Mills, who was then part of the Ford team, and was spotting animals for Colin. The chopper flew a quarter-of-a-mile ahead of the rally car, and if there were any hazards such as large animals or wayward locals in overloaded 'matatu' buses, Colin would be advised. I was privileged to be involved, and to be part of the celebrations organised by Ford boss Malcolm Wilson when Colin and Nicky Grist won the Safari, bringing the Focus its first win. In September 2007, the world of motorsport was completely numbed when 39 year-old Colin was killed after his helicopter crashed near his home in Lanark. The incident also claimed the lives of his 5 year-old son Johnny and two friends. It was, indeed, a very sad day for everyone in the world of rallying.

I had a fairly worrying time at the end of the Lombard RAC Rally at Chester in 1992, when I was asked by Dennis Adams, BBC's executive producer, to interview winner Carlos Sainz on the finish ramp in Chester's main street. As this was the last year of Lombard's long-term sponsorship of this event, you can probably imagine the razzmatazz – huge crowds, spotlights, and cameras all over the place. It was my job to greet Carlos and co-driver Luis Moya, once they had done the champagne spraying bit, and interview them for precisely 90 seconds at 8.10pm. This interview would not only be taped for the *Top Gear Rally Report* programme to be shown later in the evening but would also be going out live. I was quite relaxed, despite a burglar alarm going off at a nearby shop, but fifteen seconds before I was expecting to be cued to start, I heard through my earpiece that there had been a cock-up of some sort and I should interview the winners for another full minute. Now, a minute may not seem a long time to you, but when you are all miked and earpieced up for a live television report, it is a lifetime. Anyway, I did what I had to do, and the sequence with Carlos and Luis, who were thankfully people I knew quite well and who spoke good English, went splendidly. I was congratulated on my performance by all concerned, but it could have been a nightmare and the end of my career. I remember seeing some of the interview replayed on the BBC main news programme later that night, and reliving every second.

Among the very many *Top Gear* items I enjoyed was an entry on the Tour of Cornwall Rally where I navigated my *Top Gear* pal, Tiff Needell, on his first ever rally. I am delighted to say that we won the Ford RS2000 section of the event. Mind you, it was the navigation that did it. No, I'm only joking! Not long after, we were together in another car, joined by all the other *Top Gear* presenters for a photograph to appear on the front cover of the *Radio Times*. This was certainly an accolade for the programme, and led to an evening party at BBC TV centre in London, attended by all those who had appeared on the front cover that year. It was certainly a star-studded gathering and I was lucky to spend some time chatting to one of my heroes of comedy, Ernie Wise and his wife, Doreen. They asked me how I was getting home, and kindly offered to take me back to their house at Dorney Reach, Maidenhead (in their Rolls-Royce, I should add) where I could be collected by my driver. I didn't like to tell them that my 'driver' was a Banbury taxi queuing up at the station! It was during our conversation that Ernie suggested I should get on the cruise ships as an entertainer/lecturer – he was a great cruise enthusiast. I followed his advice.

I did not realise that Ernie Wise was something of a car enthusiast too, or that he watched *Top Gear* regularly. He asked me how we decided on items and how much rehearsal we did. Rehearsal? What's that? I told him that we usually turned up wherever we were filming with a few notes on bits of paper, and said what the director suggested in his notes. Ernie was amazed. "Oh. That's no good," he said. "You must rehearse." Of course, Morecambe and Wise were renowned for rehearsing their Christmas shows for five or six weeks, and many of their 'ad libs' were similarly rehearsed. I remember Ernie telling me that he had conceived the idea of that great 'breakfast sketch' to the stripper music, one of the greatest comedy classics of all time. "Ernie doesn't like watching that," said Doreen. "He hates the bit where he was whisking the eggs. He thinks the timing was wrong and he came in too soon." Hearing of such perfection helped me a lot in my future TV filming.

In fact, I had another amazing happening that will lead to another bit of name-dropping! Whilst filming the Manx International Rally on the Isle of Man, our cameraman Jim Knights (he of the Dr Mahathir incident in Malaysia) spotted Manx resident Norman Wisdom in a small crowd of spectators near his home in Andreas. The shot was included in my report, and I made reference to the great film star's attendance. A short time later, I received a note from him telling me that it was his ambition to appear on *Top Gear!* The following year he presented the prizes after the Manx Rally, and I was on stage with the man who was once Britain's highest earning film star. Now in retirement, Norman invited me to visit him at home in the north of the island whenever I was over there. I saw him a few times, and he proudly showed me his new BMW M3, his Rolls-Royce, and incredibly, a fast motorbike that he used to ride around the TT course, at the age of 90!

Still on the name-dropping front, I cannot resist mentioning that Pirelli invited me in 1991 to a most exclusive function in London one evening to celebrate the 80th birthday of the greatest driver of all time, Juan Manuel Fangio. I met him and shook his hand, and received an autographed menu. Stirling Moss and Phil Hill were also in attendance, and Stirling made some rude remark about me to Fangio, but I will never know what he said.

Further afield, I regularly attended the Race of Champions, at which Michèle Mouton gathered together all the World Rally Champions to drive on a fast test track in various works rally cars she had obtained from manufacturers. We filmed the very first event in France in 1988, and nearly every year after, when Michèle moved the event to Gran Canaria. Ken Pollock included the annual event in *Top Gear Motorsport*, and Michèle gave us carte blanche to film whatever we wanted. Needless to say, I found myself sitting alongside every single world champion of the first twenty years as we charged around the fast gravel figure-of-eight track. It was interesting to observe the different driving styles of the champions, none of whom frightened me, thankfully, although Colin McRae came closest! Carlos Sainz gave me one of my magic TV moments in 1996 driving a Toyota. We had cameras and microphones inside the car and I remember saying that I felt so confident as brilliant Carlos, twice world champion, knew this track like the back of his hand. At that very moment Carlos lost it, and the Toyota clobbered a bank before flying in the air, eventually landing in a cloud of dust. "What happened then, Carlos?" I asked. "Oh! I think I drive too fast," he replied, somewhat understatedly.

On a more genteel note, I filmed a huge event known as the Alpine Challenge in the summer of 1993. Over 100 Rolls-Royce Silver Ghosts assembled in Vienna to re-enact the great event run around the Austro-Hungarian Empire some 80 years before – the last time Rolls-Royce competed in motorsport. The hugely expensive vehicles came from all over the world, and were priceless. Jon Bentley, my producer, had worked hard to organise this outing, which would make a full one-hour programme and two *Top Gear* items. There was one proviso imposed by the powers-that-be in the BBC insurance division: on no account must I be allowed to drive any of the cars. I was a bit miffed by this, but as every car was worth more than a million pounds I suppose it was understandable! One splendid American owner took me in his car for a spot of filming in Croatia, and invited me to drive. I explained that I was not allowed, as I might break or crash it, according to our masters. "You can't break this baby!" he said, "Anyway, if you do, I have another two at home!"

Another favourite 'old car' event was the Claret and Classics Rally held in France. I competed in it one year, navigating for Don Barrow in his Triumph TR3, and filmed it a couple of times for *Top Gear*. Organised by the splendidly eccentric Roger Deeley, the cars rallied around the lanes of France in the mornings before visiting magnificent chateaux each afternoon, where competitors partook of their fine wines. In 1992 we visited Chateau d'Yquem, home of an incredibly expensive dessert wine, where producer Dennis Jarvis borrowed a bottle so I could do a piece to camera. I was asked to hold a small glass of the precious liquid in my hand and say how wonderful it was, and that each competitor would receive a small glass of it. I kept having a little sip between takes until the camera crew thought they, too, would like to sample it. Eventually, the empty bottle was returned to the Baron, or whoever owned the Chateau, and he went completely spare. He had not expected us to drink the stuff, priced then at well over a hundred pounds a bottle, but merely to hold the bottle up to the camera! Funnily enough, I wasn't all that impressed by the wine, and thought it tasted a bit like Dettol!

There was certainly variety in my life. I filmed in Florida at the Daytona 24 hour race, and in Jersey where I drove Bergerac's famous Triumph Roadster, which had the worst steering I've ever known. I say this as an excuse, for when trying to emulate the opening shot of the popular Bergerac series, I clobbered the camera with my offside front wheel! I filmed at the Skoda rally team headquarters in Czechoslovakia, and in Dubai where they have a very sandy rally. My biggest memory there is of filling up an extremely empty Range Rover with petrol – the total cost was £6! Another rather strange claim to fame came a few years earlier when we were filming at the Motor Show at the National Exhibition Centre in Birmingham. Mitsubishi had triple Grand National winning horse Red Rum in attendance. I thought it would be quite nice to say I had patted Red Rum, so did so. Regrettably the great animal moved as I approached, and stood on my foot! Still, not a lot of people can say that they were stepped on by Red Rum.

Speaking of large animals, producer Ken Pollock agreed that we should go out to Kenya in 1994 to film an amazing event called 'Rhino Charge,' run for charity to help preserve the magnificent beasts. The 'rally' consisted of many four-wheel drive vehicles driving over impossibly tough terrain, and made very good television. After the event, Ken decided that I should find some rhinos and stand in front of them for a piece to camera. With the help of a game warden we duly found a group not far from Nairobi, and I learnt my words and took up position. I then noticed that alongside the cameraman and sound-recordist there were two large men with rifles pointing at me. They explained that if the rhinos decided to come for us, they would shoot them. I must say, I thought that was a strange way of protecting the rhino!

I achieved a boyhood ambition of driving a fire-engine when we filmed the centenary celebrations of Dennis vehicles. I enjoyed pressing the blue button to get the sirens going, but didn't appreciate quite as much wearing an oversized yellow fireman's helmet, as when I came to the end of a very fast straight on the Dennis test-track, I braked hard, it came down over my eyes, and I sailed off into a field!

I love trucks and buses, and was thrilled to go with Richard Pearson to film *The Story of Eddie Stobart*. I was kitted out in the green uniform of their drivers, and took to the wheel of a Volvo FH12 articulated truck. It was another dream coming true. I got to know the entire Stobart family very well, and still keep in touch, although the Stobart Group is now a huge public company. I was invited to attend the Stobart 25th anniversary celebrations at the Dorchester Hotel in London, where Volvo had assembled a full-size truck inside the ballroom. Fellow Eddie Stobart spotters Jules Holland, Bernie Clifton, and comedians Cannon and Ball were among those of us entertaining. As many will know, every truck in the 2000-strong fleet has a girl's name, and I was thrilled when Edward and William Stobart offered to name a truck Emma Nichola after my daughter.

Other memorable *Top Gear* items included the Reliant Robin world championship that took place at the Mildenhall race track in Suffolk, and was a sort of demolition derby. It was a 20-lap race, and all the other hooligan drivers were told to keep away from me, otherwise there would be no programme. Needless to say, they went for me on the last lap and biffed into me as I perfected the art of driving the three-wheeler on two wheels. I rolled the car twice, but restarted the engine and finished the event amid much cheering. I finished fifth in the Reliant Robin world championship, I am pleased to say, and of course the *Top Gear* item showed my great incident in detail. It's still watched on YouTube.

Back on the trucking scene, I adored driving a 1953 Leyland Octopus up Britain's once most feared road, the pass of Shap. In pre-motorway days, the pass was a real headache for truckers going to and from Scotland, and we relived those days when I took control of the eight-wheel Leyland. I drove it up and down the pass for hours and only missed a gear once, despite there being no synchromesh on the gear box and having to double declutch all the time. You won't be surprised to learn that the only close-up shot of my feet on the pedals was that of the one gear I missed! I drove an even bigger truck when a 222-wheel Faun heavy low-loader collected some huge generators at Avonmouth docks.

They had been shipped in from Germany en route to Didcot power station in Oxfordshire. I drove this leviathan around the docks, grappling with its thirty gears, before handing over to the proper driver who would take us on to the M4 motorway. The great vehicle travelled mostly at night, resting at service stations during the day, but at one point we were still on the motorway mid-morning as we crossed a bridge over the River Avon. All sorts of officials in reflective yellow jackets were there to measure the bridge for weight stresses, and the top brass from Wiltshire constabulary were there to stop all the east-bound traffic on the motorway, as the great behemoth had to straddle the centre lane. Traffic was building up behind the obstruction and my director, Chris Richards, thought it would be a nice idea to do one of my famous pieces to camera. I stood in the centre of the motorway (in my reflective yellow jacket, of course) and was encouraged by two senior police officers, who didn't seem to mind when I fluffed my lines and the traffic queues built up even more. I heard them talking on their walkie-talkies, and can verify that the stationary traffic measured six miles when I started, but had extended to thirteen before I got my words right!

1997 was a mixture of emotions for me. In February I received an invitation to attend a reception at Buckingham Palace given by the Queen and the Duke of Edinburgh to celebrate Sport in the Life of the Nation. Top sports stars, past and present, were invited and ushered into the various grand rooms to be presented to Her Majesty and members of the royal family. My invitation specified the White Drawing Room, which was, in fact, the first room visited by Her Majesty. Maybe they decide upon the positioning of presentees by height, but all I know is that I was in among all the jockeys including Willie Carson, Richard Dunwoody, and Tony McCoy. Maybe it was something to do with horsepower, as the two rallying Simmonite sisters were also in the line-up, as was now six-time Olympic equestrian competitor Mary King, who greeted me warmly, having met me at BBC's *Question of Sport* and numerous horse events when my daughter Emma was competing. Her Majesty was, of course, very gracious, and had apparently seen our efforts on television output as she said "rallying looked extremely exciting." I later had the honour of meeting other members of the royal family who were circulating. Prince Edward was very aware of my rallying activities (and crash) with his uncle, Prince Michael of Kent, and Prince Andrew, when being introduced, exclaimed "Ah! Reliant Robins – bloody marvellous!" The whole evening was memorable, and I found it amazing that I should have been speaking to two great footballers, Sir Stanley Matthews and David Beckham, on the same evening. I understood Sir Stanley earned £20 per week as a player and travelled to matches on a public service bus. The jockeys, meanwhile, were encouraging the liveried footmen to keep our champagne glasses well filled, so when the party broke up at about ten o'clock in the evening we all skipped down the front steps of Buckingham Palace, scarcely believing our good fortune.

Shortly after the Buckingham Palace shenanigans I filmed a super *Top Gear* item around the lanes of Sussex in a Mini-Cooper. I showed off doing various handbrake turns and reverse spins, and then took a very important passenger with me as we tracked behind the camera car. This passenger was none other than John Cooper himself, who developed the Mini into a serious competition car after his long-time career running a Grand Prix team. I am lucky to have met John a number of times, and knew he appreciated the work I had done on *Top Gear*, so we had a very nice unhurried conversation. Unfortunately, during these tracking shots the heavens opened and driving conditions worsened. I could not put the windscreen wipers on, as this would spoil the spotlit shot, so I continued for about three miles driving a couple of yards away from the camera car, and could not see a thing. John never said a word about the conditions, but he must have wondered what was going on at times!

Not long after this there were all sorts of celebrations, as it was the 25th anniversary of Roger Clark's and my victory in the RAC Rally of Great Britain. Our winning car had been lovingly restored by enthusiast Tony Yendall, who brought the car up to a forest near Silverstone so Roger and I could be reacquainted with it. It became one of the most popular *Top Gear* items ever, and is regularly watched on YouTube along with many other of my items (and mistakes!). We charged through the forest as we had all those years before, and it brought back a lot of memories. Roger was experiencing bad health at the time, but still drove in his unique and brilliant way. This was the last time I saw my mate Roger. On the 12th January 1998, he died of a stroke at the cruelly early age of 58 years.

Like Roger, and many other motorsport people, I have been lucky to travel the world, and of course, I have many memories of meeting interesting people. I still travel to spectate on various world rallies, and enjoy the hospitality of Rally Travel Ltd which takes organised spectator tours to major events. David Hutchinson, Neil Prunell, and Jeff Garnett look after me well, although I was a bit concerned to be with Jeff in a taxi in Sofia, Bulgaria one evening when the taxi driver, who had no seat belts in the car, was smoking heavily, speaking on a mobile phone, and watching a film on a TV set on the dashboard all at the same time!

I have had a long association with Philip Young who pioneered the sport of classic rallying and is one of the sport's great characters – in 1988 he ran the Pirelli Classic Marathon from London to Cortina, and I was lucky to be asked to present an item on the event for a *Top Gear* special. The year after, Pirelli's marketing people persuaded big names like Stirling Moss, Paddy Hopkirk, Timo Mäkinen, and Ove Andersson to compete, and also invited Roger Clark and myself. It was a hugely enjoyable event, and we all liked our evenings around Europe. This was really when I got to know Stirling well, and I always remember him asking me which country we were in, for in those pre-Euro days he carried little bags of change, extracted from the electricity meters of flats he owned in London, which were fed by foreign students!

Philip Young organised many more of these rallies, as well as more ambitious marathons around the world. He revived the Peking–Paris event, and invited me to go out and film it, dressing me up in a Chairman Mao uniform and filming me on the Great Wall of China. Philip's fertile mind also had me riding a bicycle in Moscow's Red Square and around the Eiffel Tower in Paris before I returned to normality.

Of all the places in the world that I have visited, I think New Zealand is my favourite. The people are friendly, the varied countryside great, and it's all a bit like it was in Britain thirty years ago. I've attended the World Rally Championship event there, but in 2003 was asked if I could arrange for Hannu Mikkola to compete on the classic Otago Rally based in Dunedin on the South Island. A good Escort Mk2 RS1800 would be provided. Oh! And could I co-drive Hannu? This took quite a bit of organising with Roger Oakley and his team out there, but Hannu agreed and we went along. It was exactly thirty years since I had been in a rally car with Hannu, and I remember saying that I hoped we'd have a nice gentle drive as we were now far too old to be crashing. He agreed, but by the end of the first two days we were five minutes in the lead! Eventually we clobbered a very large rock with the nearside rear wheel, as did our friend and team-mate Björn Waldegård from Sweden. We still finished well, and after the rally I enjoyed doing my 'act' to a completely new audience at the gala prize presentation. I decided then that I wouldn't again compete in any rally car anywhere. It had been most enjoyable, but enough is enough. If I had to retire totally, then I might as well do it with the best rally driver in the world. I still see Hannu a lot, so it was not a serious parting, but I felt relieved to have got the rally out of the way, so I put on my tourist hat to wend my way home via the Pacific islands of Fiji, Tahiti, and Tonga. Well, someone's got to go to these places!

Twenty-five

Singing for my supper!

As my varied career has moved into the twilight zone I have seen a little less action, but done plenty of talking about it. Ever since the early years of my rallying, I have regularly appeared at car club dinner dances and other functions where I would sit at the top table between the chairman of the club and some lady mayoress, or whatever, enjoying fairly soggy chicken, croquette potatoes, and some over-boiled, green vegetables. I once thought of writing a book about after-dinner speaking, entitled 'The bad food guide!' I was always welcomed to these functions, but often sat next to someone who hadn't got a clue who I was. One adjacent lady diner once misread the menu and said "Oh! You're a lorry driver; that must be very interesting." I remember going to the Holiday Inn in Plymouth, arriving only just in time, having struggled through the traffic. I asked the hotel receptionist where the Plymouth Motor Club dinner took place and was pointed to the next floor. I ran up the stairs and into the first room, which was full of dinner-jacketed people and their partners taking their seats. I moved towards the top table, and was welcomed and asked to take my seat. I was slightly baffled when the person next to me asked "How long have you been in the Royal National Lifeboat Institution?" I was at the wrong dinner!

In the early seventies, after the RAC win, I had invitations from all parts of Britain, and my wife Sue would loyally come along, not knowing anyone but frequently presenting trophies. It must have been a hard ordeal for Sue who, quite understandably, never really grasped the bizarre world of motorsport. I soon realised that this was just a job of work for me, so have usually attended solo.

Bigger bookings came along once I moved to television, and there were major dinners all over the place. I had modified my act as time went on, and realised that some audiences didn't really understand rallying, but enjoyed a few one-liner jokes and a light-hearted approach. It seemed to work, and I have, in fact, spoken at over a thousand functions over the years. At Manchester's Piccadilly Hotel in the early eighties, I preceded Bernard Manning, one of the stars of the then famous show *The Comedians*. He was renowned for his racial jokes and rudeness, and stood up after I had finished and said "That was the funniest f---ing thing I've heard since *Gardeners' Question Time*!"

For many years I have been booked to commentate at various motorsport events, particularly those with a leaning towards rallying. I will never be a frenetic lap-by-lap commentator like my good friend Murray Walker, but I have knowledge of the cars and competitors and manage to slip in the odd amusing comment from time to time. I have commentated at Race Retro, Rallyday,

Silverstone Classic, Donington Historic, and the marvellous Goodwood Festival of Speed. I have, in fact, attended every Festival of Speed since the ever-enthusiastic Lord March first thought of letting racing cars charge up his garden path twenty years ago. In the early years I filmed for *Top Gear*, but for the last eight years I have commentated on the rally stage that was introduced when Lord March invited Hannu Mikkola to design a challenging and authentic rally stage in the woods of the Goodwood grounds at the top of the hillclimb. The running of the stage was assigned to top rally organiser Rick Smith of the Southern Car Club, who still runs this event meticulously with the help of 300 marshals and other officials. The event has attracted all the top world championship rally drivers, as well as the best club and classic car drivers. For all these years I have had terrific support from Conny and Carl Bailey, who have always ensured I have the right bits of paper to look at. After flogging away by myself for a couple of years, prolific motorsport author Graham Robson joined me as co-commentator, and his presence was most welcome. It was like sitting next to an encyclopedia.

A bit of public performing came along more recently when I was contacted by P&O Cruises to be a celebrity after-dinner speaker. I (hopefully) entertained passengers three or four times during a cruise, often joining a long cruise at some intermediate port. Many well-known entertainers work on cruise ships in order to entertain passengers of a certain age; they have been around for a few years but are still remarkably popular. Away from the ships, I recently met one of the new, young breed of comedians, Ross Noble, and told him about my cruise appearances, to which he cheekily said "Oh yes! I'll be doing them when I'm on the way down!"

Not long ago, I had to fly out to the Caribbean to join the P&O ship Aurora; this entailed flying to Antigua before taking a local flight to St Maarten. It was a hot, sunny afternoon when the big British Airways jet landed in Antigua, and whilst queuing for passport control I recognised two fellow entertainers also bound for the Aurora. I had previously met the brilliant cellist Andrew Skrimshire, but introduced myself to Richard Digance, an entertainer who was celebrating 40 years of performing around the world as a comedian/guitarist. Richard has done everything, including appearances at the London Palladium, at the Royal Albert Hall with Tom Jones, and numerous Royal Variety Shows and, of course, his regular Saturday night TV programmes in the eighties and nineties. Little did we know that we three would get to know each other extremely well in the ensuing 24 hours! On arrival we discovered that the local LIAT airline was involved in intermittent strikes by pilots, and no-one knew which planes were going where. Added to this, in the middle of the chaos in the arrivals hall, we could not find Andrew's hugely expensive cello, which was something of a drama, although it was eventually found. We arrived at 2.00pm, local time, but seven hours later, having consumed a few beers and packets of crisps, which was all that was available, were told that the airline would put us up in a hotel and find a flight next morning. Needless to say the taxi never appeared at our hotel, which was on the other side of the island, but we somehow got back to the airport. By now Richard, Andrew, and I were getting on really well, and there were plenty of laughs, but by 2.00pm (24 hours after we arrived) we became a little concerned as the airline folk kept telling us lies about flight times. We telephoned the P&O staff in Southampton to tell them of our plight, and that we might not get to the

Aurora in St Maarten before the 5.00pm sailing time. All hell was then let loose with phone calls back and forth, and the captain agreeing to delay the departure of the ship for another five hours. Richard then spotted a little airline manager-type person, and accosted him. It was brilliantly funny, and Andrew and I could not keep our faces straight as Richard said "Look here, I don't know whether you realise this but we three are Britain's top three entertainers! If we don't get on that ship, all the 2000 passengers will ask for their money back, and P&O will then sue your crappy little airline and you'll be out of a job!" The man scurried off, and little happened for an hour until a plane appeared, and said little man was seen pulling three passengers off it, so we could get on! Our total trip from London had taken 26½ hours! We three saw a lot of each other during the cruise, and watched each other's shows. After my performance, where I show footage on screen of my RAC Rally win, Richard commented "You say you only won that rally by three-and-a half minutes. Blimey, if you'd stopped to boil an egg, you'd have lost it!" That really appealed to my sense of humour – only a comedian would think of saying something so whimsical.

So, as you'll have gathered, I've had a varied life with more than its fair share of dramas and mayhem, and I hope I've provided a lot of enjoyment and entertainment along the way. I've met many, many interesting people during my trips to nearly 100 countries, and obviously had a lot of laughs. I've had serious points along the way also, and owe a huge amount to the settling influence of my family, Jane, Clare, and Emma, and, of course, Sue who has put up with so much to run a lovely and well-organised home for me to return to after all my activities.

Anyway, I'll leave the last words of this book to Sue, who recently said to one of our friends "What a pity he never had a proper job!"

Index